D0162443

Human Behavior in the Social Environment

Families, Groups, Organizations, and Communities

Human Behavior in the Social Environment

Families, Groups, Organizations, and Communities

Vimala Pillari
Kansas Newman College

Moses Newsome, Jr.
Norfolk State University

Brooks/Cole Publishing Company

I(T)P® An International Thomson Publishing Company

Pacific Grove • Albany • Belmont • Bonn • Boston • Cincinnati • Detroit • Johannesburg • London
Madrid • Melbourne • Mexico City • New York • Paris • Singapore • Tokyo • Toronto • Washington

Sponsoring Editor: *Lisa Gebo*
Marketing Team: *Jean Thompson, Romy Taormina, and Deanne Brown*
Editorial Assistant: *Shelley Bouhaja*
Production Editor: *Timothy Wardell*
Production: *Greg Hubit Bookworks*
Manuscript Editor: *Linda Purrington*
Permissions Editor: *May Clark*
Interior Design: *John Edeen*
Cover Design: *Roy Neuhaus*
Typesetting: *Susan Rogin*
Printing and Binding: *Malloy Lithographing*

COPYRIGHT© 1998 by Brooks/Cole Publishing Company
A division of International Thomson Publishing Inc.
I(T)P The ITP logo is a registered trademark under license.

For more information, contact:

BROOKS/COLE PUBLISHING COMPANY
511 Forest Lodge Road
Pacific Grove, CA 93950
USA

International Thomson Publishing Europe
Berkshire House 168–173
High Holborn
London WC1V 7AA
England

Thomas Nelson Australia
102 Dodds Street
South Melbourne, 3205
Victoria, Australia

Nelson Canada
1120 Birchmount Road
Scarborough, Ontario
Canada M1K 5G4

International Thomson Editores
Seneca 53
Col. Polanco
11560 México, D. F., México

International Thomson Publishing GmbH
Königswinterer Strasse 418
53227 Bonn
Germany

International Thomson Publishing Asia
221 Henderson Road
#05–10 Henderson Building
Singapore 0315

International Thomson Publishing Japan
Hirakawacho Kyowa Building, 3F
2-2-1 Hirakawacho
Chiyoda-ku, Tokyo 102
Japan

All rights reserved. No part of this work may be reproduced, stored in a retrieval system, or transcribed, in any form or by any means—electronic, mechanical, photocopying, recording, or otherwise—without the prior written permission of the publisher, Brooks/Cole Publishing Company, Pacific Grove, California 93950.

Printed in the United States of America

10 9 8 7 6 5 4 3 2 1

Library of Congress Cataloging-in-Publication Data
Pillari, Vimala.
Human behavior in the social environment : families, groups, organizations, and communities / Vimala Pillari, Moses Newsome, Jr.
p. cm.
Includes bibliographical references and index.
ISBN 0–534–35029–1
1. Social psychology. 2. Social groups. 3. Social
4. Social interaction. 5. Human behavior. 6. Social
I. Newsome, Moses. II. Title.
HM251.P536 1998
302—dc21 97–26559
CIP

This one is for you, too, Kapil

Dedicated to my wife Barbara
and my two daughters
Ayanna and Mariana

For all their support and encouragement

Contents

2

The Family 33

3

What Are Groups? 87

Organizations *129*

5 Communities 173

Preface

Human Behavior in the Social Environment: Families, Groups, Organizations, and Communities deals with theory and knowledge building for social workers.

We use the ecosystems framework as a conceptual framework for presenting information on diversity, oppression, patriarchy, and feminism. We present family development as a system of changing roles. Diverse family lifestyles include two-parent families, single-parent families, and gay and lesbian families, from various ethnic, racial, and class backgrounds.

This book considers different stages of group development and various types of group membership. Norms, group conformity, group goals, leadership, and power issues, including working in a multicultural context, are highlighted.

We also discuss social-welfare organizations as systems involving labor power and leadership in a community setting. We discuss goals of organizations, the bureaucratic environment, and communication processes, and we emphasize different types of leadership. Throughout, we discuss ethnic and racially based organizations.

This book stresses the concept, function, and structure of communities as systems, and explores different types of racial, ethnic, and other diverse communities. Each chapter offers selected case examples of individuals who experience being a member of a family, a group, an organization, or a community. The reader thus considers all sizes of systems—family, group, organization, and community—from a realistic and personal perspective. At the end of each chapter, we discuss implications for social workers working with individuals, families, organizations, and communities.

The Council of Social Work Education (CSWE) accreditation standards mandate for all undergraduate and graduate students specific content on members of ethnic minorities, women, gays and lesbians, and people with disabilities, all of whom are affected by bias and oppression. This book pays explicit attention to the patterns and consequences of discrimination and oppression.

We have aimed to present a book that can be easily understood by students at both the undergraduate and graduate levels. This book can also serve as a sourcebook for faculty who want to discuss social systems of different sizes from a life-span perspective.

Our goal is to speak directly to students and view them as active participants in search of knowledge. All chapters in the book were read by master-level students (Pillari's) and thus "pretested." Their suggestions were incorporated in the final draft of the book. It is important to incorporate such feedback because students are the consumers, the audience, the future social workers, the knowledge builders, and the torch bearers of the profession. We have therefore aimed at a writing style that flows easily and at a comfortable pace for students.

An instructor's manual and a test bank have been prepared to supplement this textbook.

The instructor's manual contains chapter outlines, summaries, key terms, suggestions for class lecturers, discussions, and other valuable aids. At the end of each chapter, the manual also presents exercises that reflect a social worker's perspective. The manual is an important tool for instructors who wish to incorporate systems concepts into their own teaching styles.

A test bank is provided for all instructors who adopt the text. The test file for each chapter consists of a variety of multichoice items (with answers) and essay questions, both conceptual and applied.

Another book, titled *Human Behavior in the Social Environment,* second edition (by Vimala Pillari), provides the life-span perspective. This book (*Human Behavior in the Social Environment: Families, Groups, Organizations, and Communities*) provides information about systems of different sizes. The life-span text deals with the developmental stages of life from conception to old age and death in a biopsychosocial framework, keeping in mind the "person–environment" fit. It is also accompanied by an instructor's manual and a test bank. The decision was made to present information in two books so that the students and faculty would have the option of using either one or both books in their classroom teaching. Or they may wish to use one in conjunction with another book, or use one as a text and the other as a supplement.

This is the final but pleasant task of thanking those who were instrumental in the development of this book. First and foremost I (VP) wish to thank Dr. Isaac Alcabes for his critical comments, thorough questioning, and complete support in the development of this project. I would like to thank my students who read the manuscript and made useful comments: Klynn David Donaldson, Ralph Laub, Todd Powers, and Birdie Rasmussen. My heartfelt thanks also to Dennis L. Welker from the Brigham Young University Media Services for his patience and prompt help.

We would like to thank the following reviewers for their valuable suggestions: Janice Adams, Indiana Wesleyan University; Anna Bowman, Goshen College; Peggy Brunhofer; Fiona Bullock, Pacific Union College; Katherine M. Dunlap, University of North Carolina at Charlotte; Mark Fagan; Marvin Feit, University of Akron; Leola Furman, University of North Dakota; Gloria Jensen; Ronald M. Katsuyama, University of Dayton; John King, University of Arkansas; Munira Merchant, Valparaiso University; Phyllis J. Peterman, Rutgers University–Newark; Frederic G. Reamer, Rhode Island College; William Roberts; Velma Scott, Jackson State University; Jerome Smith; Mary Swigonski, Rutgers University–Newark; Dan Weisman, Rhode Island College; and Walter F. Zahnd, California State University, Chico.

We also thank the members of the Brooks/Cole family for their complete support: Lisa Gebo, editorial assistant Shelley Bouhaja, Timothy Wardell, Greg Hubit of Bookworks, and Linda Purrington for her editorial assistance. We also thank Charlotte Johnson of Norfolk State University for her supportive attitude in facilitating the progress of this book.

Last but not least I (VP) wish to thank my husband Steve for his support and encouragement.

Vimala Pillari
Moses Newsome, Jr.

1

An Overview of Human Behavior in Systems of Different Sizes

Rita is crying. Her face is swollen, one arm is bleeding, and her body is shaking with sobs. She hardly looks 18. Holding her hand and sobbing loudly by her side are two young children, a 3-year-old son and an 18-month-old daughter. Rita's eyes dart from person to person on the busy street. She tries vainly to hold her tears back while she hastily and clumsily crosses the street. On close examination, you notice a bag hanging off her shoulder—a tiny baby is sleeping in it. What do you think is Rita's story? Are you curious?

Ara, a kindergarten child, is very sensitive about how she dresses. Whenever the group is in the playground, she insists on wearing slacks, as her mother has told her she must be modest. One day, in the classroom, Ara slips, tumbles, and goes sprawling on the floor. She starts to cry hysterically, saying she is a "bad girl" because she has exposed her panties to other children. She tells the teacher her mother has said there is a "bad part" under her panties where people do bad things to each other and where bad things happen. She cries violently and cannot be consoled. She also tells the teacher that she never touches herself in the bad part, as her mother has instructed her not to. Why is Ara so afraid of her own body? And her mother . . .

Let's look at Rita first. Rita is running away from her husband, who has been physically abusing her, and this time he has used a knife on her. The only obvious injury is the arm that is bleeding, but she is hurting all over. Who is Rita, and why is she in such a situation? She is an individual who grew up in a social environment that was not conducive to her growth. Every one of us is a bit like a plant that grows. When a plant receives enough water and has good soil and enough sunlight, then the plant grows up healthy. It looks up to the sun, its leaves are a healthy green, and its stem is strong. In a similar manner, what goes into children contributes to making adults who are either well adjusted or not so well adjusted. Rita comes from a family of four children. Her father was an alcoholic, and constantly abused his wife and at times his children. Rita was the youngest child and a main target of her father's temper. Rita grew up feeling this was how everyone lived. To her, home was scary. She cried quietly when she saw her mother being abused. At times, she tried to protect her mother, but always ended by getting hurt herself, as her father violently turned on her.

Rita left home early to get married. However, even before her marriage she was aware that her boyfriend, Damon, was a drinker. He called it social drinking, but she noticed that he drank far more than anyone else in the group. When Rita complained, he told her that was the way "real" men were—drinking was the in thing for men. He added that Rita's father drank, and so did his. Rita did not leave him or fight back. She accepted his explanations. After all, he might be right; her father was also a drinker.

A year after they started dating, she found herself pregnant, and

Damon married her. However, a few days after the marriage he complained that she had trapped him into marrying her. He constantly abused her verbally, saying that she was worthless and not capable of working outside the home. Rita tried to get a job, but did not succeed, because of her obvious pregnancy. She grew more and more ashamed of herself and avoided talking to her friends. Damon did not like her parents and prevented her from going home. However, one day she sneaked out of the house to visit her mother. Damon found out, and although she was pregnant, she received her first violent battering. After that, the situation got worse. Every time they quarreled, he beat her and called her a useless tramp. He threatened to kill her if she saw her parents again.

Time passed. Rita accepted the abuse as part of her life. She had a second and a third child and a miserable life. She had dropped out of high school when she became pregnant, and at this point in her life she had no support systems. The community she lived in was rough; drug dealers and alcoholics were everywhere. Apartments were overcrowded, and loud quarreling and physical fighting went on behind closed doors. The elevators stopped working, and Rita was not allowed to go out of her fourth-floor apartment, because her husband suspected that she was unfaithful to him. He used this as an excuse to batter her. Then he removed her last resort for help and comfort, the telephone in the apartment. When she asked for one, he ridiculed her about her inability to earn a livelihood; in the same breath he forbade her to leave the apartment. Rita became a prisoner in her own home. She was too scared to venture out of her home, because of the threats and battering, and her feeling of isolation.

One night Damon, in a drunken stupor, threatened to kill their second child, a daughter, hardly 2 years of age, and ran to beat her, because the child was crying. Rita intervened, and he punched and kicked her until she fainted. He stopped when he was totally exhausted. Rita did not wish to tolerate any abuse of her children, particularly as they were "innocent," and that is why now we see her in the streets. The pathetic picture she presents is that of an 18-year-old mother with a 3-year-old son and a 18-month-old daughter walking beside her holding her hand, and another baby in her arms. The 3-year-old is fussing, the 18-month-old wants to be carried, and the baby in her bag is crying. A young, battered wife running away from home with her kids. She has been planning this ever since she heard on the radio about a shelter for battered women.

Rita stops at a phone booth and calls an agency that provides temporary shelter for people, particularly women, who have been battered. Rita now receives the help she needs to get away from the abusive relationship. She is given food, shelter, and counseling to help wean her away from dependency and her lack of trust in her own judgment that had been instilled by her husband and earlier her father. For this purpose, she sits in on group meetings for abused mothers, with a social worker present, where the mothers share their pain, their fears, and their need to move on in life without their abusers. This group meeting appears to help Rita as she hears about and understands the stories of abuse. It helps her to feel part of a group of people who share similar experiences, and strengthens her determination to leave her husband permanently (although occasionally she seems afraid to do so).

Thus we notice that Rita, from an abusive family of origin, entered a similar family of procreation, and lived in a community infested with drugs, liquor, and prostitution, where networking or being neighborly was almost impossible. Isolated from her mother and her siblings and the few friends she had at school, Rita finally seeks aid from an organization where she feels safe, and where group counseling starts to help her. You can see that this individual is part of a family, a community, and different organizations such as the school system, and a social-welfare organization such as the shelter for battered women. Group work in the shelter helps Rita reevaluate her life. As for Rita, our lives are intricately intertwined with our environments, and the environment is made up of individuals, families, groups, and organizations. The families, groups, and organizations are part of the community.

Now let us look at Ara's case.

Why is Ara so afraid of exposing her panties? The child is in an organization, a school system with different types of adults and children in it. But she also comes from a home setting, a family that has profound influences on her. Ara's family is quite affluent, with a lovely suburban home. Her father is a lawyer and her mother a nurse who decided to give up her job when she became pregnant a second time. They are religious in their outlook, and active in their church. Ara's private school caters attentively to the emotional as well as academic needs of the children. In this case, when Ara begins to cry hysterically, the teacher calls the mother for a conference. After a brief discussion with the teacher, the mother relates rather hesitantly that she was raped by a neighbor when she was 9, and therefore has strong feelings about sex and sexuality. After further discussion with the teacher (a community resource), Ara's mother says she does not want her child to be unhappy and asks the teacher to arrange some help for her daughter. The mother adds reluctantly, "Perhaps I, too, need some help and some guidance, because it seems I am creating problems for my daughter." The mother also agrees to confer with the school social worker, and a meeting is arranged. After several meetings, the mother eases up on clothing restrictions and other behaviors at home and school. Although many years have passed, the mother agrees to attend a group for rape victims. Within the group discussion, the mother comes to understood her own issues more objectively, and grows in terms of sharing and self-understanding. As time passes, she becomes more relaxed and willing to deal with her daughter as a young child who needs to learn to feel good about her body and herself.

In this case we note that the individual, the child Ara, comes from a home and family where sex is viewed negatively. The child is misinformed because of her own mother's negative experiences. The mother, out of shame and perhaps guilt, which is common among rape victims, has kept her rape a secret. The community they live in is upper middle class, but through the school (an organization), the mother is introduced to a new community of social-welfare agencies where she can receive help for herself and her child, both for this problem and other social problems that might arise. Her venture into helping herself leads the mother to a self-growth group, where she learns to work on filling her own needs. She is motivated to become a well-nourished and more complete person. Even in grave difficulties, people have potential for positive growth given the right intervention. This case, too, shows the place held by a person in relation to a family, the community, and the organizations and groups that can provide help.

All people are connected to several different social systems. This book focuses on developing an understanding of families, groups, organizations, and communities, and of how we operate within them. No person can live in isolation. Our interconnectedness needs to be understood particularly by members of the social-work profession. In social work we deal with people embedded in the different environments they belong to, because it is impossible to understand issues and problems, as well as individuals' strengths and potentials, without understanding the background and environments. In *Human Behavior in the Social Environment* the main emphasis is on life-span development; in this book the focus is on systems of different sizes, such as families, groups, organizations, and communities. We reviewed the different perspectives that would make useful frameworks for understanding the different areas of study, and chose to use two points of view: (1) the strengths perspective and (2) the ecosystems perspective. We chose the ecosystems perspective, which views all size systems holistically, as an overall framework. A perspective is a way of looking at and arranging information that lets the reader connect different thoughts and ideas. The ecosystems perspective forms a broad framework for understanding the values, beliefs, and environmental factors in diverse social systems.

In addition, the strengths perspective offers a refreshing, positive way of viewing and dealing with problems. As Saleeby (1992) notes, the strengths perspective is not fully developed yet, and has conceptual gaps and practical uncertainties; nevertheless, it is founded on a solid basic assumption that all clients have strengths. Client motivation is based on fostering client strengths, and the social worker thus acts as a collaborator with the client. The environment itself also contains strengths, not merely weaknesses. This perspective does not obsess over problems, pathologies, and defects (Saleeby, 1992). The strengths perspective is an important emerging model in social work, in tune with the values on which social work is based. In the strengths perspective, there is a good fit between positive thinking and its use as a way of viewing clients and helping them in productive ways. To view knowledge and theory productively and expansively, we used the ecosystems perspective, which views people in their various settings with an awareness of the different resources available to people in families, groups, organizations, and communities in terms of the "fit" between people and environments; to view people and systems positively, we take the strengths approach.

THE ECOSYSTEMS PERSPECTIVE AS A CONCEPTUAL FRAMEWORK

We use the ecosystems perspective as a conceptual framework for understanding the different-sized systems and working within them. A conceptual framework, also described as a "school of thought," can be defined as a set of interrelated concepts that attempt to account for some topic or process (Martin & O'Connor, 1989). The ecosystems perspective is a conceptual scheme consisting of layers and sets of interrelated concepts that can explain human behavior in the context of the environment.

The purpose of this book is to introduce social workers to information and theories useful in understanding families, groups, organizations, and communities and how people fit into them, creating and changing environments for themselves and their own growth, and being influenced by them. As Winston Churchill said, "We shape our buildings and . . . then our buildings shape us."

The ecosystems perspective can help social workers arrange, integrate, and systematize knowledge about how people interrelate with each other and with their environments (Pillari, 1993).

The ecosystems perspective integrates two schools of thought, ecology and general systems theory. General systems theory applies to the entire physical world as well as the human social world. In combining an ecological perspective and general systems theory, we achieve a broader way of viewing the universe. Ecology is the study of complex reciprocal and adaptive transactions among organisms and their environments. Each organization has an "ecological niche," a particular place or environment where it is most comfortable and that is well suited for its growth and development. Boulding describes how systems change and survive depending on their own adaptability, and change, in turn, changes the niche in which they are lodged. Boulding says, "Niches continually change. They may shrink or they may expand, and if they shrink too much, species that are well adapted to a particular niche will become extinct as the niche shrinks to zero" (1978, p. 111). Thus ecology focuses on the *adaptability* of organisms and environment. For example, constant physical and sexual abuse in a family erodes productive family life, and severe constant abuse may lead to investigation and to family members being removed from the family system. The children may be placed in foster care, and the parents arrested. Thus, the home niche of this family disappears, because the family atmosphere is not conducive for the growth of the children. A person's personal niche changes, expands, or contracts depending on the other systems that inhabit this niche. There are links among systems; when one system changes, that changes other systems. For example, if a problem arises in a family system and the husband and wife (marital subsystem) divorce, that is bound to affect the children's subsystem.

Ecology is concerned with the interrelationships and connections among organisms. In describing the ecological processes, Handler (1970), a biologist, identifies three major variables: (1) the arrangement and distribution of the organisms in relation to time and space; (2) the particular way in which energy flows to different organisms; and (3) the role of the different species (in our case, different people) involved (p. 456). From a social-work perspective, we focus on an individual, a family, a group, an organization, or a community as the unit of attention for offering help, that is, the entire person–environment configuration. The ecological setting is the natural milieu in which the social worker defines and views individual family, group, organization, or community systems. Thus, in looking at a case the social worker must think in ecological terms, assessing the terrain of the system and considering indirect and direct influences on the client. Germain, thinking philosophically, highlighted two variables, time (1976) and space (1978), in working with clients. The manner in which a family organizes, uses, and responds to time, and the effects of spatial arrangements on the family, group, organization, or community, affects clients—and vice versa. For example, use of space differs in different cultures. In some cultures, all family members, such as parents, adolescents, and young children, may sleep in a crowded bedroom, and view that as normal. Similarly, time may be viewed in a more leisurely way, with people eating and sleeping as need dictates, rather than basing their lives purely on clock time, as in Western cultures.

The historical roots of general systems theory reach back to the 1920s, to the work of a biologist named Bertalanffy. Bertalanffy observed that a system is a "set of elements standing in interaction" (1967, p. 115). A closed system, in social-work terms, could be a department of social work that does not receive or accept new ideas, and does not bring innovative faculty but retains old ideas and old faculty and does not attract many new students. Funding may begin to dry out, and less and less energy may be left to fight or persuade the bigger funding system. If such a state of affairs continues, the department must close. Open systems, in contrast, allow a constant, readily available exchange of energy.

Greif and Lynch (1983) identify six basic concepts in general systems theory, applicable to open systems. The six basic concepts are those of boundaries, structure, hierarchy, transactionality, frame of reference, and time.

In the systems approach, a system is considered to have its own spatial or dynamic *boundaries,* which separate it from the rest of the environment. The boundary permeability varies. Boundaries can be rigid, flexible, or enmeshed. For example, a person with rigid boundaries may not accept new ideas as readily as a person with flexible boundaries; and when people encroach on each other's rights and overlook individuality, they are said to have enmeshed boundaries. Depending on a boundary's permeability, there may be a flow of information and energy.

Depending on the *structure* of any particular system, a *hierarchy* may arise. For example, a small system such as a family is also embedded in the larger system of the community, and both are controlled in terms of law and order by the legal system, which takes the form of legal organizations. Hierarchically, legal organizations control the behaviors of people in the community and in the family. When a person—a small subsystem—disobeys the law, he or she may be punished by the hierarchical power structure. A functional family involves hierarchical power exercised by the adult parent or parents over the children.

To work effectively with people, in the ecosystems approach, we need to look at issues in *transactional* terms. A transaction suggests multidimensional interactions and influences all players in relation with each other (Germain & Gitterman, 1996). Transactions take place not only with other systems, but also within the hierarchy of subsystems (Greif & Lynch, 1983).

The *frame of reference* indicates to the observer whether he or she is studying a family, a group, or an organization. Based on the frame of reference, social work may place special emphasis on either a family, group, or organization. *Time* can be divided into individual, historical, and social time. Individual time concerns the continuity and meaning of individual life experiences over the life course. Historical time concerns the impact of historical and social change on the developmental portrayal of a birth cohort (all people born in the same time period, such as a particular decade). Social time concerns the timing of individuals and family transitions and life events as influenced by changing biological, social, demographic, and cultural factors (Germain & Gitterman, 1995).

The system's internal operations take place through seven processes: input, throughput, output, feedback loops, negative feedback, positive feedback, and entropy.

The type of transactions that take place depend on the *input,* that is, on the different ways a system takes in energy. *Throughput* means that once the input is accepted into a system, this input is acted on, transformed, coded, and used for functioning. *Output* is the response of the system that has a direct effect on environment and acts as inputs for other systems through feedback loops. For example, 10-year-old Debbie wishes to go out and play with her friends. But the input she gets from her mother is that Debbie should first do the dishes. Through input, Debbie understands the consequences of not responding (which is punishment), and therefore her output results in immediately doing the dishes before going out to play. *Feedback loops* consist of either *positive* information that acts to maintain a system equilibrium, or *negative feedback* that disrupts the system and thus promotes change (Bertalanffy, 1956). That is, feedback has a role in input and output. If a husband becomes angry with his wife and she responds in anger, then negative input has been followed by a feedback loop and a response from the wife that is negative, too. If the wife is happy and communicates this to her husband, and he responds positively, then the feedback loop is said to be positive.

Thus communication is not one-directional but like a circular loop in which an event or process may be a cause at one point and an effect at another point. The feedback loop sweeps people up in complex social, cultural, emotional, psychological, biological, and physiological processes.

When a system begins to deviate too far from its course and is not corrected, it experiences *entropy:* The system has no energy input from the outside, and no exchange, and therefore winds down and runs out of energy. In other words, entropy is a measure of the quantity of energy not available for use (Carter & Anderson, 1990).

The internal state of the system is also determined by six principles, which include homeostasis, differentiation, nonsummativity, reciprocity, equifinality, and multifinality.

Homeostasis—balance or equilibrium—is the state at which a system is maintained. In the Maples family, for example, the father is the chief wage earner and the mother has a part-time job and cares for four school-age children. When Bob Maples is involved in a car accident, the family struggles to pitch in so that Bob, who is emotionally distraught because his friends died in the accident, need not work for a few weeks. The family supports him wholeheartedly in his grief but rejoices at their own good fortune in having him alive. The family struggles to regain balance or homeostasis that reappears when the father goes back to work.

Differentiation is the tendency of the system to increase in order and complexity over time, just as growing older entails the acquisition of more knowledge and life experiences and becoming more differentiated. In the Maples family, although Bob's temporary emotional crisis is a setback, it leads to deeper understanding among family members about pain, loss, and death and also to a deeper appreciation of the rewards of living.

The effects of what happened in this family cannot be seen from looking at isolated, fragmented components of the event. This principle, called *nonsummativity,* asserts that data collected from isolated parts of the system cannot be simply added up to represent the whole system.

In the Maples family, there is also *reciprocity,* which simply means when there is change in one system, it affects the whole system.

The principles that deal with the path or trajectory of a system include equifinality and multifinality. *Equifinality* suggests that a system can reach the same final state from a variety of different paths, and under different initial conditions. For example, when the Maples family is affected by crisis, the members need help in sorting out issues such as loss and grief. There is a great deal of mixed communication, and the family loses some balance. However, each person separately shows strength and thus helps to balance the family. A similar outcome might have been achieved by involving the whole family in an intensive counseling intervention.

The principle of *multifinality* says that similar conditions can lead to dissimilar ends. For example, in the Maples family, if the different family members had not offered support, Bob might continue to be depressed and unable to return to his job. This would affect family life and force the mother to take a better-paying job, or set the stage for divorce, unhappiness, alcoholism, and so forth. If multiple negative effects remain and if no attention is paid them, then this might drive the family toward closing itself off, and to entropy.

Seeing people in their ecological milieu (families, groups, organizations, or communities) and in their transactions lets us assess their strengths and weaknesses in their own physical, psychological, and social environments. Some of the major concepts that rule our social ecosystem are diversity, oppression, patriarchy, and feminism. Let's look at these concepts and how they interact in our social environment.

FORMS OF DIVERSITY

Human diversity includes differences arising from color, gender, sexual orientation, religion, age, disabling condition, culture, income, and class (Shriver, 1995).

U.S. society is becoming increasingly multicultural. Culture consists of patterns, explicit and implicit, of and for behavior acquired and transmitted by symbols, constituting the distinctive achievement of human groups, including artifacts. The essential core of culture consists of traditional (historically derived and selected) ideas and their attached values. Culture systems may, on the one hand, be considered as products of action, and on the other, as conditioning elements for the development of further action (Green, 1982). Culture is the acquisition of learned behavior that is shared and transmitted by the members of a particular society. It is the total way of life for a group of people.

Culture can also be classified as material and nonmaterial. Material culture encompasses people-made objects such as cities, factories, churches, schools, books, computers, painting, cameras, vacuum cleaners, and so forth. Nonmaterial culture consists of language, values, behavioral styles, beliefs, norms, customs, mores, and folkways (Light, Keller, & Calhoun, 1989; Robertson, 1989).

Cultural diversity is also based on ethnic and racial differences.

Different racial and ethnic families are discussed in a later chapter, to highlight differences and similarities. Empathy in cross-cultural social work can be enhanced by learning about how power, or lack of power, is associated with racial and ethnic identity. For ethnic groups, cultural life reinforces positive functioning through family support systems, self-identity and self-esteem, and the specific ethnic philosophy of living (Lum, 1986, p. 5).

As Pinderhughes (1982) notes, students can be helped to examine their perceptions, feelings, and behavior of themselves as ethnic persons. An atmosphere of group trust allows students to share and compare similar and different experiences. These are understood in the context of (1) the relative power of each student's ethnic group and of others, and (2) his or her own personal power gestalt. This process allows: (1) understanding of the complexities involved in cross-racial and cross-ethnic communication, (2) a recognition of one's own biases and the dynamics involved, (3) a tolerance for differences in one's own and others' perceptions and experiences, (4) an understanding of feelings and behavior in any situation that involves a consistent differential of power, and (5) an enhancement of one's ability to perceive oneself and the client accurately. Only by recognizing both our similarities and differences with others can we achieve our full potential.

Intellectual as well as emotional exposure to diverse human experience begin to make it possible for readers to view diversity creatively and deal sensitively with differences. Different types of diversity are presented throughout this book. For example, one group of people easily overlooked are the poor and frail elderly. A study done in South Florida (Rittner & Kirk, 1995) found that basically affluent communities still have an invisible population of elderly men and women with unmet social and medical needs. The poor and frail elderly people in many communities are among those who are adversely affected in periods of extended economic decline or rapidly rising inflation. Although tax and income advantages have helped preserve the financial security, property, annuities, and other holdings of some elderly people, many at lower socioeconomic levels continue to live below the safety net (Phillips, 1990). A conservative U.S. Census Bureau estimate is that as many as 4 million elderly people may live below the poverty level by the year 2000 (Rittner & Kirk, 1995). We will be discussing the elderly in various contexts throughout this book.

Gays and lesbians are another diverse group of people who can help us understand human behavior. Understanding the complexities of sexual orientation, be it gay, lesbian, bisexual, transgender, or heterosexual, can provide new perspectives on human diversity and alternative family structures. This group is also discussed in the chapter on families.

In a similar manner, we will discuss other groups and issues as we encounter them in the social-work field, to expand our understanding of diversity.

OPPRESSION

Oppression is a state of being in which an individual or group is deprived of some human right or dignity and is not given an equal opportunity to compete for available positions. Many different forms of oppression plague different groups of Americans in the 1990s, including political, economic, and social oppression. An example of oppression include the underrepresentation of racial and ethnic groups in the 1990 census. When numbers are underrepresented, that in turn affects how funds and services are allocated to a population. Oppression includes written and oral racial slurs and physical attacks on people (Atkinson, Morten, & Sue, 1993). Undocumented workers are often paid subminimum wages. Collins (1990) uses the term "interlocking systems of oppression." This approach recognizes the interrelatedness of oppressions and the interconnections among oppressions. When oppression in any institution is directed toward any individual or group, it is connected to and results in oppression in other institutions, individuals, and groups.

Gloria Yamato (1993) discusses systemic institutionalized mistreatment of one group of people by another. The oppressors have preferred access to economic resources, information, and respect, whereas the oppressed have a corresponding disability. The outward effects of oppression lead to internalized oppression: Members of the target group are so emotionally, physically, and spiritually battered that they begin to believe their external oppression is deserved and their lot in life is natural. As racism becomes comfortable in a society, it creates yet worse social problems and therefore must be attacked from all angles. Collins (1990) suggests that racism is a systemic problem; that is, when one group is mistreated, other groups will be too. Pharr (1988) speaks in terms of interconnectedness of oppressions: "It is virtually impossible to view one oppression such as sexism or homophobia in isolation because they are all connected: sexism, racism, homophobia, classism, disablement, anti-Semitism, ageism. They are linked by a common origin—economic power and control—and by common methods of limiting, controlling and destroying lives" (p. 26).

For example, often people on welfare are stereotyped as being unworthy of the taxpayers' money. Peter Swet (1990, p. 132) relates, "I was on the cashier's line at a supermarket, behind this young, healthy-looking black woman. When her groceries were rung up, she pulled out a bunch of food stamps. I said, 'Hey, get a job, I'm tired of having money taken from my paycheck for people like you!' I expected a sharp answer; instead, she looked embarrassed and said, 'There's nothing I'd like better than a job, but nobody will give me one.' 'Bull,' I shot back, then turned away. Twenty years later, I'd love to find that lady and tell her I'm sorry. Little did I realize that what happened to her could happen to anyone. It happened to me."

Oppression and discrimination are intertwined. Prejudice is an unjustified *attitude* or prejudgment of people; discrimination is an unjustified negative or hostile *action* toward a certain group or an individual (Queralt, 1996). Individuals and institutions may use decision-making procedures that may consciously or inadvertently discriminate and reinforce inequalities. For example, income differentials may cause unequal access to education even if the school system does not intend to discriminate. Also, the decision by a company to relocate may have the unintended impact of reducing access to jobs. Housing is segregated by income and by race, and not all individuals have equal access to job information. Higher-income Euro-American households tend to have greater access to job information through personal contacts than do lower-income African-American households (Cherry, 1989, p. 139).

In every chapter, we discuss different types of oppression and its effects on families, groups, organizations, and communities.

PATRIARCHY AND FEMINISM

A patriarchal society is one in which formal power to make decisions and set policy is held by adult men. Society and its institutions reflect the values and priorities of the patriarchy, which embodies masculine ideals and practices (Ruth, 1990, p. 45). Patriarchy influences all aspects of culture. Our ideas of truth and knowledge are accepted, shaped, and articulated by dominant males. Educational institutions are fundamental shapers and socializers of the roles of male and female members of society. For example, what are the qualities admired and accepted in a workplace, and what type of behavior is rewarded? The traits that are rewarded are aggressiveness, courage, physical strength and health, self-control, emotional reserve, perseverance and endurance, competence and rationality, independence, self-reliance, autonomy, individuality, and sexual potency (Ruth, 1990).

Politics, education, and the sciences reflect men's perspective; women take a secondary role. Men in a patriarchal society support one another through social, political, and economic institutions. Under this male dominance, women and others either become invisible, become estranged, or fail because of "natural inferiority" (Westkott, 1979, p. 424). In the social context of organizations, women are controlled by men and are culturally devalued if they do not measure up to the standards set up by the larger society.

The accepted role of women in men's lives is that of masculinity-validating power. For men to play their role, the women play their prescribed role of doing things that make men feel masculine. Men need women to validate their own masculinity. Their (women's) power to help men express their emotions places heavy burdens on the woman.

Women's sense of powerlessness led to the rise of feminism and the women's movement. Male experience and male behavior, particularly white male experience, are the norm by which human behavior and experience are judged (Coulter, Edington, & Hedges, 1986).

Feminism offers a different approach to understanding human behavior and the social environment. Feminism is multidimensional, and has various definitions. A comprehensive definition suggests that feminism is an entire world view or gestalt, not just a laundry list of "women's issues." Feminist theory provides a basis for understanding all people's lives, and a feminist perspective proposes to change the world politically, culturally, economically, and spiritually (Bunch, 1983). The feminist movement is one of the strongest currents of our times. Its aim is nothing less than to redefine human nature, which will have a profound effect on our culture.

The feminist movement has developed through different phases. The first phase of the feminist movement was focused almost exclusively on gaining access to areas of male power and privilege that had been withheld from women. In the second phase, women found themselves reclaiming aspects of themselves that they felt had been lost in the first phase of the battle for equal rights. A psychological shift, a concern for what goes on inside, took place (Peay, 1994). Meanwhile, feminism continues to recognize women's persistent inequality. The central definition of feminism entails the conscious, explicit awareness that women are denied equal rights, opportunities, and access to goods and services. Feminists seek to build an egalitarian system that provides every person, irrespective of biological sex, maximum human freedom and dignity. Ultimately, as Norman and Wheeler (1996) comment, we are able to understand each other because of our human homogeneity, but social workers must also be able to assess and intervene with clients as distinct individuals, keeping in mind that gender, socialization, and subgroup cultures make all people different. They continue by saying that the broad effects of gender, race, or socioeconomic status should be evaluated in the most person-specific context possible.

Later chapters discuss the inequalities women face, as well as help develop a psychological understanding of women.

We discuss diversity, oppression, patriarchy, and feminism within the ecosystems perspective. All chapters discuss current topics, such as AIDS among heterosexuals and homosexuals, the developmentally disabled, and women's issues.

An ecosystems perspective offers a holistic view of people and environments as a unit; neither can be fully understood without the other. In the ecosystems perspective, all relationships are characterized by continuous reciprocal exchanges, or transactions, where people and environments can influence, shape, and change each other. At the end of each chapter we present implications for social-work practice. Now we will look at the individual as a unit and transactor in the small family system, as a unit in the group system, as a member of an organizational system, and finally, as a member of a community.

TRANSACTIONS BETWEEN THE INDIVIDUAL AND THE FAMILY

Families are systems with subsystems and rules and regulations of behavior used to control and maintain the system. When families communicate, they process information and use it to implement rules and regulations. Families may follow unwritten rules. Let us look at one individual in a certain family, the father. For example, when the daughter's dog has dirtied the carpet, the father may convey this message to his wife who, in turn, asks the daughter to clean it up. The communication pattern is indirect, because the father does not directly tell his daughter what to do. Perhaps this father is ambivalent about parenting, sees himself as only the wage earner, and leaves the control and disciplining of children to the mother; or maybe he is uncomfortable with telling his daughter what to do, or perhaps the daughter doesn't listen to him. Thus, when he does communicate, his tone of voice may carry the message "Although I would like you to do something, I am really not sure that you will do it without creating a fuss, so it is not really worthwhile to ask you to do anything as you may not listen." Styles of communication evolve around such family norms and regulations. In Chapter 2 we discuss the developmental life cycle of the family, social class and family life, and forms and types of families. We also discuss some crucial problems that affect families and have implications for working with families.

Here, as an introduction to these family issues, we discuss the role of the individual, a member of a family. For example, each family member develops a basic pattern of functioning within the family group that extends to participation in the broader society. This is the story of John. "After dating Alice for a couple of years, he married her when he was 20 years of age. He was happy for about three years and then matters began to change. He found her parents and siblings were interfering in his life. They questioned him on his behavior and on things which he felt were none of their business. Of course he was dating other girls on the side, but what was wrong with that? After all, his father had done the same and his mother hadn't seemed to mind; the role of a woman was to please and satisfy her man." (Pillari, 1994, p. 149). When we look at John's life, we become aware of the multiplicity of factors that influenced him. These included his own modes of feelings, thought, and action, as well as the cultural, economic, and political contexts in which his family functioned. In this case, the family member, a male child, learns a pattern of behavior by absorbing the rules and regulations of behavior that had been played out in his family of origin. Family members evolve and grow differently in families, depending on their family of origin and their own needs and desires.

In one family Pillari (1994) studied, the female family members had a hidden agenda. Women family members were loyal to each other, and this was related to the way they felt about men. They married men with chronic problems like alcoholism, and this in turn caused enough problems to help the women regroup themselves in the family. In this family, the men were the scapegoats and played their roles very well because these were their designated roles even before they married. One man, who started to drink at a young age, was told in the family that he would not amount to anything, and he did not. In his marriage, too, he was seen as being a no-good person, and thus he continued his life as an alcoholic until his death. As Emily, his mother-in-law, commented, after the death of her third husband, to whom she had been married for five years, "I was happy to see him go. He was a problem, and a troublemaker and it was such a relief." He was such a scapegoat in the family that even after his death, Emily's sisters and her daughters got together and talked ill of him. About the money her husband left for her, Emily commented sarcastically, "It was not much. It paid for his funeral." She ended her narration of her life with her third husband by saying that there was nothing left of the marriage except the bad feelings between herself and *his* daughter (Pillari, 1994).

All family members play different roles in the family. Children can get inducted into roles. Jerry was the family savior, and his induction took place when he was very young. He remembered that when he was 5 years old, his parents had a serious fight, and his mother, Cheryl, decided that she did not wish to live. Severely depressed, she locked herself in her bathroom and cut her wrist with a razor. Her husband, Arnold, could not rescue her, because the bathroom door was locked. So he broke the glass window of the bathroom and instead of going in by himself, he sent Jerry through the window, and ordered him to persuade his mother not to kill herself. Jerry was shocked to see his mother in a pool of blood, but he took on the responsibility and persuaded her not to kill herself. Thus began his induction into the role of family savior (Pillari, 1991).

Depending on the needs and desires of the family, individuals play different roles and seek to "fit" into the family system. This is where people begin to work out their basic needs, sense of self, and feelings of security and insecurity. The manner in which a family functions and deals with its members depends on both internal family conditions and external demographic and economic situations. Family systems deeply influence when people leave home, marry, give birth to their first child, space the births of subsequent children, or send their children to work or to school. Such events are timed by an internal clock of family traditions as well as by external pressures such as the job market and economic needs.

Historians find that these processes have varied among different socioeconomic and cultural groups under different circumstances. As Longres (1990) notes, in feudal times most peasant families lived in villages, the social unit around which all family life was structured. Neighbors, relatives, and friends lived close by, and the households impinged on each other. Village norms and traditions were upheld, and the village had considerable authority over families. Marriage was prefaced by collective forms of courtship; the villagers strongly controlled mate selection. The roles of men and women were complementary: Each sex had its own functions to perform. Women were subordinate to men. Social authority was not merely invested in men, however; the work of women was necessary for the survival of the family and the village.

In villages, children were needed for economic survival. Despite a high mortality rate, therefore, families continued to have a large number of children. Older children were often sent away from home to be apprenticed in a trade. The responsibility of child rearing was vested in the village, and a child's failure to heed could lead to severe punishments and sanctions. Poster (1978) concludes that, unlike today, "The child was not trained to defer its gratifications, to accustom itself to a clocklike schedule of rewards, to face the world alone and be prepared to make autonomous decisions, to regulate emotional energy for a competitive struggle against others. Life for peasants had a fixed pattern, governed by innumerable traditions which were not even to be questioned by individuals" (p. 188).

Thus, in history and today, the role of individuals in families varies, depending on the needs of the family and environmental factors. At times the needs of the family, particularly in dysfunctional families, may be so intense that the person fulfills those needs and sacrifices him- or herself for the sake of the family. Often a balance is achieved between the external needs of the family and the internal functioning of the family.

THE INDIVIDUAL IN THE GROUP

Just as the individual in the family learns family rules and ways of behavior, so does the member of a group. There are different types of groups (discussed in detail in Chapter 3). Groups have norms, standards, and ways of behavior. Natural groups consist of people who have similar backgrounds: the same socioeconomic class, religion, race and ethnicity, and so forth. In this book we discuss race and ethnicity as they affect communities, because communities are larger and encompass more variables than families.

An individual may join a group for many reasons, including self-growth, working through some issue such as alcoholism or drug dependency, and so forth. There are groups for children, adolescents, adults, and the elderly. Individuals are also exposed to groups at different institutions, including schools, workplaces and recreational clubs.

For example, let us look at a group for children of divorce. Such groups are often organized to help children in elementary schools, because divorce is frequent. Children of divorced parents may face a number of social and personal problems.

Jon's parents have just divorced. Jon feels lonely, and also feels responsible for the divorce, although of course he is not. Because Jon feels responsible for the divorce, he experiences divided loyalties, does not know how to deal with parental conflicts, and fears the loss of family stability. A teacher who sees that Jon's ability to focus and concentrate on school work has declined tremendously decides that Jon needs to become a part of a group setting where he can work at his issues.

Jon's needs are assessed based on topics such as divorce, stepfamilies, death, stress, and friendships. The classroom teacher, who is also a trained social worker, holds about six 30-minute meetings in a week, for six weeks. A needs survey is done, and the children are asked to think about issues and respond realistically to the teacher.

This survey helps the children take an active role in discussing their current concerns. The selection of students to become members is based on their willingness to participate. Jon wants to participate, so the teacher gets permission from the parent through a signed letter.

The group creates its own rules; Jon is an active participant. For example, children can remain silent in the group if they need to. As the children make up their own rules, this keeps them involved and creates a "we" feeling.

The group leader helps the children understand that they are special people and they are all right and that children, like adults, can learn to cope with difficult times. For example, Jon is told that the divorce was between his parents but that no one is divorcing Jon. Moreover, Jon, the child, did not cause the problems between his parents and therefore he is not responsible for the divorce. Finally, as he is not responsible for their problems, he cannot fix them. This approach takes a great load off the child.

This intervention group offers Jon and other children like him support when they need it, to let them know they are not alone, to teach them coping skills, and also to reinforce the child's need to talk to teachers, parents, and others. It is also intended to help children of changing families explore ways in which they can express and deal with their feelings.

A focus of this group meeting is to help Jon and others develop rather than to provide only therapeutic help. In such sessions, according to Corey (1990), the interviews and group process are structured minimally, to allow free range to the learning process. However, the initial session is clearly structured so that the children will understand the purpose of the group. The teacher, a social worker, plays the group leader and facilitator, and helps children understand why they are in the group.

Children such as Jon are helped to use positive adjectives to describe themselves. The children define their own families. What is a family? Questions such as "Who am I, and who lives in my house?" become important guides for these children. Each child describes how it feels for him (or her) to be in his particular family. Jon says that his parents quarreled a lot, and then suddenly, when his father left, everything became very quiet. But his mother is either angry or sad, and she is also moody and does not spend much time with Jon. Other children describe their own family stories and compare similar situations. The children are asked to make three wishes that they would like their parents to know about. One includes the feeling game, where Jon and other group members describe how they feel about their family situation. Jon wants his parents to get back together, and this wish evokes similar feelings from the other children. Children also express feelings about wanting a peaceful environment again in their lifetime.

The children decided what they wanted each parent to know, and this included discussing their uncomfortable feelings about being in a new family and their feelings about a new stepparent. Children are sometimes forced to make adjustments before they are ready and they may be uncomfortable, not having dealt yet with their own emotions.

Jon and his group members discuss and attempt to understand what they can and cannot control in the family. They realize that they can control their own behaviors but not those of others. The group worker leads Jon and the others through the process of understanding how they can control their own feelings. The children are told again and again that this is not their own divorce but that of the parents.

In the final session, the children work with the tasks of termination. The children discuss their own feelings and what they have learned from the sessions. The final session is celebrated with cupcakes and potato chips to highlight their progress and the success of the process. At this point, many parents who have seen the positive effect of such help are willing to enter therapy for the sake of the child or for themselves (Corey, 1990).

In a similar manner, it is possible to set up groups for the elderly, for adolescents, and for adults. In these groups, when a person becomes a member, remember that each has special needs and group members may be suspicious of working together unless the group leader can explain the purpose of the group.

For example, when working with adolescents either in institutions or creating special-interest adolescent groups, certain rules should be followed. The rules for group workers include being able to adapt to different settings, such as mental-health clinics, community centers, public schools, residential facilities, and family-service agencies. Most of these groups are personal-growth or self-exploration groups, and the age of the group members is between 15 and 18 years. These groups work at providing self-acceptance and self-growth, developing a genuine caring for others, learning to be sensitive to the needs of parents, and so forth.

Basic ground rules must be created for such adolescent groups: All members should attend all the meetings and commit to be a member of the group for a certain amount of time. The topics for group discussion may include alcohol and drug abuse, communicating with others, defining sex roles, exploring identity issues, discussing conflict with parents, and learning how to live with and appreciate parents.

When 16-year-old Kirk enters the drug rehabilitation program, he is afraid he may not be able to cope with others or deal with his own emotions in the group. But in a pregroup interview, the caring social worker immediately has a positive effect on Kirk. At first, Kirk is resistant, but as he sees others work on their own issues, he becomes involved and decides to work more effectively as a member of the group.

There are also groups for adults and for college students, for weight loss and control, for substance abusers, for incest victims, for personal growth, and for recreation. There are AIDS crisis groups and women's support groups. These are all theme-oriented groups, and the topics reflect the life issues of different groups of people, depending on the ages and occupations of the members.

For example, in a group for AIDS patients, Ken is angry that his life is complicated by a myriad of psychological problems on top of physical complications (Spector & Conklin, 1987). Many issues surround AIDS, and the group worker must educate him- or herself about the problem. The worker must explore the stigma of AIDS with such clients and create a support group where members feel comfortable dealing with it. Group members need to be able to vent their anger. People suffering from AIDS often also stigmatize themselves and have self-destructive beliefs, but by sharing fears they can come to realize that they are not completely alone. In the group, Ken talks about his feelings of helplessness, social stigma, guilt, shame, isolation, anger, anxiety, and concerns related to clients' identity and intimacy. As he slowly becomes an active member of the group, Ken discusses some of the topics that really bother him. He discusses his grief and loss, assertiveness training, family issues, spirituality, medication, health, nutrition, and exercise. The members learn and discuss how to have safer sex and how to handle living wills, legal issues, depression, and other mental-health concerns.

In groups for the elderly, the orientation is different, as are the norms and rules. While in institutions or in day-care centers, the elderly may take medications that interfere with their ability to be fully present or aware in a particular place. Regular attendance may be a problem because someone may fall ill or may have an appointment with a doctor, and so forth. Yet the elderly need a great deal of support and encouragement and also have a great need to be listened to and understood, and such groups can be valuable forms of social work.

At first Mr. Katz, in his late 70s, does not quite understand why he is in the group, but as time passes it becomes clear to him that there is a purpose in it. Initially, he addresses all his issues to the group leader and some of the other group members do not talk at all. But as time passes they become more comfortable and find it easier to talk, to reach out. Mr. Katz listens and models himself after the group leader, whom he likes. The group leader also allows time for reminiscing and gives them opportunities to draw pictures and paint and so forth. Sometimes Mr. Katz enjoys and participates fully; on other days he is not active, but both modes seem acceptable to the group leader. Slowly the group members begin to enjoy each other's company, so they attend more regularly. They talk about their sorrows and their happiness, and feel glad they can socialize and ventilate safely in a group setting.

Groups are built to cater to the needs of a special group of people. Goals and work activities are designed to fill these needs. In some settings, group meetings are mandatory—in correctional institutions, court-ordered group counseling for couples with marital problems, and so forth. The social worker encounters many groups in dealing with clients, and needs to understand the various types and the dynamics of each.

THE INDIVIDUAL IN ORGANIZATIONS

One well-accepted definition of an organization is a system of roles graded by authority. Talcott Parsons (1960) defines organizations in the following manner:

> Organizations are social units (or human groups) deliberately constructed to seek specific goals. Corporations, armies, schools, hospitals, churches, and prisons are included; tribes, classes, ethnic groups, friendship groups, and families are excluded. Organizations are characterized by: (1) divisions of labor, power, and communication responsibilities . . . ; (2) the presence of one or more power centers which control the concerted efforts of the organization and direct them toward its goals . . . ; and (3) substitution of personnel. (p. 17)

Every person carries within his or her mind a set of images or metaphors about the nature of people. The manner in which organizations and systems in societies are fashioned and managed are directly related to these images. Morgan (1986) suggests that there are implicit metaphors and images that shape the way we think and see the world around us and how they influence us, as follows.

Organizations can be seen as *machines*. All elements of organizations—people, equipment, materials, processes—are like interrelated parts of a machine, arranged in a highly routinized pattern to be efficient and predictable. In this mechanistic way of viewing organizations, people can be seen as appendages of machines. This metaphor reaches its ultimate expression when robots replace human beings, as actually now can happen.

Viewing organizations as *organisms* is another metaphor. Like organisms, organizations can interact with their environment for growth, adaptation, and survival. Just as organisms seek the proper fit with their environment, so too must organizations.

And organizations can be viewed as *brains*. Like brains, organizations can be creative, inventive, flexible, and resilient. Organizations are information processing, communicating, and decision-making systems. As in the brain, information can be converted into thoughts and actions. Like brains, organizations can be self-regulating, self-learning systems.

Organizations can also be seen as *cultures* that have shared unique beliefs, values, symbols, routines, and rituals. Just as the cultures of societies differ, a person can experience different organizational cultures. This metaphor helps us recognize that the organization creates and imposes its culture on organizational members.

Organizations are also seen as *political systems* in their inner workings and their interactions with the environment and society. Organizations represent power, which gives us insight into the power-seeking and -wielding behavior of individuals within an organization and into the behavior of organizations themselves. Organizations are seen as arenas where people can express their desire or need for power and control. Organizations compete, collaborate, compromise, accommodate, and avoid each other in the pluralistic drive to share, hoard, accumulate, and distribute power.

Moreover, organizations are seen as *psychic prisons,* created and sustained through conscious and unconscious processes. Organizations are often patriarchal structures dominated by traditional male values. These self-contained patterns imprison people and shape the ways in which organizational members see and act while interacting with the environment.

Finally, organizations are *instruments of domination*. Historians and sociologists often imply that organizations are used by a selfish elite to impose their will on society. In this sense, organization, class, and control are closely related. There are many negative effects of organizational life on employees, such as occupational hazards and diseases such as "workaholism" and conditions related to physical and mental stress, substance abuse, and even suicides. Although this metaphor may be highlighted especially by "radical" organizational analysts, all organizational analysts can recognize intended and unintended results of organizational formation and management.

Let's see how a particular agency that offers counseling services functions as an organizational unit.

Let us walk through a human-services organization with Harry, the manager. Managers like Harry who take a systems perspective tend to see the organization more as a process than as a structure. Harry is aware that structural changes affect and are affected by changes in all other components of the organization. He is also aware that the goals and activities the organization chooses will be affected by environmental factors that are quite often beyond the organization's control.

Thus systems theory suggests that environmental factors affect both the human-services program as a whole, as well as individual clients. Using this idea, Harry has developed structures that reflect relationships between his agency and other systems as well as those within the agency. He uses the systems approach to coordinate his agency with community groups, funding sources, government agencies, other helping agencies, and educational and professional institutions. His strategies are designed to facilitate the progress of individual clients through the system. Harry found ways to link clients with various services, to follow up on clients as they move into other systems, and to communicate with referring agencies. These links are planned as carefully as communication within the program itself.

Harry has found out that the systems approach encourages human-service professionals to think of themselves as part of a network. The resulting sense of totality can serve the individual client in a coordinated way, and also helps keep their agency's programs from being buffeted by external events. It clarifies the basic program goals, and helps the agency find ways to unify efforts in reaching various goals (Lewis, Lewis, & Souflee, 1991). As a key person in a well-structured organization, Harry is well liked and respected.

Let's look at another snapshot of a person functioning in an organization system. Mariana closes the door behind her and walks quickly down the hall to meet with Dr. White, who is the president of the hospital. She is elated and confused, and also a bit in shock. She has had outstanding success in working with the hospital's employee assistance programs (EAPs) for local companies. Dr. White has just offered her the position of director of program development for the hospital. She must start work immediately. Mariana is caught by surprise, but she is ready to accept the position on the spot. It is the crowning achievement for all the work she has done for the hospital and its people. She picks up the phone to inform and talk to her family before accepting the position. Her reaction to Dr. White's offer is complete joy. The goal that she has struggled so hard to reach in this organization is finally in her grasp and in her hands. And she feels she knows exactly what changes she will—and will not—make in the programs to develop the whole hospital system.

Last but not least, organizations may appear to be impersonal, but the individuals set the tone and create the atmosphere. Harry and Mariana are not just acted upon, or contained like goldfish in a larger bowl; they are making their mark on the organization, which is strongly colored by their flair and personality.

THE INDIVIDUAL IN THE COMMUNITY

Individuals can also become members of different types of communities. Communities are social systems distinguished by the personal or affective ties among their members. They are groups of people with a common identity and bond to one another through regular interaction. Communities may occupy a specific geographic area, engage in common activities, and organize in ways that adapt to the environment as a means of meeting common needs. They include individuals, groups, families, and organizations they form to meet their needs. Space or place communities are contained in a particular geographic area. There are also non-place communities such as ethnic and racial communities, which share a common cultural heritage, history, and background. Others include the business and academic communities (Carter & Anderson, 1990). Some are natural communities, such as ethnic and racial groups; some belong to a particular sex, such as lesbian or gay communities; and some are selective communities based on class or religion.

Belonging to a community creates a feeling of togetherness and comfort. Erika, who is 17, is a member of a Puerto Rican family and lives in a community that consists chiefly of Puerto Ricans. Her family doctor lives in the same neighborhood, which is very friendly. When Erika goes to school, she speaks English in her classes but switches back to Spanish as soon as she leaves the classroom. When the family came to the mainland of the United States, she still had a strong accent and was more comfortable speaking Spanish. She still speaks Spanish at home and to her neighbors.

One day, on her way home from school, Erika is caught in an accident and hurts her leg. Her father rushes her to the local hospital in their community, where Erika receives medical attention and is then sent home. Her mother shops in the local grocery store and brings invalid Erika all her favorite foods. While she stays home, her friends in the community come to visit her and talk to her about what is happening in school, the neighborhood, and the movies, as well as the local teenage gossip. When she asks for help with her homework, someone in the community helps her.

When she gets better, her family decides that she should first visit the local church before she goes back to school. In her church (Catholic) the priest says the church members had been inquiring about Erika, because she had not been to church in four weeks. As Sunday mass is an important part of their life, Erika wants to know what she can do to make up for not coming to church. After a brief discussion with her priest, Erika decides on her own to help in the children's Sunday school classes.

Thus there is a great deal of homogeneity in the community and a network of caring. The togetherness is facilitated by shared ethnicity, language, and religion.

Let's look at another community, in a small Anglo town. The pattern is to reject outsiders who were not born in the area and to maintain strong prejudice against other ethnic groups. Families have lived in the area for a long period of time and have found their own niche. The professionals socialize exclusively with similar people, and businesspeople do the same. Church attendance is important; when someone does not attend, members check, inquire, and help out if there is a problem such as illness or death in the family. Adult daughters are encouraged to get married, and sons provide for parents and siblings, particularly sisters. Families do not encourage sons to marry. A son's marriage is tolerated if the woman is from the same community; if not, she is subtly rejected. Men are the financial providers, while women are the pillars of the community, because of the active social roles they play in "keeping the family together." This entails having up-to-date information about relatives and friends. The community follows a number of proverbial rules that include "Walk with your head held high in the community," "Never share your family secrets," "Don't wash your dirty linen in front of friends or relatives," and "Always be pleasant and give the appearance of happiness."

John, a young businessman in this community, falls in love with a woman from outside of the community; worse still, she does not even live in the same state. His family receives the news coldly. His mother is aghast—he is the family's chief provider. She keeps referring him to girls in the community: "They are good girls, and we know all about them." Finally, she tells her son's fiancée, Gayle, that she'd better watch out for John because there is a possibility that he has high cholesterol and high blood pressure, and many men in the family have died of heart problems.

A social worker who belonged to this community—for example, in the local hospital—would not have a problem developing a relationship with clients here. However, social workers who enter the community from outside would not be easily accepted, and would be given only superficial information until they were. Such a community says, in effect, "Prove yourself—we'll decide."

In the United States a number of communities exist in relative social isolation. Segregation based on social class and ethnic groups may cloister a community. Each community has a unique culture, constituted by its values, norms, and traditions; religious denomination; and lifestyles. Religious groups show differences in attitudes, child rearing, sex, and marriage. For example, some fundamentalist and Baptist communities express conservative views, condemning premarital sex, abortion, birth control information for teens, divorce, and new roles for women.

Another type of community is the rural community. Rural communities often feel the impact of the larger political and economic environment. For example, rural communities in Alaska and other Western states have been changed drastically by the boom-town phenomenon as the search for new sources of energy continues. And in the 1980s, rural farm communities suffered poverty as a result of several years of drought, falling farm prices, increased costs, and cutbacks in federal subsidies. Farmers and their families faced farm auctions, foreclosures, and corporate takeovers.

Rural communities experience many different kinds of stressors, such as malnutrition, substandard living conditions, maternal and infant mortality, unemployment and underemployment, poverty, water pollution, and increases in divorce. Other stressors include social isolation, because of the nature of the setting. Yet despite all their problems, many people share a sense of identity and relationships that represent significant coping resources for the community. The rural helping network draws on extended families, relatives, friends, and neighbors as well as social exchanges through church members, volunteer firefighters, school-based parent groups, and adult-led youth groups. Although they may lack services, rural communities survive because of their networking.

In Chapter 4, we focus on communities. The communities in which people live are their major social context. An individual's attitudes, values, needs and problems, strengths, and resources are all linked with the community life. Social workers should consider clients' cultural uniqueness and their status in society as a community in assessing problems and devising interventions.

IMPLICATIONS FOR SOCIAL-WORK PRACTICE

This chapter introduces the reader to different areas of study in this book. Individuals come from families, groups, organizations, and communities. Social workers occupy many different positions and work with and on behalf of different groups of clients dealing with different types of issues. For example, an administrator who is putting together a program for an inner city must function differently from an administrator who works in a suburb. Working with families can be a different experience for different workers, but understanding families is crucial for offering any type of help. Added to all human experience are issues of race, ethnicity, class, religion, and different family lifestyles. How social workers use sensitivity and respect depends on their knowledge and understanding of different families and their own self-awareness.

Social workers deal with individuals, groups, organizations, and communities, and the roles of various people in each system. The information in the next chapters is presented to prepare new social workers to understand systems of different sizes. Social workers assess case situations and follow through on the plans for help. The ecosystems approach helps social workers look at people from a person–environment perspective and thus to keep in mind the mutual influence and transactions among people and their environments. We discuss in detail the different environments of which people are members, highlighting the characteristics of families, groups, organizations, and communities.

Understanding different systems such as the family and organizations can help social workers process clients' needs more accurately. They can assess clients through three subprocesses: (1) understanding the client's background and history, (2) identifying problems and needs, and (3) identifying strengths and resources. The information presented in the following chapters fleshes out the knowledge you will need to make assessments this way. When organizations, communities, groups, or families are assessed, it is always important to see the individual or groups of individuals as the recipients of the services offered. The needs and issues clients present are the result of transactions between them and the individuals and groups that make up the environment. The problem analysis is based on the state or condition of a system, and the analysis continues to function between the system and the environment in which the system is embedded. Without considering the transaction between the two, any help offered would be incomplete.

SUMMARY

All people are connected to systems of different sizes. The ecosystems framework is used for this book. This framework is useful for understanding and working with different-sized systems such as the family, groups, organizations, and the community. The ecosystems perspective integrates two schools of thought—ecology and general systems theory.

Ecology is the study of complex reciprocal and adaptive transactions among organisms and their environments. Ecology is concerned with interrelationships and connections among organisms. The social worker views and defines the family, group, organization, or community systems in the broad ecological setting.

General systems theory is not a body of knowledge, but a way of thinking and analyzing that accommodates knowledge from many disciplines. The ecosystems approach orders and organizes the multiple, transacting ecological variables. The six basic concepts of general systems theory are applicable to open systems; they include boundaries, structure, hierarchy, transactionality, frame of reference, and time. Systems have their own spatial or dynamic boundaries, which may be rigid, flexible, or enmeshed.

The internal functioning of a system takes place through input, throughput, output, and feedback loops. Energy input, throughput, and output cycle through a feedback loop. When a system deviates a great deal from openness, entropy ensues, because not enough energy is available for use.

The internal state of a system is determined by the following dynamics. *Homeostasis* is the balance or equilibrium at which a system is maintained. *Differentiation* is the tendency of the system to increase in order and complexity over time. The principle of *nonsummativity* asserts that data collected from isolated parts of the system cannot simply be added up to represent the whole system. The principle of *reciprocity* asserts that elements are interrelated. *Equifinality* suggests that a system can reach the same final state from a variety of different paths and given different initial conditions. *Multifinality* says that similar conditions can lead to dissimilar outcomes. The ecosystems perspective as a conceptual framework gives the practitioner an expansive understanding of the social environment in which all human beings exist.

Four concepts used in this book, and with which social workers need to be familiar, are diversity, oppression, patriarchy, and feminism.

U.S. society is becoming more and more diverse culturally. In cross-cultural social work, social workers need to understand the relative power status of ethnic groups and their own power gestalt. Successful cross-racial/cross-ethnic communication includes recognizing one's own biases, tolerating differences, understanding feelings and behaviors, and enhancing people's ability to perceive themselves. Some examples of diversity include the elderly and the gay and lesbian populations.

Oppression is a situation in which an individual or group is deprived of some human right or dignity and is not given equal opportunity to compete for available positions. Different types of oppression and their effects on families, groups, organizations, and communities are discussed in later chapters.

Formal power—decision making and policy making—is held by adult men, and our institutions clearly reflect the patriarchy, which embodies male ideals and practices. Women are forced into a secondary role. The feminist approach offers an alternative to patriarchy, a different approach to understanding human behavior and the social environment. Feminist theory, one of the strongest currents of our times, provides for understanding all people's lives. Acting on a feminist perspective can affect the world politically, culturally, economically, and spiritually.

These different concepts of diversity, oppression, patriarchy, and feminism are viewed within the ecosystems perspective. An ecosystems perspective offers a holistic view of people and environments as a unit, and neither can be fully understood without the other.

Transactions constantly take place between an individual and the family. Families are structures with systems and subsystems, and rules and regulations of behavior. Depending on the needs and desires of the family, individuals play different roles and fit into the family system. This is where people first begin to work out their fulfillment of basic needs, sense of self, and feelings of security and insecurity.

Just as individuals learn family rules and ways of behavior in a family, so do individuals as members of groups. Groups have norms, standards, and ways of behavior. When an individual joins a group, he or she does so for many reasons. These may include self-growth and working through issues such as alcoholism and drug dependency. Groups are built to cater to the needs of a special group of people. The goals and work activities are oriented to the needs of group members.

Individuals are also members of organizations. One definition of organization is that it is a system of roles graded by authority. Organizations are social units that are deliberately constructed to seek specific goals. Organizations are characterized by division of labor, power, and communication. Morgan (1986) suggests that implicit metaphors and images shape how we think and see the world around us and how the world influences us. Organizations can be seen as machines; as organisms; as brains, because they are creative, inventive, and flexible; as cultures; as political systems; as psychic prisons; and as instruments of domination. Finally, organizations may appear impersonal, but the individuals set their tone and create their atmosphere.

Individuals are also members of communities. Communities are social systems distinguished by the personal or affective ties that their members share. Members of communities have a common identity and bond with each other through regular interaction. Communities may occupy a specific geographic area, engage in common activities, or have some form of organization that makes the community adaptive to its environment as a means of meeting common needs. Space or place communities are contained within a specific geographic area, and nonplace communities, such as ethnic and racial communities, share a common cultural heritage, history, and background. Others include business communities, academic communities, and so forth.

SUGGESTED READINGS

Ballou, M. (1995). Women and spirit: Two units in psychology. Special issue: Women's spirituality, women's lives. *Women and Therapy, 16*(2–3), 9–20.

Harvey, A. R. (1995, January). The issue of color in psychotherapy with African Americans. *Families in Society, 76*(1), 3–10.

Lenton, R. (1995, July). Power versus feminist theories of wife abuse. Special issue: Focus on the Violence Against Women Survey. *Canadian Journal of Criminology, 37*(3), 305–330.

McMahon, A., & Allen-Meares, P. (1992, November). Is social work racist? A content analysis of recent literature. *Social Work, 37*(6), 533–539.

Schlesinger, E. G., & Devore, W. (1995, March). Ethnic sensitive social work practice. The state of the art. Special issue: Social work with minority and ethnic groups. *Journal of Sociology and Social Welfare, 22*(1), 29–58.

Smuts, B. (1995). The evolutionary origins of patriarchy. *Human Nature, 6*(1), 1–32.

SUGGESTED VIDEOTAPES

American exposé: End of the road. (1993). Word Inc. Educational Video Network, 1401 19th Street, Huntsville, TX 77340. 28 minutes.

Going international, Part 3: Beyond culture shock. (1983). Griggs Productions, 5616 Geary Blvd., San Francisco, CA 94121. 29 minutes.

On equal terms: Sex equity in the workforce. (1987). Centre Communications, 1800 30th Street #207, Boulder, CO 80301. 28 minutes.

South America: Content of diversity. (1995). Word Inc. Educational Video Network, 1401 19th Street, Huntsville, TX 77340. 20 minutes.

Workforce diversity: The corporate response. (1993). General Telephone. Advantage Media Inc., 2226 Devonshire St., Chatsworth, CA 91311. 24 minutes.

Working together: Managing cultural diversity. (1990). Crisp Productions. AIMS Media, 9710 Desoto Ave., Chatsworth, CA 91311-4409. 25 minutes.

REFERENCES

Atkinson, D. R., Morten, G., & Sue, D. W. (1993). *Counseling American minorities: A cross-cultural perspective.* Dubuque, IA: William Brown.

Bertalanffy, L. von (1956). *General systems theory.* In L. von Bertalanffy (ed.), *General Systems Yearbook of the Society of General System Theory* (Vol. 1). Medical Social Work Section.

Bertalanffy, L. von (1967). *General systems theory.* In N. I. Demerath III & R. Paterson (eds.), *System, change and conflict.* New York: Free Press, p. 115.

Boulding, K. (1978). *Ecodynamics: A new history of societal evolution.* Beverly Hills, CA: Sage.

Bunch, C. (1993). *Going public with our vision.* In V. Cyrus (ed.), *Experiencing race, class and gender in the United States.* Mountain View, CA: Mayfield, pp. 388–393.

Carter, R. E., & Anderson, I. (1990). *Human behavior in the social environment: A social systems approach* (4th ed.). New York: Aldine de Gruyter.

Cherry, R. (1989). *Discrimination: Its economic impact on blacks, women and Jews.* Lexington, MA: Lexington Books.

Collins, P. H. (1990). *Black feminist thought: Knowledge, consciousness and the politics of empowerment.* Boston: Unwin Hyman.

Corey, G. (1990). *Theory of practice of group counseling* (3rd ed.). Pacific Grove, CA: Brooks/Cole.

Coulter, S., Edginton, K., & Hedges, E. E. (1993). *Feminist scholarship and the "invisible paradigms."* In V. Cyrus (ed.), *Experiencing race, class and gender in the United States.* Mountain View, CA: Mayfield, pp. 243–244.

Germain, C. B. (1976, July). Time, an ecological variable in social work practice. *Social Casework, 57*(7), 419–426.

Germain, C. B. (1978, November). Space, an ecological variable in social work practice. *Social Casework, 59,* 15–22.

Germain, C. B. (1991). *Human behavior in the social environment.* New York: Columbia University Press.

Germain, C. B., & Gitterman, A. (1996). *The life model of social work practice* (2nd. ed.). New York: Columbia University Press.

Green, J. W. (1982). *Cultural awareness in the human services.* Englewood Cliffs, NJ: Prentice Hall.

Greif, G. L., & Lynch, A. A. (1983). The eco-systems perspective. In C. H. Meyer (ed.), *Clinical social work in the eco-systems perspective.* New York: Columbia University Press, pp. 35–71.

Handler, P. (1970). *Biology and the future of man.* New York: Oxford University Press.

Janchill, Sr. M. P. (1969, February). Systems concepts in casework theory and practice. *Social Casework,* p. 77.

Lewis, J., Lewis, M., & Souflee, F. (1991). *Management of human service programs* (2nd ed). Pacific Grove, CA: Brooks/Cole.

Light, D., Keller, S., & Calhoun, C. (1989). *Sociology* (5th ed.). New York: Knopf.

Longres, J. F. (1990). *Human behavior in the social environment.* Itasca, IL: Peacock.

Lum, D. (1986). *Social work practice and people of color: A process stage approach.* Pacific Grove, CA: Brooks/Cole.

Martin, P. Y., & O'Connor, G. G. (1989). *The social environment: Open systems applications.* New York: Longman.

Morgan, G. (1986). *Images and organization.* Beverly Hills, CA: Sage.

Norman, J., & Wheeler, B. (1996). Gender-sensitive social work practice. *Journal of Social Work Education, 32*(2), 203–213.

Parsons, T. (1960). *Structure and process in modern societies* (Vol. 2). Glencoe, IL: Free Press.

Peay, P. S. (1994, July–August). What do women want? *Common Boundary,* pp. 22–34.

Pharr, S. (1988). *Homophobia: A weapon of sexism.* Inverness, CA: Chardon Press.

Phillips, K. (1990). *The politics of rich and poor.* New York: Random House.

Pillari, V. (1993). The eco-systems perspective as the conceptual framework. *Newsletter* (Ethelyn R. Strong School of Social Work, Norfolk State University), *6*(1), 8.

Pillari, V. (1991). *Scapegoating in families: Intergenerational patterns of physical and emotional abuse.* New York: Brunner/Mazel.

Pillari, V. (1994). *Family myths in family therapy.* Newark, NJ: Jason Aronson.

Pinderhughes, E. (1982). Afro-American families and the victim system. In M. McGoldrick, J. K. Pearce, & J. Giordana (eds.), *Ethnicity and family therapy.* New York: Guilford Press.

Poster, M. (1978). *Critical theory of the family.* New York: Seabury Press, p. 188.

Queralt, M. (1996). *The social environment and human behavior: A diversity perspective.* Boston, MA: Allyn and Bacon.

Rittner, B., & Kirk, A. B. (1995). Health care and public transportation use by poor and frail elderly people. *Social Work,* 40, 365–374.

Robertson, I. (1989). *Society: A brief introduction.* New York: Worth.

Ruth, S. (1990). Issues in feminism. In V. Cyrus (ed.), *Experiencing race, class and gender in the United States.* Mountain View, CA: Mayfield, pp. 148–149.

Saleeby, D. (1992). *The strengths in social work practice.* New York: Longman.

Shriver, J. M. (1995). *Human behavior in the social environment.* Boston: Allyn and Bacon.

Spector, I. C., & Conklin, R. (1987). AIDS group psychotherapy. *International Group of Psychotherapy, 37*(3), 433–439.

Swet, P. (1993). "We're not bums." In V. Cyrus (ed.), *Experiencing race, class and gender in the United States.* Mountain View, CA: Mayfield.

Westkott, M. (1979). Feminist criticism of the social sciences. *Harvard Educational Review, 49*(4), 424–430.

Yamato, G. (1993). Something about the subject makes it hard to name. In V. Cyrus (ed.), *Experiencing race, class and gender in the United States.* Mountain View, CA: Mayfield, pp. 132–134.

2

The Family

The word *family* means different things to different people. Traditionally, a family is a sanctioned, long-term, legal, and social relationship to have and bring up children and to meet the physical, emotional, and sexual needs of the married couple. However, as Meyer (1990) comments, "It is a phenomenon of our times that people have discovered so many other ways to come together as 'family.'" To understand and help these people, Meyer argues, we need a more comprehensive and more contemporary definition when we think of families. She offers the following: "Two or more people who are joined together by bonds of sharing and intimacy."

Thus the family is an extraordinary microsystem of which we are a part. It is the web into which, with few exceptions, everyone is born, lives, and dies. The few exceptions include babies who are the result of very casual sexual encounters who are abandoned in unlikely places like a trash can or a public restroom, or left in the care of hospital nurseries. Most infants end up in the legal custody of families, natural or adoptive. The families people are born or adopted into are called *families of origin*. This is the first social institution a person normally encounters. And most people eventually create a family of their own, the *family of procreation*.

Jenny is 3 months old when she begins to view human contact with anticipation and pleasantness. As she grows older, she learns to understand that she has a mother, father, and older sister. By the time Jenny is 3 years old, she is aware of certain basic family rules, such as telling an adult when she wishes to go to the bathroom when they are in the car, rather than wetting her panties. She follows the rule that when in church she should not distract people and be as quiet as possible until they leave and then they will have a good lunch with ice cream for dessert.

Thus a child in a family learns ways of behavior through rules set by parents and through examples set by parents and other family members of different ages and genders. Although environmental influences vary, the family continues to be the primary miniature society into which a person is socialized. It is a microsociety where acceptable, and sometimes unacceptable, behavior is played out.

Families result from one or more types of bonds: marriage or cohabitation, childbearing, and kinship. We have a variety of family forms today. Families are based on genetic and/or social ties, and include economic rights and responsibilities. In families, children learn about relationships and learn to be loved—or not loved. The family is the web in which the person becomes inextricably intertwined with family history.

Family ties have the force of law and tradition behind them. Membership carries a number of benefits and responsibilities. Most people spend their lives in families and take part in an active kinship system. In families we satisfy our needs for identity, relatedness, intimacy, and growth; in short, most deeply felt human qualities are lived through within families.

The family can be a great place to be. As Mead (Mead & Hayman, 1965) said, "As in our bodies we share humanity, so also through the family we have a common heritage . . . the task of humanity. This is to cherish the living, remember those who have gone before, and prepare for those who are not yet born" (p. 11). Some families, however, depending on the manner in which family life is lived out, have negative effects on their members, as we often see in the field of social work.

For example, 40-year-old Stella's mother Leslie (age 65) lives in Stella's house as her dependent, along with Stella's grown-up, unmarried sisters. At age 10, Stella was involved in a car accident in which her father and brothers were killed instantly. Stella feels guilty that she survived. Leslie continues to blame Stella for the car accident, which happened 30 years ago, saying that if Stella had not been crying, her father might not have wanted to take her out for a ride!

Stella has developed a strong feeling of guilt and believes that she is responsible for her father's and her brothers' deaths, although she knows that her father had other business to take care of that evening. A strong love–hate bond has developed between Stella and her mother, Leslie. At times she cries, "I want to hit my mother, but I can't. She is a phony and a bitch just like I am." Stella is afraid of her mother's sharp tongue, because Leslie retaliates quickly, but at the same time Stella is aware of her dependency on her mother's acceptance and approval (Pillari, 1991, p. 54).

Learning to live with a person you do not love or respect, and learning to live with a person you *know* does not love or respect you, as Stella lives with her mother, is like learning *not* to live. It means learning to talk in frightened whispers, to deny what you feel, to hate without showing it, to weep without tears, and to hide that the shame you are living in is your family reality (Pillari, 1991).

FAMILIES AS SYSTEMS

Families can have such profound effects on family members because they are part of a family system. Why is the family called a system? Families are systems because the different members of the family are linked. Hartman (1981) describes it as a "social service agency in meeting the social, educational and health care needs" of its members. A family might also be described, paraphrasing Bertalanffy (1934), as a dynamic order of *people* (along with their intellectual, emotional, and behavioral processes) standing in mutual interaction.

The family is made up of *subsystems*—pieces of a larger system and at the same time complete in themselves. Let us look at a family that consists of a father, a mother, three children, and a grandmother. Each family member is a subsystem with his or her own needs and goals, contributing to the family and drawing on family resources. Family members are related to each other, and two or more can also form a subsystem. For instance, all the children may form a sibling subsystem, where they fulfill needs for peer relationships and communication through conversation and playing games together. A sibling subsystem may involve learning and following family rules and learning to grow in a family. The father and mother may form a parental subsystem, functioning in terms of procreation, adult companionship, and providing for the family. The son or the daughters and the father or the mother could also form a parent–child/children subsystem. Thus a number of subsystems can be part of the family system. Different subsystems contribute to the outlook of the whole family system.

Because the family is a system, the social-work practitioner must understand the individuals in relation to what goes on in the family. It is in this family setting that children learn ways of behavior and also develop their own self-esteem, depending on how they give and take in such situations. Families also have implicit and explicit rules that govern roles, power, and authority. The family provides information about different forms of communication, ways of negotiating, and also ways of solving problems.

The family is an evolving system, and expands and contracts depending on the needs, roles, and responsibilities of different family members. It evolves from a small unit of one or two adults or children and constantly changes based on family lifestyle, number of children, roles, and rules. As noted, it resembles a miniature society with more or less freedom to be what the person wishes to be, depending on how the family system has evolved. Dependency and interdependency, and satisfaction of needs and desires, also characterize the family as a social institution.

In the family social institution, certain ways of behaving are accepted. As members of patriarchal society, for example, family members take on gendered roles and power relationships. Social workers, however, need to avoid stereotyped thinking, which can block accurate, individualized assessment. In moving toward nonsexist ways of working with families, the social worker needs to consider gender equality and social oppression of women. Becoming aware of these factors can help practitioners value all family forms and develop sensitivity to the cultural differences. Globally and nationally, raising everyone's consciousness about the rights of women and men in families would be a good start toward solving social ills. Sexist social mores and moral attitudes affect the behavior of both men and women. It is important to encourage social workers to think, feel, and function in nonsexist terms and to strive for objectivity in working with families. Depending on their own upbringing, life experiences, and role in society, people will favor traditionalism or change. We seek, in this chapter, to present materials from a perspective that is useful in viewing family roles and to encourage functioning with sensitivity and empathy for sexual/social roles.

The family is a social institution because it brings values and authority to bear on collective behavior. Values imply that certain kinds of behaviors are preferred, and authority uses sanctions and other forms of control when someone fails to conform (Longres, 1990). Social institutions are governed by rules and laws and ways of behavior that are traditional in society. The intertwining of broad societal values and family life affects the formation of families and the assumption of family roles. As the broader society has changed, family lifestyles have also changed.

Recent changes in family living trends have also affected the functions filled by families and the development of family members. Cherlin (1988) identifies a number of such trends:

A larger number of men and women today live together before getting married.

Men and women are getting married later in life.

More married couples are having fewer children, and in some situations, none.

The number of unmarried women with children has increased.

More wives and mothers with very young children are employed outside the home.

More marriages end in divorce.

Single-parent families have increased.

Remarriage among adults is now more likely than widowhood to follow divorce.

Remarriage rates have declined, especially for women.

All these factors indicate that the family is moving away from the traditional type of marriage and family that consisted of two parents—a husband and wife—and children. Changes in society influence the family in a number of different ways. It is safe to say that the family as a social institution is here to stay, although like other human systems it is constantly changing.

Certain families come into special focus for social-work practitioners, because the changes that affect all families hit these families hardest. Because of the constant difficulties that assault poor families, recent federal legislation as well as the media have cast a spotlight on programs designed to support such families so that they can remain together safely. These services are delivered under a variety of program titles —family-based services, family-preservation services, and intensive family-preservation services. These programs share a number of features such as emphasizing family strengths and resources, providing intensive intervention focusing on the whole family, and delivering a variety of services to support family functioning (Berry, 1994).

FUNCTIONS OF THE FAMILY

The family has always performed a number of functions, from providing food, clothing, and shelter, to procreation, education, socialization, recreation, and production of goods and services. From time to time a variety of family functions have been taken over by the government or other organizations. However, some of these functions are now being reclaimed by families. For instance, earlier in this century the birthing process was taken over by the formal health care system in our culture, but recently more provision has been made for rooming-in facilities, at-home childbirths, and the participation of the father and the other children. Also, the terminally ill are beginning to be treated more humanely. They are allowed to go home or enter a hospice setting before death. And although home schooling was once not allowed, it is becoming more common. Parents are tutoring their children at home either because the school is located far away, the classrooms are too crowded and the student does not get what he or she needs at school, or the parents have a different philosophy of education from the school. One client and her friend started home tutoring because the local school was dangerous, young children being hurt or threatened with guns and knives in school. The family is a source of basic education and a significant factor in influencing its members, for good or bad. Children learn from parents in countless ways. Parents in turn also learn from children; through these transactions, both grow and change.

The functions of the contemporary American family can be divided into (1) manifest or overt, concrete functions; and (2) latent or subtle (but important) functions.

Procreation and Socialization

The *manifest functions* in the family relate to system maintenance. The family system is maintained by procreating, socializing, and providing food, clothing, shelter, and medical care. A good family offers a safe and healthy home environment, and an emotional climate in which the emotional and developmental needs of all its members—men, women, and children—are met.

The family is the place where children are born and reared. In contemporary society, day-care centers and schools also help socialize the child.

Emily was born in a small middle-class family to an unmarried teenager. When Emily was hardly a week old, her mother gave her up for adoption. Her adoptive parents were upper-middle-class professionals. Although they cared intensely for their Emily, she spent much time outside the home. By the time she was 2 years of age, she was being cared for in day-care centers and with baby-sitters for long hours. By the time she was 3, she knew what would make her baby-sitter angry and how to behave while around her. One day Emily is screaming and running in the playroom, talking and yelling at her toys, while the baby-sitter is on the phone. Emily does not heed the baby-sitter's requests to be quiet. She is shocked when the baby-sitter starts to beat her, at first mildly and then violently. She warns Emily that if she tells her parents, she will be punished more severely the next time. Emily is too scared to complain to her parents. Her fear takes the form of painful stomachaches when the baby-sitter comes. Emily also starts to have nightmares and cries in her sleep. Her parents attempt to console her without knowing the reason for her fears. Emily, who is usually outgoing, starts to cry when she sees strangers, and becomes less and less sociable and more withdrawn. Not knowing or understanding Emily's background, her parents send their daughter for counseling, thinking that her withdrawal might have something to do with her heredity. In this case, however, Emily's development is being affected by the abuse suffered from her baby-sitter.

The *latent functions* of the family include the socialization of its members by perpetuating the norms and values of the larger society. This can include positive values such as honesty, caring, and achievement as well as negative values such as ethnocentrism, racism, and sexism.

Racism is behavior learned from families and in many school settings. Historically, Goodman (1964) indicates that racism develops in three stages. Children first learn to distinguish between skin colors, and negative feelings are attached to color differences. Then a racial orientation develops. In the final stage, full-fledged positive or negative attitudes develop.

Sexism is also an outgrowth of family upbringing. Scanzoni (1982) notes that from very early in life boys are treated differently from girls at home. Boys are generally socialized to be aggressive and active, while girls are expected to be passive and well-behaved. Traditionally, parents treat boys and girls differently from the time they are born. At a young age, boys learn that crying is "sissy," and boys do not cry. Girls are not encouraged to fight back or to be aggressive. Boys can be punished physically, often by fathers, whereas girls are disciplined by withdrawal of love and psychological punishments. For example, Johnny falls down, scrapes his knee, and begins to cry. His father pats him on the head and comments that he should not cry because "it's sissy." When his daughter Joan cries, however, he kisses and consoles her. Thus as early as 5 years of age, boys and girls have been socialized into gender roles.

Gender-role expectations are somewhat dependent on the culture of the family and the environment. Andy's single-parent mother, a young, naive professional, has decided to bring up her son (1) to learn to view sex differences positively and (2) to become a nurturing and caring person. To help him understand that all people are created equal, she occasionally dresses him in pink and takes him to her workplace to show him where and how she works. However, a week after he is sent to an upper-middle-class kindergarten, Andy tells his mother that he will not wear pink, because he is told in school that it is a "girl's color." The mother sees that her son has to deal with the outside world, and thereafter takes a more realistic attitude to child rearing.

Clearly, socialization takes place not only in the home setting but also in schools and day-care centers and other places to which the child is exposed.

Production and Consumption

Production and consumption are functions carried out by the family, as well as by society, to satisfy the needs of the family members. Today, in most families, the wife/mother (usually the chief caretaker) continues to be the chief producer, in terms of taking care of children, cooking, cleaning, and so forth. Because material goods are available in stores and home deliveries are declining, the caretaker is also the shopper and the provider of transportation. She provides most services (not paid) for the rest of the family. The *productive* functions in the family are related to transportation, gas, water, electricity, and other such utilities (Cowan, 1983).

Another essential productive function in the family is gainful employment outside the family. To a large degree economic productivity by family members becomes the scale by which their role and status in society is determined.

For example, Janet is the mother of four sons. She has a part-time job where she works as a salesperson. The rest of her day is spent in taking her children, who vary in age from 8 to 14, to ball games and all kinds of after-school practices, including guitar lessons, soccer, and debate activities. Her husband works full-time and thinks that his wife has a lot of time at home, until one day when he is off work, and Janet is sick. He takes over her responsibilities that day and begins to understand that being a housewife is as taxing as his job, except her job as a mother and a wife is unpaid—and would almost be impossible to pay in terms of dollars and cents.

The family is also a *consumption* unit. There is a direct relationship between production and consumption. The larger society produces, and the family—the smaller social unit—consumes. Goods include food, housing, furniture, household gadgets, clothes, and cars. Services include medical and school or training services, repairs, and a variety of helping services such as daycare. Consumption also takes the form of social and cultural activities, such as going to theaters, concerts, and sports (Cowan, 1983). Social activities intertwined with cultural activities include camping; family get-togethers; and family, community, state, and national celebrations. Thus the family plays a very important role as a consumer in the economy of a society.

The Family as an Emotional System

The family also performs a number of *affective functions* for members. Generally, the family is the place where members can relax, rest, and express genuine feelings, unless the family is dysfunctional and cannot contribute to the well-being of its members. If the outside world is harsh, the family is the shelter for emotional support and caring among its members. Because of this shelter, family members behave differently with each other than they do with others. Sociologist Talcott Parsons (1964) noted that there is a difference between a public world, which is an impersonal, economic work world, and the private, personal family world, in which feelings and relationships are paramount. The family is expected to offer moral support to its members and to create an emotional climate conducive to growth and development. However, although the family may be idealized as a haven from abuse and impersonal, uncaring behaviors of the outside world, families are not always ideal, as seen in the following example from *Scapegoating in Families* (Pillari, 1991):

> While married to Tom, whom she claimed she did not love, Andrea gave birth to Nick. However, Nick was not her husband's child but the child of her lover, Richard, with whom she had been involved briefly; and she claimed she did not really love Richard either. Later she divorced Tom and married Peter. Neither Peter nor Nick knew that Nick's father was not her first husband, Tom; Andrea kept this information to herself.
>
> Andrea and Peter developed grave marital problems, and Nick, intensely disliked by his mother, was scapegoated in this situation. Nick visited Richard (his real father) once a year, but he did not know that this man was his "real dad." Nick assumed that he was visiting an uncle, a fabrication kept up by his mother. When Nick was 13, the scapegoating took a turn for the worse: Andrea's second marriage was crumbling. Nick heard the silent message "Rescue us" and accordingly started to act out by getting into trouble at school and at home.
>
> Amid all this commotion and pain in the family, 10-year-old Donna, the child of Peter and Andrea, was viewed as the "good child." She did very well in her role, as did her older, 13-year-old scapegoated brother, Nick, who was the "bad child." Donna had no friends and never showed any affect during the family therapy sessions, yet the parents continuously claimed that she was a "wonderful child." Donna was the exalted one and the family's darling, and she always had her way. She instructed herself to dissolve into tears or to take the disposition of a martyr, whichever action suited the situation. This behavior kept her out of trouble with her parents. Nick was the one who had to be "fixed," and even though he was the one who had been at a disadvantage all his life, he continued to be the recipient of the family anger and pain. (pp. 14–15)

Thus this family had two sets of rules, one for Nick and the other for his sister. Growing up in families can be painful, and this was true for Nick. His emotional experience in his family was one of deprivation and emotional abuse.

THE FAMILY AS A SYSTEM OF CHANGING ROLES

As we are all aware from our experiences, families are constantly changing. Children are born, grow up, and move out. For some, growing up is smooth sailing; for others, the journey is quite turbulent. Parents may or may not grow old together. Families may or may not have adequate environment supports and financial resources at different points. Each of these circumstances makes different demands on the family and its members, and requires different types of role performance to fulfill family functions.

That the family is a *system of roles* becomes clearer when we look at the life cycle of families. This theoretical formulation for understanding families is based on the historical work of Duvall and Hill (1948); Hill and Rogers (1964), who refined it; and Carter and McGoldrick (1980). Although some argue that the sequential way of viewing families does not deal with all life events, it is still the best way of understanding growth and development and life issues and also nondevelopmental crisis. Issues that are more common to development in contemporary families such as unmarried teen parenthood, births to middle-aged first-time mothers, and so on are discussed here as issues in development that can occur at any point in a person's life.

With divorce, a nondevelopmental feature of contemporary family life can alter the family situation at any point; then the concept "family" takes on a new meaning. Whether single parenthood becomes a permanent lifestyle or new family members are added, such as a stepparent (with or without children), the picture of the family changes. Similarly, accidents, terminal illness of a family member, and the birth of a mentally or physically challenged (disabled) child create new and different problems for the family. The family must develop coping and adapting skills to deal with these issues, which vary depending on the developmental stages of the family members.

A marriage can occur at different points in a person's life, and chronological age may have very little significance to the tasks that a person faces in marriage. For example, a girl who marries as a teenager takes on the burdens of parent and homemaker earlier in her life than a woman who marries in her 30s. Although there is a big difference in age, the tasks each faces may be similar. The older person may be more mature and function well as a parent, or more set in her ways and less able to adapt to change. For example, 18-year-old Meena, an Asian, has an arranged marriage and became the mother of two children in her late teens, whereas 18-year-old Phyllis, from the Midwest, is a high school graduate and has not experienced her first serious romance. However, Phyllis is eager to enter the world of college and perceives the world as being open to her and all her needs. There is a sense of beginning for her, whereas Meena feels more settled in her role as wife and mother and participates constructively and contentedly in those roles.

For study purposes and for understanding the life cycle of the family, we will present the developmental tasks of both traditional and alternative families. Social workers deal with the reality that family structures and dynamics serve both adaptive and survival purposes. Changes may be orderly, gradual, and continuous, or they may be sudden, disruptive, and discontinuous.

The Beginning Family

Before a couple marries, if the marriage is to be successful, they must understand each other's cultural background. Donald and Jessie have dated for a period of two years, have attended couple communication classes, and went into counseling to understand all the implications of getting married. When they decide to wed, they feel they have made the right choice and have good parental support. They have had some preliminary discussions on finances and division of work in the house. Unlike couples who marry hastily and without thinking through issues, this couple has an excellent chance of making the marriage work, because they enter it as responsible adults.

However, people frequently marry for other reasons, too. A woman who becomes pregnant by her boyfriend may wish to marry him; a person may marry for the initial excitement of it; a person may marry to get away from home; and so forth. Marriage also happens because a person is coerced into it, as in Nina's case.

Nina comments, "I did not want to marry my husband. He drank a lot and had a vicious temper, but I was too afraid to say no because I thought he would come after me and kill me. . . . That's why I am with you, I am still afraid of him, although he can be nice. At times he hurts me and the children badly." Thus a family can be built on various foundations. In some cases, the power of differences in gender can be played out, even before marriage, in the form of domination, authority, and submission.

And marriage can turn sour, too. Ricky is a professor who married his former student, Rita, after she obtained her master's degree. He knew her for eight years as his friend's wife before he married her. He says that her former marriage turned sour and she cried on his shoulder while breaking away from her former husband. However, as soon as Ricky married Rita he began to abuse her, ridiculing her and the problems of her earlier marriage she had discussed with him. He has used every situation and incident she shared with him as ammunition to put her down and make her submissive. Meanwhile he has taken complete control of the money and developed his power over her.

In a two-parent family, the first stage of the family life cycle begins with marriage and continues until the first child is born. This involves the couple functioning as a dyad, a couple system. This stage also involves *boundary negotiation* between the two individuals and between the couple and the extended family. A boundary can be defined as rules and regulations that symbolically separate the system from the rest of its environment. In other words, boundaries are the family system's ways of presenting *permeability* or *nonpermeability* to each other and the outside world. Boundaries are highly permeable when thoughts and ideas are exchanged between people, and not nearly as permeable when people do not exchange ideas. This notion is equivalent to Germain's (1991) concept of the interface; she talks about the family and the environment engaging in reciprocal exchanges and also "interpenetrating" each other (Gordon, 1969). From a family therapist's perspective, Minuchin (1974) discusses the complex process of negotiation on three fronts. First is the couple subsystem, where the husband and wife develop a series of mutually satisfying patterns of communication. That is, the spouses must develop a way of seeing themselves together as a couple coming from two different families but with their own space and identity as a unit. To be successful, they must separate themselves to some degree from the family of origin and other family systems. Second, they negotiate new boundaries and modify their relationships to accommodate the new marriage relationship. They renegotiate relationships with siblings, in-laws, and divorced spouses and separate from the families of origin, that is, parents and other family systems, which might involve ex-boyfriends or ex-girlfriends. To suit this new dyad, a new couple also must organize and regulate work as well as leisure activities and commitments.

Dick and Trish have just married. He is an only son, and his sister resents his marriage. She makes unkind comments to her new sister-in-law, and Dick does not know how to handle the situation. When the marriage starts to show wear and tear within two months, he tells his wife that he will distance himself from his sister to help his marriage survive. Dick, who had worked 12 to 14 hours a day, begins to cut down in order to spend more time with his wife. Both of them work at involving each other in common and shared leisure activities.

Negotiation between members of couples also involves mundane issues like whether the toilet seat be left up or down, and how to share the cooking and cleaning. Also during this first period, the couple's upbringing and environment affect communication. Communication styles, power issues, and relationship structures become more firmly established now. Patterns of communication arise in the early relationship between the couple, and may become established even before they are married. In some new marriages, there may be unresolved issues that the couple has not worked through or negotiated before they begin to think about having children. If boundary negotiations have not taken place, such a new marriage may not easily resolve issues of power and control.

For instance, Johnny and Jill were married for about a year and lived with Johnny's mother before they moved into a new apartment. Jill's mother-in-law visits them every day and is very critical of the daughter-in-law's ability to decorate, cook, and keep the house "clean." This makes Jill angry, but Johnny does not interfere. Instead he turns his anger on Jill for her outbursts. Jill has become progressively more resentful of her mother-in-law and angry with her husband for overlooking her needs and desires in her own home. Jill has a demanding, high-status job, and when she is out of the house Johnny's mother comes in to rearrange the home to make it "nice" for her son. Without working through this issue of renegotiating boundaries, Jill becomes pregnant, hoping this will ease the tense family situation. The unmet challenges lead to more problems and eventually to a bitter divorce. In a marriage, the need to create boundaries with each other and with people outside the marriage cannot be overlooked or minimized.

The Infant Family

The infant family begins for an average married couple with the birth of the first child and continues while the child is at home and until he or she becomes a preschooler ready to go to school. The birth of a child is a momentous turning point in the life of the couple. Parenthood means having almost everything in the family revolve around the care of the new baby, including feeding, diaper changing, nurturing, and comforting. It means late-night feedings, soothing the child when it cries or does not sleep at night, and caring for each other, the child, and the extended family. New factors in the relationship include how responsibilities and caring are shared in the family. How will the family implement personal and family goals? The three-member family system may create some problems: The mother may spend more time with the child and exclude the father, or the father may spend more "free time" outside the home and arouse resentment in the mother. Sometimes, of course, (still rarely) the father may be the primary caretaker and the mother may be the chief wage earner outside the home.

In the expanded family system, power sharing becomes a major concern. Becoming parents entails additional negotiations as family members and redefining power and functions to meet the new demands. Minuchin (1974) notes that new subsystems come into play—a mother–child dyad and a father–child dyad—changing the relationship to the outside world as well. Again the couple renegotiates with the extended family in terms of boundaries and relationships with grandparents, aunts, and uncles.

Another aspect of development is that both parents may work. Young babies are dropped off at day-care centers, and the parents often must work through feelings of separation, loss, and guilt. The type of facilities available and the kind of care offered are important. According to recent U.S. Department of Labor statistics, only 25% of infants and toddlers are cared for by their parents; 27% are with other relatives, 7% are at home with a sitter, 26% are in day-care homes (usually run by a woman who takes a few children into her own home for payment), and 16% are in large day-care centers (Clarke-Stewart, 1993).

Do infants and children who attend day-care centers suffer in any way compared to the children who stay at home with a parent? Research suggests they are not necessarily damaged by the experience (Clarke-Stewart, 1993; Scott & Eisenberg, 1993). For instance, infants who attended high-quality day-care centers were no less securely attached to their mothers than infants who were raised at home. Thus quality day-care becomes an important necessity for the well-being of children. Yet despite a growing percentage of women in the workforce, putting infants in day care is still controversial. Also, people need good-quality *affordable* child care. Leaving children with a qualified (certified) day-care person in the child's home is an attractive alternative but not readily available, especially for low-income families. And many poor people, especially in rural areas where there are no day-care centers, find relatives, baby-sitters, and extended neighborhood networks to take care of children. If any trained family day-care providers or child care centers are available in the rural areas, geographical access (transportation) as well as cost may make them prohibitive.

Finding an acceptable baby-sitter for a child is difficult. Most parents feel conflict about leaving the child in the home and care of another person, and experience a great deal of anguish and guilt in doing so. Separation issues may have to be handled by parents and the child even while the child is very young.

Sheila, who had envisioned staying home with her first baby, found that she had to go back to work immediately (after a month) because the bills soared sky high. Leaving the baby with a sitter made her uneasy and suspicious. She would suddenly leave her desk to call the baby-sitter to check on her, and made at least three sudden visits a week to "catch" the baby-sitter not being nice to the baby. Sheila's behavior chiefly reflected her own sense of inadequacy and guilt in leaving her newborn baby with a sitter, as she struggled with her own pain of separation from the child. Quality child care continues to be a problem for many working parents at different economic levels. Parents struggle to find the best care within their budgets where they can feel sure that their child is well taken care of.

The Preschool Family

The preschool family is the family in which the oldest child is 3 to 5 years of age. For quite a few families, this is the first separation from the chief caretaker and is an adjustment period for both parent and child. At this stage the parents face a number of parenting challenges. Often siblings also need care. Parents must work hard to provide for the children, to simultaneously have time as a couple, and to fulfill extended-family obligations, which may include occasionally caring for an aged or ill parent. A child of this age does a great deal of questioning and is very curious about sexuality. Each parent's responses to children at this stage of development reflects his or her own upbringing. Socialization begins to take place in two ways—that is, the parents socialize the child, and in turn the child quite effectively "socializes the parents." During this period, everyone grows up a little bit (Okun & Rapaport, 1980).

With additional children, sibling relationships become important. Minuchin (1974, p. 59) notes that the sibling subsystem becomes "the first social laboratory in which children can experiment with peer relationships." Children generally experience their first social contact with siblings and form their first miniature society. This process continues as children grow and become adolescents. Meanwhile, structural change and boundary negotiation continue to take place among siblings and parents. Younger siblings now treated as "babies" are looked on differently as they grow older. Siblings play, take sides, and learn about rules and regulations in their relationships with each other. When relationships are created between siblings, the process of creating the relationship depends on what the rules and regulations are in the family and how power is distributed among parents and children. Minuchin calls attention to *generic* and *idiosyncratic* constraints. Generic constraints are rules of family organization that pertain to power structure; idiosyncratic constraints are the unique individual expectations and intentions of each family member. Role patterns are either explicitly or implicitly formed. These role patterns are carried along by children and the parents. Long after children leave the parents, they often continue to play these roles.

For example, Cynthia is the oldest child in the family, and the parents use her appropriately to "mind the other children" when they are not home. However, Cynthia's powers are limited to disciplining her younger siblings by sending them to their rooms, and she cannot punish them physically. When the parents come back home, they take over their responsibilities and Cynthia is immediately placed back in her role as a child in relationship with her siblings. Thus Cynthia's role is formed both explicitly and implicitly in her family, and this process reflects the pattern of power and responsibility in the family. An example is that of a mother who becomes the chief person in touch with the adult children. The father's expression of caring may not be as verbal or direct, but this does not mean that it does not exist. The father may continue to be the chief wage earner, and often carries a great degree of power. He may do things such as play cards every Sunday with the "boys" or go fishing and so forth. The development of such patterns is based on a specific family's matrix of values, expectations, and intentions.

The School-Age Family

The school-age family stage begins when the first child enters school full time and ends when the last child is still in school but has reached puberty. During this period, there is a great deal of system adjustment.

When the last child is no longer at home, the mother who has been a full-time housewife has time on her hands. Often such women, who are in the minority, decide to take on new jobs, go back to school, or go back to an old job that they once enjoyed doing. Or they may work because they need the money. This may stress children, because a caretaker who was habitually home to receive the children is no longer there. Often arrangements must be made to send the children to a baby-sitter or to a friend's home until parents can get home. The manner in which this is resolved depends on how parents communicate and negotiate with each other. This is a period of adjustment for both the mother and the father. Problems and conflicts that have not been resolved between the couple while children are growing up create barriers and play an important part in the adults' ability to renegotiate. When renegotiation is done amicably, rich dividends can be reaped from sharing financial, social, and parenting responsibilities. Such sharing helps cement the relationships among the parents and the children.

During the school-age years, parents must provide active support to their children and to the teachers, if the children are to achieve their full potential in school. Some special programs have been developed for children most likely to be seen in social-welfare settings. In 1965, the quality preschool education program called Head Start began admitting children at 3 and 4 years of age. This two-year program helps children do better even later, in high school, than nonparticipating children (Germain, 1991). When parents become involved, the gains children make continue throughout the schooling of the child.

The Adolescent Family

Before the first child leaves home, the family system is at its largest. Regardless of how old the parents are, the adolescent now brings in another world view. The adolescent's interests may vary from college to vocational training school. Sexuality and steady intimate relationships, and sometimes, the use of drugs and alcohol, may play a part in a young person's life, depending on family training and the community environment. The adolescent begins to challenge the parents' rules and standards around privacy, friends, dating, time curfews and other matters. Parents struggle to maintain a balance between open communication and privacy, and between firmness and flexibility in negotiating acceptable behavior. Whether parents are in their 30s or older, adolescence is a time for testing limits. Adolescents are no longer children, but they are not yet adults. Their emerging sexuality may bring unresolved sexual issues of the parents to the fore. In some cases, envy complicates relations between parents and children of the same gender.

Shelly is 16 and in therapy along with her parents. The first session is a surprise for the social worker. Mother and daughter both look very young and dress alike. In short denim skirts and white blouses, with flowing blonde hair and similar gestures, they could be mistaken for sisters. The daughter indicates many problems with her mother, including the fact that the mother spends an inordinate amount of time socializing and, in this case, competing with her daughter for boyfriends. The daughter has tried to run away from home but was caught. The father, who is also in the session, is distant, and the mother and daughter either ignore everything he says or respond sarcastically. The mother apparently does not love her husband (and vice versa) and seems to be more invested in her daughter. The daughter and mother fight with each other about clothes, makeup, and the daughter's boyfriend, whom the mother seems to like a little too much. Sexuality, youth, and unmet needs seem foremost in the mother's mind, as in the daughter's. Adolescence in the daughter has brought forth repressed feelings and unresolved issues of the mother to the forefront and escalated the problems of growing up for both. In this family, unlike others, the generation gap is too narrow rather than too wide. The mother is using her daughter's own adolescence to work through some of her own issues.

One of the biggest problems most adolescents face is being able to separate and yet be emotionally connected to the family. There is a great deal of ambivalence on both sides, and conflicts are created both in letting go and holding on. Parents want their children to be grown up and mature, but they fear the loss they must eventually suffer. In a similar manner, children fear and love their independence. They wish to be accepted as nearly adult, but fear the responsibilities of adulthood.

The Launching Family

The launching stage is the time for the family to let go of their young adult children. The child differentiates from the parents, and parents and children decide it is time to "let go" of each other. The manner in which the young adult child who leaves home copes with the outside world is based on what he or she learned at home, both good and bad.

Every time Linda and Tony fought it was a signal for their 5-year-old son, Randy, to act up and draw attention to himself. As an adolescent, 16-year-old Randy successfully gets himself into all kinds of trouble in school, resulting in his inability to leave home. His parents, who have a history of conflicts, are unhappy with Randy and his behaviors but are also pleased to keep him at home as he is easily triangulated (made to be the third person in conflicts) between them and thus maintains the unhealthy family dynamics. A young person who has grown up fairly well adjusted in a family does not internalize the problems of the family but tries to be objective and helpful whenever possible.

During this period in the life cycle, couples face the prospect of being alone with each other for the first time in twenty to twenty-five years. The older couple again renegotiates roles, and the wife who is working may choose a new career or resume an old one and find other activities. There is a renewal of the couple relationship, and the wife or husband may develop a new interest in sex. At times a couple who stayed together for the sake of children begins to move away from each other. They may maintain their psychological distance, or may divorce. Or they may live together because it is convenient; each one does her or his own thing. Some women lose interest in sex, due to misinformation about sexuality after menopause, and some men may report a decreased interest in sexuality because they have invested energy in vocational and avocational pursuits. Help is available for such problems.

The Postparental Family

For a long time, the stage when all the children left home was called the *empty nest* stage. The implication was that the children had left home, and now the parents were lonely and lost without the children while they lived out the remainder of their lives. It was assumed that there was also a great degree of emptiness and dissatisfaction in the relationship with each other. However, it has become evident (Houseknecht & Macke, 1981) that this is not true. Happily married couples are in fact happier still with the leisure time and discretionary money available to spend on themselves. Houseknecht and Macke conclude that greater cohesiveness and affection characterize marriage after the children leave home, especially in satisfactory marriages. The couple are free from financial burdens, and this gain outweighs the loss of the parenting function (Okun & Rapaport, 1980). During this period, the older couple may take on the role of grandparenting and renegotiate boundaries with their children as they enter the new family system of their children's homes. Neugarten and Weinstein (1964) identified four major roles of grandparenting: (1) Some formal grandparents leave parenting to the children and do not see the grandchildren frequently. (2) Some grandparents are fun seekers and have a good time with their grandchildren. (3) Others play surrogate parents and take care of the children. (4) Finally, some see children only as a necessity during festive times such as Christmas and Thanksgiving. They exchange gifts, but have little other contact.

The Aging Family

The aging family stage commences when retirement begins for one or both partners, bringing a major role change in their marriage. At this point, if both partners are alive they must adjust to being together more often. They must also rely on and adjust to income limited by savings, pensions, the family, or the government. Beside adjusting to changes in status, they may also need to adjust themselves to inevitable health problems and develop a clearer understanding of the medical benefits to which they are entitled. Many aging people have children and grandchildren, but often retirement entails some loneliness and the feeling of not being useful in society. People, especially men, who do not have any hobbies or interests apart from family and work, may find this period difficult. Men who have worked all their lives often feel lost and may develop major emotional and economic problems that challenge the relationship. Becoming old is ironic, comments Froma Walsh: "We dread growing old almost as much as we dread not living long enough to reach old age" (Walsh, 1980, p. 197).

Another area of interest for aging parents is their grandchildren. To manage the effects of increasing divorce, grandparents have fought for and received grandparent visitation rights for children living with former daughters-in-law or sons-in-law. This can be a source of great comfort for the child and also help him or her deal with the trauma of the divorce. Other grandparents are physically and emotionally overburdened by the care of their grandchildren.

According to the Profiles of Older Americans survey (AARP, 1992), 74% of men over age 65 who were studied lived with their spouses, whereas only 40% of their female counterparts lived with their spouses. About 44% of women lived alone or with nonrelatives, compared to 18% of the men. Only 41% of the women were married, but 77% of the men were. Almost 50% of the women were widowed, but only 15% of the men were.

Depending on the families' values, the elderly may or may not receive help from adult children's families. In some cases they may become disabled, and they may have to move to a child's home. An adult child may become the most important person in the older person's life. Thus roles may be reversed between elderly parents and their adult children, the parents becoming increasingly dependent.

Another factor that affects the elderly couple is the loss of a spouse. Women are four times more likely to become widows, and at an earlier age than men, and they also live longer than men. The sense of loss women feel contributes to their disorientation and loneliness. Studies show that many widows experience marked fluctuations in financial resources for years after widowhood (Zick & Smith, 1991; Bound, Duncan, Laren, & Olenick, 1991). Death and suicide rates also increase among both men and women. This is especially true for men; often the woman keeps in touch with family and social community, especially after retirement. The first difficult task is to loosen bonds, accept the fact that the spouse is dead, and change shared experiences into memories. Feelings of loss and grief should be expressed overtly. Second, within a year attention turns to the demands of everyday functioning, such as self-support and household management. This adjustment is difficult, because it is hard to be alone. Within a couple of years the person moves toward the third phase, which emphasizes new activities and interest in others.

Remarriage is an option for the elderly. However, many remain unmarried and identify themselves as widows or widowers. Most widowers remarry, whereas the vast majority of widows live alone (U.S. Bureau of the Census, 1992b). In recent years, a small number of elderly people have lived together without marriage. Cohabitation has fewer economic and legal constraints, although a certain degree of social stigma attaches to this lifestyle. A crucial factor in the success of a remarriage is the relationship with adult children and their approval. Concerns about inheritance and disloyalty to the deceased parent may affect the decision to remarry, and it is best to work these issues through before a marriage.

NONDEVELOPMENTAL CRISES

We have looked at developmental stages from the viewpoint of a two-parent family. However, a number of *nondevelopmental crises* can upset family equilibrium at any point in the family life cycle. Such events may begin with one family member and quickly impact the emotions and transactions of the rest of the family.

Divorce

Divorce can happen at any time, although it generally occurs within the first five years (the second largest number of divorces occur in middle age). Divorce takes its toll on all family members, including spouses, children, and extended family. For the couple, this period is characterized by ambivalence and shifting moods of guilt, anger, sadness, depression, and fear. When the divorce takes place, the couple must negotiate emotional and physical separations to establish a favorable climate for legal and other types of negotiation. Often divorce takes its toll of children as well, as they become torn between conflicting loyalties. As a result some act out in classroom situations or do poorly in school. Absence of fathers—which is more common than absence of mothers—harms children, especially sons. Lack of child support creates not only financial strain but also bitterness in both custodial parent and children, which can injure their relationship with the noncustodial parent. The age of children, working capacity of the ex-spouses, socioeconomic class, reasons for divorce, and willingness or unwillingness of the divorced parents to cooperate all affect both parents and children. The cycle of poverty into which women and their families are pushed after divorce has been labeled "the feminization of poverty," and threatens both social equity and the children's futures.

Terminal Illness

A terminal illness in one member often has different impacts on different family members and their ability to cope. Living with a person who is dying, whether adult or child, is painful. It often drains the family members, particularly the chief caregivers, as they live through the process of dying with their loved one. The emotions aroused in different family members may include anger, sorrow, and hurt. Unless family members can express their feelings and thoughts to each other, they are likely to feel isolated and distant at a time when they especially need closeness.

Although death has been a taboo topic, this situation has slowly changed, and people now speak more openly about death and dying. However long a terminally ill person lives, the other family members must continue to live and cope with their own developmental tasks and issues as well as the implications of an impending death.

Forty-year-old Shriver, who suffers from headaches, is suddenly diagnosed with a malignant brain tumor and told he has only six months to live. His wife of 10 years is devastated as she and their children watch the man slowly, steadily, and very painfully die. He loses his cognition and falls into a coma, in which he stays for nine days before dying. It is agonizing for family members to see the changes in his behavior and thinking, as they grapple numbly with the implications of his death. His children respond to his death with a great deal of depression and only slowly begin to adjust to the new single-parent lifestyle of their mother. The mother attends a group for grieving and mourning the loss of a spouse. The oldest (17) son by a previous marriage, takes on a role protective of his mother and younger siblings, ages 8 and 5, while each adapts to a changed lifestyle. How family members cope depends on relationships in the family and on the emotional climate.

Death of a child at any age, from childhood to young adulthood, is likely to have a profound effect on the marital relationship. Sometimes it leads to divorce, as parents unable to take or bear the pain begin to blame each other for the death of the child. Sometimes the death may bring the couple closer together and have a profound, positive effect on how they treat the rest of the children and each other. In some families, one or both parents continue to live in a state of permanent mourning, carrying the burden of unresolved grief and guilt forever.

When 5-year-old Jamie drowned in the ocean as the family was swimming on a balmy Sunday afternoon, the family, shocked and numb, returned home. After months of blaming and fighting and crying, the couple decided to get therapy, to work through their anger and the pain of losing their child. After two years of intensive help, the couple was able to resolve their feelings and pay more sensitive attention to their other children and their needs.

Mental and Physical Disabilities

When children are born with a severe mental or physical disability, it causes the family a great deal of grief. Mothers and fathers tend to respond differently when they learn of the child's handicap. Mothers usually react more emotionally and express their feelings openly, whereas fathers tend to show concern about the long-term financial and social implications.

Schultz and Decker (1985) divide parents' responses into stages as follows: (1) awareness, (2) denial, (3) recognition, (4) search for a cause, (5) search for a cure, and finally (6) acceptance. However, not all individuals follow this pattern. Regardless of the response pattern, this crisis affects the family profoundly. It is estimated that the stress in such a marriage is three times more than normal, and the desertion rate by fathers is twice as high as the national average (Love, 1973). When there is a mentally disabled or severely physically disabled family member, expenses are higher and most family activities are curtailed. A veil of despair, confusion, and disappointment may descend on the family. The family also suffers from chronic sorrow, which persists as long as the child lives. At times the child may grow into adulthood and outlive the parents. In such circumstances, the situation must be restructured. With increased community awareness has come increased availability and coordination of services for such people.

If the children are not completely disabled, they can attend public schools. In 1975, the U.S. Congress passed the Education for All Handicapped Children Act, which required schools to provide appropriate education for such students. How do disabled children fare in this situation? Mixed results are reported from studies of developmentally disabled children who have been integrated into regular classrooms through a practice called *mainstreaming*. Compared to similar students who attend segregated special classes, these youngsters generally fared better academically and socially, but sometimes they did not (Buysse & Bailey, 1993; Madden & Slavin, 1983). However, these children rarely showed an increase in self-esteem, because their classmates seldom choose them to be their friends or playmates (Guralnick & Groom, 1988).

Having a child who is permanently dependent affects the developmental stage of the couple. The manner in which the crisis is viewed depends on and reflects the developmental stages of the individual family members and family subsystem. One major issue such families frequently face is whether to place the highly disabled child in an institutional setting either on a temporary or long-term basis. Working on this issue causes the family a great deal of stress and pain.

Other nondevelopmental crises, including domestic violence and alcohol and substance abuse, which have a negative impact on the growth, development, and well-being of the family, are discussed next.

FAMILY PROBLEMS AND VIOLENCE

Family violence, a major social problem in America, can be subdivided into spousal abuse, child abuse, and elder abuse. By some reports as many as 60% of all couples have been involved in at least one incident of domestic violence. The incidence is even higher if we include severe physical punishment of children. The actual incidence is unknown, because most family violence is not reported, and because society did not focus on abuse within the family as a major public concern until quite recently.

Spousal Abuse

It is hard to assess the number of people who have been abused, because many do not come to a shelter, are not aware of services, and suffer in silence. Abusive or violent behavior among people who are married, living together, or have an ongoing or prior intimate relationship is called *spousal abuse, battering,* or *domestic violence.* This occurs in all races, ethnic groups, religions, age groups, lifestyles, and income and educational groups. About 95% of the victims are women (Diehm & Ross, 1993). Also, women more often than men may suffer serious injury as victims of domestic violence. The Federal Bureau of Investigation reported in 1986 that about 85% of the people arrested in the category of criminal offenses against family and children were men, and about 62% of those arrested are 25–44 years old (U.S. Bureau of the Census, 1988). Men are abused as well, but the number who report abuse is not as large. Abused men may share some of the same fears that women victims experience. Also, because society is paternalistic, it is far more difficult for a man to report abuse, so more such abuse may exist than suspected. Spousal abuse also occurs in the form of psychological abuse and exploitation. Partners who abuse rarely do so not just once, but as a pattern.

Battered Women

An estimated 4 million or more women are beaten by their partners each year. For these women, home is no longer a sanctuary but a trap for physical and emotional abuse. Many women do not leave abusive situations, because they do not have a choice or do not know there is a choice. Sometimes they try, but the resources they turn to—family, clergy, lawyers, police, and even social agencies—may not provide adequate support. A study of 6,000 shelters in Texas found that on an average the women contacted five different agencies before receiving help for leaving home and becoming a resident of a shelter (Diehm & Ross, 1993).

Women endure physical abuse for a number of reasons. A woman may believe it is her duty to maintain the marriage because of religious, cultural, or other socially learned rules. She may suffer to keep her family and her children together despite all the pain she endures. She may be financially dependent on her husband and may face severe economic repercussions if she leaves. And battered women may face severe physical abuse or even death if they try to flee from their partners.

Today, after a great deal of education of the public and public officials, domestic violence is defined as a crime throughout the United

States. However, the actual number of people who are abused still remains elusive, because not all women report.

Police response has changed significantly in recent years. In 1985 a battered woman in Torrington, Connecticut, won a multimillion-dollar settlement for the failure of the police department to protect her from her husband's violence. The case of *Thurman* v. *Torrington* was a catalyst in the state's passage of the 1986 Family Violence Response Act, which mandates arrest in domestic violence when a probable cause exists (such as previous incidents of battering). In many jurisdictions, courts can order batterers to attend special counseling programs under conditions of probation. The effectiveness of these programs is not easy to measure, and little information is available.

To prevent battering, society must reshape the cultural patterns that indoctrinate men and boys into roles that encourage violent behaviors. Also, society must acknowledge the economic factors that trap women in potentially lethal situations. Other contributors to violent behaviors include genetic makeup, chemical and physiological dysfunction, family history, and trauma. Men must learn that violent, abusive, controlling behavior is not only unacceptable but illegal. To break the cycle of violence, society must provide financial support for services to battered women, strong criminal-justice response that holds abusive men responsible for their behaviors, and most important, social activism to improve the status of women.

Child Abuse and Neglect

Child abuse involves an act perpetuated against a child. *Child neglect* involves abandoning responsibility for the well-being of the child by not making physical and emotional provisions for the child's growth into a healthy human being. Deprivation of necessities is found in 56% of accounts of all child mistreatment, as compared to minor physical injuries, which accounted for 15% of abuse, and major physical injuries in 2% of the cases (U.S. Bureau of the Census, 1988).

A conservative estimate says that about 20 out of every 1000 children experience abuse or neglect. Reported incidents seem to have leveled off in the past few years (Kinard, 1987). Abuse has no boundaries, and is found in all socioeconomic, racial and ethnic, and religious groups. Young people may be abused in institutional settings such as residential treatment homes for children, the military, groups of choir boys, and day-care centers. However, it is easier to obtain statistics about the lower class, so poorer people are probably overrepresented in terms of statistics. Most abusers of children are natural parents, both mothers and fathers. However, the abuser is often a stepparent.

Child sexual abuse is different from but closely connected to physical and emotional abuse. The criteria for sexual abuse is that it is committed by men or women who are five or more years older than the abused or who have physical contact of a sexual nature with a child not yet of consenting age, or if they use force or coercion (Conte, 1987). Child abuse rates are difficult to determine. Some sound research studies show that about 20% to 30% of adults were sexually abused as children before their 18th birthday. It is very clear that sexual abuse of children is a significant and relatively common problem of childhood (Conte, 1995). In one, unfortunately not unusual, case that came to light in the May 1, 1993, *Virginian-Pilot & Ledger-Star,* a reporter tells the haunting stories of a landlord's sexual abuse of his own daughters. Five daughters in their early adulthood and middle age brought charges against their father, who sexually abused all of them for years and also made one of the daughters pregnant. One of the daughters said,

> We would try to go to sleep, but you heard him in the bathroom, running and running the water. . . . Your heart would be racing because he'd be in his underwear, and the light would click off, and he'd be on his way to our room. Tears would fill my eyes because I was praying hard, "Lord, don't let it be me." But you never knew who it was going to be. He would just walk through the room and tap you on the shoulder, and you knew what you had to do. (p. A8)

In the majority of the cases that become public, sexual abuse takes place in the home and is perpetrated by men (fathers, stepfathers, grandfathers, brothers, and friends of the family). Cole and Putnam (1992) say that victims experience depression, guilt, learning difficulties, sexual acting out, running away, somatic complaints (such as headaches and stomachaches), hysterical seizures, phobias and nightmares, compulsive rituals, self-destructive behaviors, and suicide. The effects plague the victims even when they grow up, when they take the form of negative self-image, depression, and sexual problems.

Elder Abuse

There are no adequate statistics on elder abuse. Usually abuse is reported by the elderly themselves. Such abuse includes psychological and financial abuse and physical neglect. Direct physical abuse is less common, less reported. The elderly may be afraid of retaliation, and may be dependent on the abuser for care. They also feel shame, and do not wish to admit to outsiders that they have been abused by their children. They fear being institutionalized and leaving personal relationships in the family and in the neighborhood.

The information available shows that victims tend to be women, as more of the surviving elderly in a population are female, especially widows who live with their adult children. Many of the abused have physical and mental disabilities and may be bedridden. They depend on family members to meet their basic needs. Two contradictory studies assert that women are the abusers and that middle-aged men are the abusers (Star, 1987).

Domestic Violence and Drug Abuse

Fairly often, child abuse as well as spousal abuse is connected to drinking alcohol. Alcohol use, like use of other drugs, means different things to different families. To children it may mean being quiet so that the parent can sit in front of the TV until he or she falls asleep. It may mean learning to talk in whispers or tiptoeing around the house while the drunk or drugged person falls asleep. It means learning not to irritate or aggravate an adult family member because in a drunken state the "person is capable of anything." Alcohol and drugs can harm families when they become a way of life and then a family crisis. However, drinking and at times using drugs is well accepted in our culture. When they become a way of life, drugs affect the person's relationship with the family and are a symptom of the couple's relationship strategies. In this section, we view alcohol and drug abuse from a perspective of spousal and child relationships, and will not discuss teenagers in this context.

Using drugs and alcohol gives a particular family member a powerful tool for controlling interpersonal relationships. Unless families learn to deal with it, substance abuse will continue to dominate family relations and will help the person avoid taking responsibility. A person who uses any mind-altering substance avoids responsibility implicitly by saying, "I am on drugs/alcohol, and therefore I decide what goes on in this family. And when I am not in my senses, I am not responsible for the consequences of my decisions." Alcohol and drug abuse is closely related to spousal, child, and elder abuse, and provides the same "excuse from responsibility" in each type of violence.

FAMILY DIVERSITY

Our society is becoming more and more aware that there are other forms of family living than the two-parent, heterosexual family. Each form entails certain advantages and disadvantages. Diversity in families is related to socioeconomic, cultural, and individual differences.

Social-Class Differences

Social scientists believe that the type of family life a person leads depends on the socioeconomic status of the family. Classes can be classified as the very poor, the working class, the middle class, and the rich.

Families in Poverty

Some families have incomes below the official poverty level, which is set every year by the federal government on the basis of household income and the consumer price index. In 1987, about 10.9% of all families and 13.6% of all populations were considered to be under poverty level. Those who made an income of $11,203 for a family of four were considered to be at poverty level. This income level did not include noncash benefits such as food stamps, Medicaid, and subsidized housing (U.S. Bureau of the Census, 1988) and the poverty rate has risen considerably. In 1969, 15.6% of all children were poor (Danziger & Danziger, 1993). In 1991, 21.8% of all children were poor (Sawhill, 1992). According to the U.S. Bureau of the Census *Current Population Reports,* in the United States 8.5% of white and 26.4% of African-American families live below the poverty level. This change represents an increase in poverty rates of 40% since the late 1960s, when the War on Poverty was being waged. Of great concern is the high rate of poverty for children raised in single-parent families. It is estimated that 61% of all children in this group will be poor throughout most of the early years of their childhood, and only 7% will escape poverty altogether (Committee on Ways and Means, 1992). Single parents made up 27% of families with related children in 1992, a rise from 22% in 1982. Eight million households are headed by single women, and 1.5 million are headed by single men. Policy analysts focus on three factors increasing poverty among children: demographic changes, economic conditions and changes, and changes in government spending on social welfare programs (Jones, 1995).

Another group of people affected by poverty are the elderly. Of the elderly (age 65 and older), 12% live in poverty, and 19% have incomes just above the poverty level (U.S. Bureau of the Census, 1991b). Certain groups of older people are extremely hard hit by poverty; women, people of color, very old people, rural residents, and elderly people who live alone are all more likely to be poor. Of African-American older women living alone, 76% are poor or nearly poor. African-American women make up 60% of the total African-American aged population (U.S. Bureau of the Census, 1989a, 1989b). About 49% of women age 85 or older living alone are poor, and women represent 72% of the over-85 population (U.S. Bureau of the Census, 1989a, 1989b).

Poverty makes older people dependent on family members for financial survival, and if they have no family they depend on state facilities or programs. Often the poor elderly go without heat, food, and other necessities, even housing, to get by (Motenko & Greenberg, 1995).

Also people at the poverty level, irrespective of race, tend to have a high divorce rate. There are very young teenaged parents, the equivalent of children having children. All these factors lead to a high incidence of single-parent families. Often in such households the father is absent. The argument can be made that this absence is a reasonable adaptation to the economic insecurities that confront such people. For example, is it a reasonable adaptation for a father to absent himself from the home if that is the only means by which his family can qualify for public assistance? Or to refuse a job because a minimum-wage job without health benefits would jeopardize qualification for Medicaid coverage? Likewise, a single mother may refuse a minimum-wage job because there is no way to provide day care for her infant children. A teenage girl may become pregnant to escape an unpleasant or dangerous home life. A high school dropout may be frustrated with the "put-downs" of schoolmates, educators, and others who have neither the time nor the inclination to respond to special problems. All these strategies may be reasonable adaptations to economic insecurity. From the safety of a secure middle-class economic and social status, these tactics may appear maladaptive and self-defeating, but from the perspective of the person in the situation, they may be not only reasonable but practical.

Stack (1974) indicates that the value placed on children—the love, attention, and affection children receive from women and men, and the web of social relationships spun from the birth of a child—all underlie the high birthrate among the poor. In such families, the household often centers around networks of two or more households, and these usually consist of relatives and sometimes friends as well. Thus a domestic network is created and works as an extended cluster of kin related chiefly through children but also through marriage and friendship and who pull together to provide domestic functions and services to each other. As Stack (1983) states, in African-American urban neighborhoods these networks are usually formed around women because of the role they play in child care, although sometimes men play a positive role in these networks as fathers of the children and contributors of resources.

The Working Class

Working-class families' ideals differ from those of the middle class. In the working class, family members are sent out to work in order to bring home money, and this helps keep the family from getting into financial problems. Working-class men and women judge their marriages not in terms of how much happiness they receive in the marriage but rather how they fulfill their primary role in maintaining the family. A hierarchical arrangement is more common in working-class families: The man is usually accepted as head of household, and the mother as homemaker and caretaker. The woman may work side by side with her husband, but she plays a different and more traditional role at home. In such a household, there is not much compromise in roles. However, as Rubin (1984) notes, working-class women in the labor force do not "want" to work, so much as they feel obligated and "have to work" to assure the solvency of the family.

Economic insecurity—a fact of life among more and more middle- and working-class people—is related to the restructuring of the economy that eliminated so many jobs. For example, in Buffalo, the flour and steel industries and to a large degree the automobile industries are gone, and in Norfolk, Virginia, many defense-related jobs have been lost.

The Middle Class

Rapp (1982) says that the middle class (the most numerous) is defined as owning "small amounts of resources that gives them control over their own working conditions." Middle-class norms and values dominate our thinking. The category of middle class can also be seen more as a lifestyle than as a particular income level, with emphasis on education, career, culture, place and type of residence, and child-centeredness. Husband and wife view each other as being more equal than in upper or lower classes. Often the woman, a "supermom," must wear several hats as mother, homemaker, and career woman, causing her severe stress. Often both parents work outside the home, and an agreement must be reached about how family members will share household chores. Physical punishment for children is avoided, and the parents try to bring up children by loving and nurturing them unconditionally. Middle-class people maintain friendship networks that are both a symbol of status and a set of connections to use in order to get ahead in their careers. Children are socialized to think in terms of moving ahead rather than falling lower into the working class or into poverty.

Families of the Rich

Families that earn at least $75,000 per year and control 16% of all income in the United States constitute 5% of the population and are generally considered rich (Plotnick, 1987; Plotnick, 1995). These people hold high executive jobs in large corporations or own businesses and/or professional practices. Being rich is connected to how much wealth a person has, but even more to what a person is currently earning. Not much is known about the rich, as few researchers have studied them. Rapp notes that such families are male dominated, but women hold a central role. Usually such families have household help, leaving the wife with time for social events and civic duties. Upper-class families have traditionally represented the "ideal" of family to the rest of society, and they profoundly influence the perceptions of the wife's role. In a growing group of very wealthy families, both the spouses have successful careers, which place them in the upper-class bracket. Such families also have live-in help and child care that lets the woman advance in her career.

Interestingly, delinquency is more common among the poor and the very rich than among the middle class or the working class. However, delinquent children of the rich are less likely to be caught and prosecuted; they also don't seem to be punished as severely by the courts. When such delinquents are caught, they may receive what appears to be preferential treatment by the authorities if their families intervene and provide legal and financial support (Patterson, Kupersmidt, & Vaden, 1990).

In a very interesting article called "The Truth about Growing Up Rich," Sallie Bingham (1993) talks about the role of rich women in the family. She remarks that very few people think of rich women as being "highly vulnerable." She says that in reality most rich women are invisible. They are the faces that appear behind well-known men, floating to the fore infrequently, yet they are big contributors—often anonymous—to approved charities and organizers of fund-raising events. "Rich women have been so well rewarded by an unjust system that we have lost our voices; we are captives, as poor women are captives, of a system that deprives us of our identities" (p. 111). Bingham continues that most rich families work on the English system, which favors male heirs. There is an assumption that daughters in rich families will marry well and be taken care of, for life; and the men will do the work of the world or the family and should be compensated accordingly. When a rich man dies and his will is read, the women inherit the houses, furniture, and jewels, and the men inherit cash, stocks, and securities. The upbringing that makes rich women quiet and inconspicuous prevents them from fighting for their own inheritance. Instead, the women gratefully accept what is offered. "The slave mentality abounds in the palaces of the rich, even when the slave is decked in precious attire. We are dependent, after all, on the fickle goodwill of those who will never proclaim us their heirs" (Bingham, 1993, p. 111).

Single-Parent Families

There are two types of heads of single-parent families: those who are single and give birth to children by choice, and those who become single parents accidentally, through unplanned pregnancy or divorce. Problems faced by both types are similar in many ways, particularly in regards to money. Two of the biggest problems most single parents face are economic problems coupled with an overload of responsibilities.

Of poor people in the United States, most are women and their children, as noted earlier. The government's annual redefinition of the poverty level reflects the increased cost of living and decreased value of the dollar. Thus, for example, families of four were considered impoverished in 1970 if they had an income of $3,968 or less, whereas in 1992 the figure was $14,463 (Wright, 1993).

There are, further, many major income discrepancies among racial and ethnic groups. In 1991, on an average, Euro-American families earned $37,773 per year, Hispanic families earned $23,887, and African-American families earned $21,585. The incomes of 13.1% of all Americans were below the defined poverty level in 1989. Among African- American households, 29.5% could be classified as poor (Barncik & Shapiro, 1992). According to Barncik & Shapiro (1992), among 64 million children, 46.6 million (73%) are living with two parents. This figure included almost 80% of Euro-American children, 66% of Hispanic children, and 38% of African-American children. The rest of the children were members of single-parent households (U.S. Bureau of the Census, 1993).

The children who live with single parents are often from poor homes. According to Tidwell (1997) about 53% of African-Americans live with their mothers only, compared to just 18% of white children. The overall African-American birth rate exceeds the white rate by about 6 percentage points, while the out-of-wedlock birth rate among African-Americans is three times the corresponding rate for whites. The African-American infant mortality rate is 2.5 times the rate among whites. The poverty rate among African-American families is three times the rate for white families. The racial gap between African-Americans and Hispanics is somewhat lower, with African-Americans being 2.6 times more likely to be poor (Tidwell, 1997).

The impact of poverty on children is shocking; while mothers are working or looking for work, children are left unsupervised and easily fall into bad company. Often the single-parent mother is overloaded with cooking, cleaning, and keeping food on the table. She has hardly any time for socializing with the children. Discipline is administered through quick and at times harsh physical punishments.

The stereotype of the poor person has had a long life. Often poor people are seen as being African-Americans living in urban areas and dependent on welfare to provide for them and later their children. It is true that poverty hits the oppressed more frequently, but the stereotypes blame the victim, not society.

Why is there is so much poverty among women? The theory of the feminization of poverty, advanced by sociologist Diana Pierce, explains that for the past 15 years several social and economic factors have converged to produce this situation. These factors include the weakening of the nuclear family, the rapid growth of female-headed families, the continuing dual-labor market that actively discriminates against female workers, and a welfare system that works at keeping its recipients below poverty level. In addition, women shoulder time consuming yet unpaid domestic responsibilities, particularly women who provide child care as well as hold outside jobs. A growing trend in terms of unemployment—continuing discrimination on the basis of age, race, and sex —and the changing nature of the economy have both affected single mothers and their children. A fundamental change in the family structure through divorce, death, marriage, birth, or a child leaving home affects women more severely, in terms of economics, than men in the family. Women who remain married have a better economic status than those who divorce (Sidel, 1993).

Teenagers who are not married have experienced a sharp rise in birth rates in recent times. Between 1980 and 1990, the rate of births to unmarried women between the ages of 15 and 19 has increased dramatically. From 1980 to 1990, births to unmarried women in this age group rose to 33%. In the age group 20 to 24, the increase was 70.2% from 1980 to 1990 (Committee on Ways and Means, 1993). Adolescents (15–19 years) who became pregnant obtained about 399,200 abortions, compared to 467,485 live births in 1985 (Committee on Ways and Means, 1993). The economic and social costs of birth are tremendous. It is estimated that 53% of these teenagers receive Aid to Families with Dependent Children (AFDC), food stamps, and Medicaid. Such babies suffer high medical risks, low birth weight, prematurity, mental retardation, and various physical disorders. They also grow up in impoverished one-parent homes. Often teenagers are not prepared to be parents with mundane day-to-day responsibilities. They also face anger and resentment from boyfriends, school authorities, and often parents. Very few teenagers receive support or help with their dilemma. The young new parent has problems adjusting to a child with very little support. Often the biological father of the child does not support the child and the mother ends up as a recipient of public welfare. Frequently the birth of one child leads to the birth of other children, and single parenthood becomes a way of life for quite a few women. In such homes, the likelihood of child neglect and abuse increases, as the young parent is overwhelmed by her responsibilities (Moore & Burt, 1982).

Sexual activity, pregnancy, abortion, and childbearing among teenagers are hotly debated topics on the public policy agenda. Over the past 10 years, the proportion of teens who have had sexual intercourse has increased, as has the number of births to teens. Between 1986 and 1991, the teen birthrate increased by 24.5% (Moore et al., 1994), with increases in the birthrate occurring among both younger and older teens, in almost all states across the nation, and among non-Hispanic whites, non-Hispanic blacks, and Hispanic race/ethnic groups.

Besides the burden of economics, early sexual activity increases exposure to sexually transmitted diseases and HIV infections. According to Moore, Blumenthal, Sugland, Hyatt, Snyder, and Morrison (1994), few Americans feel that childbearing among adolescents is desirable, yet public efforts to prevent pregnancy and other results of sexual activity have not been especially promising. Rigorous evaluations of existing programs and policies are limited, but among those that have been assessed only a small number demonstrate large or long-term impacts on sexual or contraceptive behavior. Also, public funding for contraceptive services declined 30% during the 1980s (Gold & Daley, 1991). In fact, net of inflation, 37 states experienced a 50% or greater decline in public funding between 1979 and 1990 for contraceptive services for at-risk women (Moore et al., 1994). With fewer resources available, many providers have had to reduce the scope of services they offer and have eliminated certain services altogether (Sugland, Moore, & Blumenthal, 1994).

Karla was 14 years old when she became a mother for the first time. From the beginning, her parents have treated her pregnancies as a curse, and she has reacted with anger and guilt. Her grandmother is her only support system. By the time she is 19, Karla has developed a pattern of having babies. She is the mother of four, the sole wage earner, and the chief caretaker of her children, although her grandmother pitches in fairly frequently. Overburdened with family and financial problems, Karla at times rages and abuses her children, although this is mostly unintentional. The frequency of her outbursts has increased as she endures the burden of parenting and poverty. In many ways having sex and having a temporary companion is the only pleasure she finds in her dreary life. She gives in to men easily and often has impulsive, unprotected sex, and thus becomes pregnant again and again. Although it is easy to be judgmental about her lack of responsible behavior, to her it makes sense. Why use birth control when it costs money and you do not have anyone in your life? But when someone comes along and is nice to her, it leads to unplanned sex, which in turn leads to unplanned pregnancies.

Another group of people who become single parents either permanently or for some period of time in their lives are divorced women. In most cases women retain custody of the children. The divorce rate in the United States has risen sharply, perhaps because the reasons for divorce have changed. According to Gigy and Kelly (1992), divorce is no longer restricted to severe problems such as nonsupport, alcoholism, or abuse. Now couples divorce because they feel the marriage lacks communication, emotional fulfillment, or compatibility. Women tend to have more complaints than their husbands do, and more frequently initiate the breakup (Gigy & Kelly, 1992; Gray & Silver, 1990). Contrary to popular belief, the largest incidence of divorce—about 40%—is in the first seven to nine years of marriage, when couples are in their 20s (Yarrow, 1987). Generally it has been estimated that three-quarters of all divorced men and two-thirds of divorced women will remarry (Cherlin, 1992).

One-parent families, usually headed by mothers, carry the burden of different types of responsibilities. These include being solely responsible for the emotional support and physical care of children. Child-care and parenting responsibilities also limit women's employment options both within and after marriage. Another heavy burden that lurks over their heads is financial responsibility. Despite laws requiring noncustodial parents to share the financial responsibility of caring for the children, there is a great degree of noncompliance with child-support orders. Even if paid, the amounts typically do not cover the costs of caring for the children, especially as they get older.

Spousal support is rarely granted and is actually paid in about half of those cases. A very large percentage of divorced women are employed and overloaded in the roles they must play. The money women make is still not equivalent to what men make for the same jobs: Today women make about 70% of what men earn (Rowe, 1995). Gender discrimination is thus obvious. Also, these jobs offer little opportunity for advancement. The hours are generally inflexible, particularly in lower-level jobs, and so a mother must go to great lengths to coordinate her work and family life.

Being a single parent includes taking on the role of both mother and father and carrying out responsibilities accordingly. At times, the overworked and exhausted mother needs time out for herself and may or may not be successful in getting it. If she dates while her children are young, she feels guilty about taking time away from them. Societal rules make it easy for people to point fingers at single parents when children have problems.

In a social-work classroom, a student related a case of a single mother who had just moved from the Northeast to Norfolk, Virginia. She had two jobs and three children to take care of. Her youngest child had problems fitting into the new school, and repeated phone calls to the mother did not bring her to the school, because she was new on the job and could not leave her workplace. Upon hearing the story, one student commented self-righteously that the mother should be reported to Child Protective Services because she was not being a caring parent. The student eventually withdrew her statement, but it illustrates the tendency in our society to "blame the victim." The mother was in a new area, with no support system, working two jobs, and with three children to provide for. She felt she had to fulfill her obligations at work so that she could provide for her family. The assumption that a mother should always be available is unrealistic.

Today we are realizing that such parents (usually women) need help. Social agencies are beginning to develop counseling and ancillary services that reach single parents and help them meet their responsibilities. These include self-help and support groups, divorce mediation, parent–child play groups, family life education, and parent-aid programs.

The third group of single parents are those who are not poor and make a conscious choice to have a child outside of marriage. Their reasons are varied: Perhaps the biological clock is running out and the woman wishes to be a parent and experience mothering. Usually such women are mature, understand the responsibilities, and are financially able to support a family.

Some single fathers are happy to raise their children when the mother does not contest their role as the chief caretaker. Of course, single men wishing to start a family have fewer options than do women. Adoption and surrogacy are possible, but there are many barriers facing single men—gay or not, in a relationship or not—who try to pursue these options.

Stepfamilies or Reconstituted Families

One out of every two marriages ends in divorce, according to the U.S. Bureau of the Census (1992a). And in many homes, one parent is neither a biological nor adoptive parent.

In the United States, it is estimated that 17.4% of all married-couple families with children are stepfamilies, that 19.1% of all children under the age of 18 live in stepfamilies, and that 12.7% of all children are stepchildren (Fine, 1995). The term *blended* has been used to describe such families, but that description evokes *The Brady Bunch,* where everybody gets along beautifully. "Blended" implies that two families and their offspring become blended into one. The term is misleading and does not always reflect psychological reality. Stepfamilies are reconstituted, and are never completely blended; children experience invisible and divided loyalties between the natural absent parent, living or dead, and the stepparent. Such loyalty, if well placed, should be fostered and encouraged so that the stepchild of a very loving and caring stepparent does not feel disloyal to the natural parent.

In stepfamilies, a number of authority and control issues must be worked out. Often, two adults from two families must compromise two sets of rules in running the household and caring for the children. Reconstituted families must work hard to make the family group function together. Stepparent and sibling relationships within such families can be awkward and difficult, especially when children have two different homes. Cherlin (1988), who studied remarriages, notes that the growth of relationships in such families

> seem to be moving in the direction of expanding the concept of family to include steprelationships and other quasi-kin ties. Indeed, family ties after remarriage often extend across two or three households. The result is that our commonsense equation of "family" and "household" often breaks down. The basic question of what constitutes a family and what its boundaries are becomes less clear.

Let us look at some issues faced in a stepfamily. After a divorce, many children feel grief and anger; they fantasize that the absent person will come back and they will live happily ever after. When a stepparent enters the picture, he or she is resented because children see the new parent as taking over the role of the absent parent and precluding his or her return. The biological parent's interest and love for the new partner can make matters worse, particularly when children are practically strangers to the new parent. The situation affects the new couple in many ways. Social workers helping stepfamilies in family sessions say that some of the terms frequently used are "confusion," "jealousy," "guilt," "alienation," "walking on eggs," and "not as good." Very rarely do people use words such as "challenge," "love," and "parental happiness."

There are countless negative stereotypes of stepfamilies. As one 7-year-old said to her stepmother, "You can't be my stepmother, you're not mean enough" (Visher & Visher, 1988). Often stepfamilies who want social approval pretend that they are nuclear or biological families. Stories such as *Cinderella, Snow White and the Seven Dwarfs,* and *Hansel and Gretel* aren't much help, particularly when they are read to children at a young age and instill notions of "evil stepmothers."

Stepfamilies have insiders and outsiders. That is, each parent has had a relationship with his or her own children from birth, and the stepparent's experience in beginning a parental relationship with a school-age child or a teen is very different. They must deal with what has already been established. The new parent must find his or her place in the already formed structure before attempting changes, because if he or she suggests too many changes, it may be viewed as intrusion by the other partner's children.

When two people marry, and each one has been a parent in another marriage, power issues come into play. Each parent has developed patterns in terms of rules, norms, customs, and routines that have shaped each family's ways of living. Remarriage means a readjustment on everyone's part and learning to accept differences. Loss of grandparents or in-laws may create feelings of relief or loss, as well. Boundary problems and feelings of closeness or distancing may start to appear.

Extended Families

When people immigrate to the United States in groups, they often do not know anyone beside people from their own land of birth. They help each other out, maintain relationships with their relatives, and care for and nurture each other in times of need. Some three-generation families live together or in separate homes but close to one another. There are ethnic groups from Europe, Asia, Haiti, and the Caribbean and Latin America who develop natural systems of family support, keeping to their own cultural and social traditions. However, such extended families are overlooked and not recognized as legitimate by the U.S. government in terms of housing, taxes, and Social Security. This curbs the development of extended family systems. Mizio (1974) states that this limitation adds to poverty and unemployment, and also limits culturally congruent formal resources. For a long time even social workers have not recognized these culturally congruent relationships, although it is finally dawning on us that extended families are a way of life in many cultures.

For example, let us look at the role of the grandmother in the African-American middle-class family. The grandmothering years call for women's continued investment in work and in other activities while participating in the lives of their children's children. Timberlake and Chipungu (1992) say that grandmotherhood involves moving beyond the direct generativity and two-generational concerns of parenting, to the mediated interpersonal relationships and three-generational concerns of being a grandparent. Relationships with grandchildren strengthen the unity of the past, present, and future that first emerged during motherhood, and also satisfy the needs of the women to connect with the past and anchor themselves beyond their own lifetimes (Timberlake, 1980). This is also a strong way of relating and using cultural communication among different generations of people. Grandmotherhood represents the culmination of socialization processes that began in childhood and provides a social identity for the members of African-American families (Martin & Martin, 1978).

Gay and Lesbian Families

The number of people living in gay and lesbian families is unknown because these couples and their children are not accepted as families in the larger society. Until recently this problem was hidden, and gays' and lesbians' civil rights were encroached on by straight people. The overt and serious attempt by gays and lesbians to become part of the larger society will be described in greater detail later. Gay and lesbian families perform the same functions as other families, including housework and child rearing, beside other arrangements in terms of role allocation and decision making in the home. For example, a young doctor in a lesbian family mentioned that she and her lover had no rigid rules of behavior, as may apply in a heterosexual relationship. They "made up rules and roles" as they went along, and this to her was creative and fascinating, because they were not tied to any specific behaviors. More recently, positive changes have been taking place for lesbian and gay couples, which are being recognized more readily as embodying a valid lifestyle. In its 1986 policy statement, the American Civil Liberties Union advocated the recognition of gay and lesbian marriages and provision of economic benefits for life partners, similar to those enjoyed by heterosexual couples, such as health insurance, death benefits, and visitation. In 1989 San Francisco began providing official certification of gay and lesbian relationships (Germain, 1991).

Lesbian and gay couples meet each other's needs for support, a loving home, and understanding, which are the same as for heterosexual couples (Patterson, 1992). Normally both partners work outside the home, although there may be a difference in the type of employment and the level of income each brings into the relationship. In these relationships, roles tend to be based on personal interest and ability. The ability to choose roles is experienced as a source of strength by many couples. Gay and lesbian couples generally seek more egalitarian relationships than heterosexual couples, with lesbian couples perhaps being the most egalitarian (Peplau, 1991).

Long-term relationships, common for years among lesbian women, are becoming increasingly common among gay men. For many people, the spectre of AIDS has encouraged the formation of monogamous, lifelong partnerships.

Gay and lesbian families reach agreements on shared and private-time activities, participation in monogamous or nonmonogamous sexual relationships, and the issue of "coming out." American society is still judgmental, as evidenced by the military's don't-ask-don't-tell policy, so a couple should discuss these problems. They need to know if coming out would cause internal problems and threats to employment and friendships, or problems with child custody and child rearing for those couples with children from a previous relationship.

Cindy is married and the mother of three children. After her divorce, she becomes involved in a lesbian relationship, and her ex-husband contests her in court for the custody of the children on the basis that she is not a "fit" mother. In the early 1980s, he receives custody of the children, even though he is not fully available to care for the children. The court's decision might be different today.

The child-rearing tasks and issues faced by lesbian and gay parents when there are children from a prior marriage, or conceived through artificial insemination, are in many ways similar to those of stepparent families. However, social ignorance and lack of tolerance by others can make parenting a difficult situation for same-sex parents. Some special issues that gays and lesbians face with reference to child rearing are how to open communication and "come out" to children, help children deal with differences and stigma, and (in divorce situations) deal with the divorced parent and with grandparents, who may be hostile to the lesbian or gay relationship (Goodman, 1980).

There is a great deal of *homophobia* in American society. Homophobia hurts far more individuals than those against whom it is directed. Like racism and sexism, it is an expression of hatred; it harms the perpetrator as well as the victim. For example, insecurities, fears, and sexual hangups may lead straight men to participate in gay bashing, which in spirit resembles the lynching of another era. Another example is a poll taken of GIs at two U.S. Army bases in Texas in December 1993, where 45% of those surveyed said they would quit if forced to serve alongside openly gay men and women. Researcher-sociologist Charles Moskas believes these numbers may be inflated but they cannot be verified because the Pentagon currently forbids researchers to ask military personnel their opinions about homosexuality (Moskas, 1993, p. A1).

Racial and Ethnic Families

In a multicultural society diversity affects the lives of all people. In the United States, families have been studied from the perspective of broad racial and ethnic categories—Euro-American, African-American, Hispanic, Asian-American—often overlooking the enormous diversity within each of those groups. Sometimes ethnic and racial differences are considered abnormal, because on the surface some groups do not resemble "mainstream" America. However, with an increasingly global economy and greater amount of everyday contact between people from different groups, it is important to understand and appreciate cultural differences.

In recent years Hispanic and Asian immigration has increased. The rising birthrates in these groups and those of African-Americans relative to the Euro-American population have decisively altered the racial and ethnic balance of the United States. Countless languages, religions, and value systems have come to the United States. It used to be that Native-American Indian tribes and nations represented the most notable examples of cultural diversity. But as the United States has become more multicultural, the cross-cultural mingling of heritages has become a unique and positive characteristic of American life. On the other hand, there remains a great deal of mistrust, resentment, and hostility among different ethnic and racial groups. Some would still prefer to assimilate all groups into that Anglo-Saxon or Euro-American Protestant "melting pot," or keep them out altogether. As the twenty-first century begins, racial and ethnic diversity is increasingly important in defining our future (Song & Kim, 1993).

African-American families Andrew Billingsley comments that African-American families should be understood in their own variation and complexity today, rather than in the context of white, middle-class society. This perspective indicates that the African-American community is large and diverse, and incorporates a number of different lifestyles. For example, in a single-parent family, a woman alone doesn't necessarily take care of her children by herself. In all likelihood, she has the help of a mother, an aunt, a grandmother, or a brother. Also, a number of households may combine to form a domestic network. Billingsley writes that African-American families are adaptive. In a special effort to meet the needs of their members, they adapt their structures and patterns according to the pressures and opportunities available to them in society. Grandmothers play an important role in the lives of their grandchildren, as noted earlier. Both directly and vicariously, they face the inevitable challenges and crises of rearing a new generation in a new era (Bengston, 1987; Meade, 1971; Timberlake & Chipungu, 1992). In addition to providing basic child care and homemaking services, grandmothers offer stability and structure by guiding, teaching, and influencing their grandchildren and by forming affiliations with other families and groups.

However, families headed by single women are not without problems. Regardless of why they are single, female householders earn less than males, and the high poverty rate among female householders has not changed much. As Billingsley (1992) notes, many single mothers in this community operate just above poverty level but are self-supporting. Some single mothers are able to obtain a high school diploma and have family support, welfare benefits, jobs, and career goals, which suggests that understanding and supportive human resources are available.

Basing his conclusions on a decade of studies, Billingsley found that a higher proportion of African-American families revealed egalitarian couple relations than did families in the nation as a whole. In African-American families, tasks and roles are interchangeable for men, women, and children in ways that differ from the traditional white family. Family members do each other's work, often in patterns of collaboration not generally appreciated outside the African-American community. Also, among African-American married couples women often assume the role of provider. They make a greater contribution to the economic viability of the family than do women in the nation as a whole. Their role is highly accepted and supported by the African-American man. Also among working couples, black men provide much greater help to their wives with housework and child care than do husbands in the majority culture (Billingsley, 1993). Even so, however, the women do a great deal of housework and are more likely to be overburdened by these tasks than are men.

As Billingsley (1993) discusses, certain distinct pathways to upward mobility appear among African-Americans. The African-American middle class is characterized by its origin in the African-American working class, generally in the previous generation. Most middle-class African-Americans are first-generation, precariously middle class, and are characterized as being more dependent than independent, more often employees than employers, with relatively little accumulated wealth. "Moderate and even high salaries and income will not automatically translate into wealth, which refers to the net value of assets over liabilities. Still, the black middle-class family is a major achievement sustained by education, two earners, extended families, religion, and service to others" (p. 287).

The family is a primary unit of the African-American church. The historic African-American church was a gathering of families and extended families that worshiped in a sanctuary they created for themselves. When they died, they were buried in a churchyard hallowed by the memories of past generations. There has always been a symbiosis between the African-American church and the family, which is mutually reinforcing and creates the primary identity for most African- American families. Its most crucial role is to bolster the personal and cultural identity and the self-esteem of African-American youngsters at all socioeconomic levels (Lincoln & Mamiya, 1990).

Hispanic families The Spanish-speaking people of the United States —Puerto Ricans, Mexican Americans, Central and South American Spanish-speaking groups, and Cubans—have their family history embedded in kinship systems that offer reciprocal support and obligations. In Mexican-American families, when people talk of the immediate family, they are referring to extended kin, including aunts, uncles, grandparents, cousins, and in-laws, as well as coparents and godparents.

For Puerto Rican families living on the U.S. mainland, the nuclear family is becoming more prevalent. However, a great deal of value is attached to strong and intimate relationships with kin and companions, including parents and godparents, witnesses to marriage, and close friends. Many single parents and common-law couples are among the most impoverished Puerto Ricans, but they maintain strong ties to the households of relatives and companions. Tienda (1989) indicates that the socioeconomic situation of Puerto Ricans has become more precarious than that of African-Americans. A high level of residential segregation contributes to their deteriorating social situation. Housing barriers, similar to those facing poor African-Americans, block many from access to quality schools and good job opportunities (Santiago, 1992, p. 109). In the Puerto Rican community, high value is placed on family unity, welfare, honor, commitment, obligation, and responsibility. The family guarantees protection and caretaking for life as long as the individual stays within the system. Leaving the family implies taking a grave risk (Garcia-Preto, 1982, p. 70).

Sharp distinctions between the roles of men and women in Spanish-speaking cultures are characterized by the terms *machismo* and *Marianismo*. A double standard prevails: Husbands can be with other women, but wives must suffer in silence and remain faithful (Ghali, 1982).

There is also a great belief in kinship ties and reciprocal support and obligations. *Hijos de crianza* means "children of upbringing" and refers to the practice of assuming responsibility for a child, without blood or even friendship ties, and raising this child as one's own. In this situation there is no stigma attached to a parent relinquishing a child for the sake of its future or taking in a child who has been given up. It can be a temporary or permanent arrangement (Mizio, 1974).

Despite proximity and interdependence, the hierarchical structure of the Latino family is very clear. Rules govern age and gender roles, and family members must follow them (Falicov, 1982). Most children live with their parents until marriage and maintain a close connection during adulthood. The parents continue their parental and grandparental functions, so most do not experience an "empty nest" stage (Falicov, 1982).

Latinos come from over 20 different countries in Central and South America and the Caribbean. The largest groups in the United States in 1990 were Mexican American, 64%; mainland Puerto Rican, 10.5%; and Cuban American, 4.9% (U.S. Bureau of the Census, 1991a).

Despite a great degree of poverty, Spanish-speaking people, except for mainland Puerto Ricans, have a high level of two-parent families. In 1990, 72% of Mexican-American families and 77% of Cuban American families were married-couple families, as compared to 79.9% of non-Latin white families and 57% of mainland Puerto Rican families (U.S. Bureau of the Census, 1991a, 1992b). The family is an institution of central importance within Latino (Spanish) cultures and an important source of safety, security, and comfort.

Latinos of Mexican descent are the largest minority group in the United States. The most important organization for this group is the family. Chicano families are usually headed by both a husband and a wife, and they are likely to be large. One-third of Chicano families have four or more children. The majority of Mexican-Americans are from poor or working-class groups, usually rural or of mixed Spanish and native Indian descent (Falicov, 1982).

Middle-class and upper-middle-class Chicano families are markedly different in circumstances and value orientation. The nuclear family usually lives in a separate house but close to the extended family, and thus preserves its own boundaries and identity. Boundaries are flexible, however, and may allow the inclusion of grandparents, uncles, aunts, cousins, and children whose parents are dead or divorced. Because children live with their parents until marriage, boundary and loyalty issues erupt early when new families are formed. The extended kin network is both horizontally and vertically interdependent, and addresses common issues of child care, financial responsibility, and the stress and strain of new marriage.

About 1 million Cuban Americans live in the United States (Queralt, 1984), and the number has been increasing. The degree of support that Cuban families receive is less than among Puerto Ricans and Mexicans. Nuclear families have been the norm among white Cubans since the process of acculturation. Cubans also maintain ties with their families of origin, but the ties become most evident during crisis periods. The status of the woman is higher among Cubans than among other Latin American groups. However, traditional gender roles are still more pronounced among Cubans than among Anglos (Queralt, 1984).

Native-American Indian families Native-American Indians come from ethnically and culturally varied backgrounds. For example, the Mohawk, Navajo, and Klamath groups differ more than do the Italian, German, Irish, and Polish.

In line with the cultural diversity of the western hemisphere, almost all variant rules of marriage, including incest prohibitions, post-marriage residence customs, and in-law relations, were followed by Native North American societies. Native-American Indian marriages took many forms, including monogamy, polygyny and polyandry. Polyandry was rare and usually fraternal. It happened under special circumstances, such as when an older brother became ill or disabled, prompting the marriage of a younger brother to an older brother's wife.

Polygyny was common among Native-American Indians of the Plains and Northwest Coast, occurring in more than 20% of marriages. *Monogamy* was the most exclusive form of marriage, found among certain northeastern agriculturalists such as the Iroquois and the Huron. Matrilocal postmarital residence and matrilineal descent were common among the agriculturalists in eastern and southwestern America, where women played a major role in food production. With the intensification of agriculture, as in Mexico, men became the predominant food producers, and postmarital residence and rules of descent shifted to patrilocal and patrilineal patterns, as in Europe.

Price (1977) notes that menarche was often celebrated in Native-American Indian societies with some ceremony. The onset of menstruation was considered dangerous for a girl, as she was then thought to be in close contact with the supernatural. The manner in which she conducted herself would determine her behavior for the rest of her life. During this time of isolation she fasted and learned the ways of a dutiful wife; she ended her "taboo" period by bathing and dressing in new clothing.

Native-American Indians tended to marry early, between 15 and 20 years of age. Premarital sex was allowed, provided it did not violate the rules forbidding incest, endogamy, or adultery. Premarital pregnancies were accepted; but the child was reared by the mother's kin.

Customs such as bride price and bride service were practiced among the Native-American Indians who lived on the Great Plains and the Northwest Coast. In an interfamilial exchange marriage, a daughter could marry the son of another family with few formalities, in places such as the Great Basin and the subarctic regions. A son or daughter could be adopted, inherit family property, and carry on descent among the sonless families that existed in several patrilineal groups. First cross-cousin marriages were permitted and even preferred in some strongly lineal societies in which the father's brother's daughter or the mother's sister's daughter was in a different descent line from the groom. This pattern was common among wealthy, matrilineal fishing societies such as the Tlingit, Tsimshsain, and Haida of coastal British Columbia and the Alaskan Panhandle (Price, 1977).

The colonizing Europeans did not approve of the Native-American Indian lifestyles, and Christian missionaries made sweeping changes in their lives. Today Native-American Indians largely follow Euro-American norms. Monogamous, patrilineal, nuclear families dominate (Price, 1981). Respect for kinship persists, although the kinship groups such as lineages and classes have been abandoned. The elderly are respected, but it is not uncommon for tribal elders to lose status and feel a sense of disaffection and alienation. There are great differences among the cultures and family living patterns of different tribes or nations, as well as between Native-American Indians living on reservations and in cities. The Native-American Indians who live in the cities have largely been assimilated. The Native-American Indians living on the reservation tend to follow the old ways, with very little input from the outside world. They speak their native languages and follow their own religion and ways of behavior, making a conscious effort not to assimilate into the majority culture. As long as they continue to live on reservations, they might maintain their way of life, but as they move into big cities and become part of the American scene, there are bound to be overt changes in family lifestyles.

Asian-American families Most Asian Americans consider family life extremely important, and family ties are strong. Throughout Asian cultures, the family is considered more important than the individual. For example, in the Japanese culture the term *kenshim* expresses the renunciation of selfish desires in favor of common family interests. In all Asian cultures, the family is seen as multigenerational and includes extended kin (Isisaka & Takagi, 1982).

Asian cultures place high value on hierarchical organization of the family, stressing responsibility for family obligations based on status and role in the extended family. Interdependence and mutuality is a way of life. As in most cultures, males are more valued than females. Ryan (1992) notes that traditional values of the Asian Americans have provided them with a structure and a strong sense of moral values.

Asian-American families cannot be separated from their cultural precedents. A large number of immigrants read and attempt to understand the American way of life. This helps them adjust to cross-cultural experiences. Most Asian Americans also feel a deep sense of identity with their cultural past and make a conscious effort to perpetuate it. Such cultural persistence is particularly strong in marriage. First-generation immigrants face a heightened sense of vulnerability, as they suffer from both deep-rooted cultural barriers and their own unfamiliarity with social resources.

Acculturation in America has brought about changes for the younger population, especially for the younger generation born in the United States. It has weakened the traditional social ties and gender roles, and increased stress on all the family members. Asian Americans experience unique problems with reference to language and cultural factors, and also stereotypes about them as visible minorities (Song, 1993).

Although the first generation maintains a great deal of the old culture and may appear to be a "closed group" in which intermarriage is controlled by ethnic community preferences, this picture is changing. The incidence of intermarriage among children of Asian immigrants is very high, and with such intermarriage cultures assimilate and intermingle, moving closer to nuclear, monogamous family patterns. Extended-family relationships continue to exist in many Asian-American families. Doting grandparents, large family gatherings, outings, and vacations often include many in-laws. In these gatherings, the "successes and failures" of friends and acquaintances are told and retold, becoming a part of family folklore and serving as models for the younger generations. Acceptable standards of behavior and acceptable norms are discussed in conjunction with everyday happenings, jokes, and gossip (Kitano & Kikumura, 1977). The traditional values of Asian cultures provide the society with a social structure and a strong sense of moral values. In many traditional families, men discipline the children, so children perceive them as somewhat distant and difficult to approach. Traditional culture views the mother as highly devoted, nurturing, and attached. It is not culturally sanctioned for parents to leave children in day-care centers, but a working mother may leave her children with a close relative (Ho, 1987). Small children are pampered, protected, and showered with love. Some young Asian children may appear to be overprotected and overdependent by Euro-American standards, but this is not generally a problem as it remains within the limits set up by the culture. As children grow older, they are expected to exhibit increasingly formal behavior, including respect for authority, strict obedience, politeness, and high achievement in school.

Like many other ethnic and racial groups, Asian Americans believe that problems should be resolved within the family. The culture views problems as failure to fulfill moral obligations (Ho, 1987). According to Shon and Ja (1996), Asians may feel they have failed if they turn to any outsider for help, including social workers and other human-service practitioners. Therefore they do not seek help until they have exhausted their resources. If they have no internal resources, they may turn to their traditional healers for help. Only after every resource has been exhausted do they seek help from Western practitioners. They tend to be obedient and unquestioning and look up for guidance and direction, which places a great deal of responsibility on the social worker (Chao, 1992). It is important for the worker to capitalize on their strengths rather than focus on their weaknesses.

Many Asian Americans have adapted to the new culture and defined new roles for themselves. Some disadvantages of acculturation are that it may weaken traditional social ties and norms of interdependence and mutuality, especially for younger people. Where an extended family and its resources are lost, a family of parents and children stands alone emotionally, economically, and socially.

IMPLICATIONS FOR SOCIAL-WORK PRACTICE

Many differences affect the developmental stages of families and individuals, and there is also a social history behind all families. Understanding different developmental stages helps the social worker understand when to intervene and how. Intervention must be based on understanding of social-class, ethnic, and racial differences in a society. Cultures cannot be understood from a narrow perspective. Work with a traditional Native-American Indian family differs from work with an African-American family. Forms and styles of family living also differ. For example, living in a two-parent home differs from living in a single-parent family. Advantages, issues, and problems in such homes vary. Contemporary society advocates monogamy and a move toward equality between partners. However, social workers need to be aware of differences in cultures, such as levels of authority claimed by men in some groups, before advocating change. The aware social worker must work within cultural restraints, remembering that there are common human experiences, emotions, and needs.

The challenges of working with single parents are many. Often they are overloaded with responsibilities as they play the role of two parents to a child, with the added responsibility of a full-time job. Helping such a family function effectively in promoting the physical, emotional, and social growth of each member requires not only clinical skills but an awareness of laws, social policies, and social programs in such areas as family leave, family child care, and adequate health care for mothers and their infants.

The ability to understand and work empathetically with different lifestyles is essential. To promote strong, positive family relationships, the worker needs to respect social, cultural, religious, ethnic, racial, biological, sexual, and psychological differences as they influence marital lifestyles and family structures. The law, of course, sets limits on the acceptance of alternative lifestyles; for example, this society does not tolerate bigamy, incest, withholding of medical care from sick children, ultraharsh physical punishment, or keeping children out of school. It is important for the worker to remember that families come for help because they need services, not to have their values questioned. This is particularly true of families that do not conform to mainstream rules and regulations of behavior. For example, a social worker was screening a client for the purpose of helping. The client, who had a homosexual lifestyle, said, "I know who I am, but I have problems in my relationship with my partner. I hope you will not use religion to make me feel guilty or use it to want to make me change. . . . I am tired of such counseling." Clearly, this client has had unpleasant counseling or therapy experiences.

When families seek help, they usually do so because they are dissatisfied. They may be unable to resolve family problems within the spousal relationship, draw boundaries for parent–child relationships, or solve problems among three-generation families or with adult children who have not learned to deal with issues and are tied to the family of origin in ways that do not encourage growth. Some family problems may require the intervention of law enforcement officials. The law requires the social worker to inform the police in cases of severe battering of a spouse, child, or elderly family member. In working with a family dealing with or contemplating divorce, which affects both adults and children, the worker must learn to help the different subsystems of the family reach their goals. Some families must deal with terminal illness and death. Effectiveness in helping requires understanding the role and position of the terminally ill—or deceased—person in the life of the family and the developmental stage of the family. Nondevelopmental situations such as physical and mental disabilities present many emotional, relational, economic, medical, legal, and other implications that the worker needs to understand in order to help.

Sexual abuse of children is both a family and a state problem. The law requires that it be reported for court action before social-services help is offered.

All plans for family intervention should follow a rational assessment of a situation in which the family is involved as fully as possible. In setting goals and providing services, social workers need to keep in mind the ideals and aspirations of different families. We need to work at making individuals and the social system more supportive of each other within the framework of the family's own ideals and aspirations.

SUMMARY

Families are microsystems of society, and they can be seen as systems because they create linkages between different members of the family. The family has undergone a number of changes through the years and means different things to different people. Traditionally it is a long-term legal and social relationship in which to raise children and meet the physical, emotional, and sexual needs of two people.

Families perform both manifest and latent functions. Manifest functions include procreation and socialization, production and consumption, and emotional development and support. Latent functions of the family include perpetuation of the norms and values of society.

The family is a system of changing roles where children are born, grow up, and move on. Roles and lifestyles can change in an orderly fashion, or changes can be sudden, disruptive, and discontinuous. Family begins with a couple getting married, followed by the birth of the first child and the responsibilities of parenthood, which include sharing and caring for family members. The preschool family begins when a child enters preschool; this is an adjustment period for both parents and child. The school-age family starts when the child or children enter school on a full-time basis and continues until puberty. The adolescent family may face chaos as a child begins to mature physically and emotionally and to question the authority and boundaries created by parents. The launching family is ready to let go of their young adult children as they leave home to attend college or take up a job and learn to cope with the outside world by themselves. The postparental family is the adult couple facing life by themselves. Depending on their relationship with each other through the years, this could be a happy or an unhappy time. The aging family begins when one of the two retires and grandparenting becomes a new role.

A nondevelopmental crisis is a serious problem that can upset the family equilibrium. Such a situation might be a divorce, terminal illness, mental or physical disability, child or elder abuse, and domestic violence. In divorce, the parents must negotiate emotional and physical separations. In terminal illness, the patient can have an impact on different family members and their ability to cope and adapt to this painful experience. Severe mental and physical disabilities in children can cause a great deal of grief to parents and siblings. Parents react in different ways; their coping abilities include awareness, denial, recognition, search for a cause, search for a cure, and finally, acceptance. Family violence is a major social problem in the United States. In spousal abuse there is a pattern of physical and/or psychological abuse and exploitation. Battered, violently abused women require financial support and services to break the cycle. Child abuse involves a negative act against a child, that is, withholding or failing to provide something a child needs. Abuse may be physical, psychological, or sexual; it has no boundaries and is found in all socioeconomic, racial, ethnic, and religious groups. Elder abuse is becoming more widely acknowledged and includes psychological, financial, and physical neglect. Domestic violence and drug abuse are closely interrelated; in homes where physical or sexual violence occurs, alcoholism and drug use are usually present as well.

Family diversity involves socioeconomic, cultural, and individual differences. Social scientists believe that the type of family life a person leads is related to socioeconomic status, which can be classified as the poor, the working class, the middle class, and the rich.

Another common family type is the single-parent family. Some women give birth or adopt children by choice; others become single parents either accidentally or through unplanned pregnancy or divorce. One-parent families are usually headed by mothers, who bear sole responsibility for the emotional and physical care of children. These responsibilities can limit women's employment opportunities and place heavy financial burdens on them. Today awareness is dawning that single parents need help, and social agencies are beginning to develop new counseling and ancillary services to meet their needs.

Finally, a third group of single parents, usually slightly older and not poor, are those who make a conscious choice to bear children outside of marriage.

Many divorced people remarry, so very often one parent is not biologically related to the children in the home. Many Americans live in stepfamilies, where children from two different households may experience invisible and divided loyalties. Stepfamilies have insiders and outsiders. Power issues come into play because each parent has developed rules, norms, customs, and routines. Members feel losses in terms of in-laws and grandparents, boundary problems, and closeness and distancing.

Extended or three-generational families may live together, as among some ethnic groups that immigrated from Europe, Asia, Haiti, the Caribbean, and Latin America. These culturally congruent relationships are a way of life in many cultures.

Gay and lesbian families are making strong efforts to become a public part of the larger society. Gay and lesbian families perform the same functions as other families, including housework and child rearing.

The United States is a multicultural society encompassing many different racial and ethnic groups. As the twenty-first century begins, racial and ethnic diversity will have increasing importance in defining our future.

African-American families incorporate many different lifestyles. Although female heads of families have their problems, many form domestic networks with relatives such as a mother, aunt, grandmother, or brother. African-American couples seem to have more egalitarian relationships than do other American couples. There are distinct pathways to upward mobility among African-Americans. The family is also closely connected to the African-American church.

Hispanic families are embedded in kinship systems that offer reciprocal support and obligations. The Hispanic group includes Puerto Ricans, Mexican Americans, Central and South American Spanish-speaking groups, and Cubans. Among Mexican Americans, immediate family includes aunts, uncles, grandparents, cousins, and in-laws. A great deal of value is attached to strong and intimate relationships with kin and companions. The hierarchical family structure has strict rules governing age and gender roles, and family members follow them. With acculturation, Cuban Americans have increasingly adopted the nuclear family structure.

Native-American Indians come from very different cultural backgrounds. Despite assimilation into the larger society, they show great respect for kinship, although the kinship groups as lineages and classes have been abandoned. Elders are still respected. Native-American Indians who live in the cities, where there is a great deal of assimilation, differ greatly from those who live on reservations, who tend to follow their own culture intimately, with very little input from the outside world.

Asian-American nationalities differ greatly. Family life is considered extremely important, and family ties are strong. In the younger generation, acculturation has weakened traditional social ties and has increased stress among all family members. As visible minorities, some Asian Americans experience unique problems, particularly racism and underemployment.

SUGGESTED READINGS

Briggs, H. E., & Koroloff, N. M. (1995, August). Enhancing family advocacy network: An analysis of the roles of sponsoring organizations. *Community Mental Health Journal. 31*(4), 317–333.

Lant, J., & Alford, K. (1995, September). Art in existential psychotherapy with couples and families. *Contemporary Family Therapy: An International Journal, 17*(3), 331–342.

Mausner, S. (1995). Families helping families: An innovative approach to the provision of respite care for families of children with complex medical needs. Special issue: Social work in pediatrics. *Social Work in Health Care, 21*(1), 95–106.

McCluskey, U., & Miller, L. B. (1995). Theme-focused family therapy: The inner emotional world of the family. *Journal of Family Therapy, 17*(4), 411–434.

Unrau, Y. A. (1995, Fall). Defining the black box of family preservation service: A conceptual framework for service delivery. *International Journal of Family Care, 7*(2), 49–60.

Weiler, J. B. (1995). Respite care for HIV-affected families. *Social Work in Health Care, 21*(1), 55–67.

SUGGESTED VIDEOTAPES

Family and survival. (1986). Multimedia Entertainment, Films for the Humanities and Sciences, 11 Perrine Rd., Monmouth Junction, NJ 08852. 52 minutes.

Healing from childhood sexual abuse. (1994). Laura LeMarr, Filmmakers Library, 124 E. 40th Street, Suite 901, New York, NY 10016. 29 minutes.

Impact of divorce on family. (1990). Meridian Education Corporation, 236 E. Front St., Bloomington, IL 61701. 16 minutes.

Impact of single parenting. (1990). Meridian Education Corporation, 236 E. Front St., Bloomington, IL 61701. 16 minutes.

Incest: The family secret. (1985). Canadian Broadcasting Corporation, Filmmakers Library, 124 E. 40th Street, Suite 901, New York, NY 10016. 57 minutes.

Sociological imagination: Social class. (1991). Dallas Telecourses, RMI Media Productions, 1365 N. Winchester St., Olathe, KS 66061. 19 minutes.

REFERENCES

American Association of Retired Persons (AARP) (1993). *A profile of older Americans.* Washington, DC: Author, p. 4.

Barncik, S., & Shapiro, I. (1992). *Where have all the dollars gone? A state-by-state analysis of income disparities over the 1980s.* Washington, DC: Center for Budget and Policy Priorities.

Bengston, V. (1987). Parenting, grandparenting and intergenerational continuity. In J. Lancaster, J. Altman, A. Rossi, & L. Sherrod (eds.), *Parenting across the lifespan.* New York: Aldine de Gruyter, pp. 435–456.

Berry, M. (1994). *Keeping families together.* New York: Garland.

Bertalanffy, L. Von (1934). *Modern theories of development: An introduction to theoretical biology.* London: Oxford University Press.

Billingsley, A. (1992). *Climbing Jacob's ladder: The enduring legacy of African-American families.* New York: Simon & Schuster.

Bingham, S. (1993). The truth about growing up rich. In V. Cyrus (ed.), *Experiencing race, class, and gender in the United States.* Mountain View, CA: Mayfield.

Bound, I., Duncan, G. J., Laren, D. S., & Olenick, L. (1991). Poverty dynamics in widowhood. *Journal of Gerontology, 46,* S115–S124.

Bureau of Statistics, U.S. Department of Labor (1993). Washington, DC: U.S. Government Printing Office.

Buysse, V., & Bailey, D. B. (1993). Behavioral and development outcomes in young children with disabilities in integrated and segregated settings: A review of comparative studies. *Journal of Special Education, 26,* 434–461.

Carter, E. A., & McGoldrick, M. (1980). The family life cycle and family therapy: An overview. In E. A. Carter & M. McGoldrick (eds.), *The family life cycle: A framework for family therapy.* New York: Gardner Press.

Chao, C. M. (1992). The inner heart: Therapy with Southeast Asian families. In L. A. Vargas & J. D. Koss-Chioino (eds.), *Working with culture: Psychotherapeutic interventions with ethnic minority children and adolescents.* San Francisco: Jossey-Bass, pp. 157–181.

Cherlin, A. (1988). Women and the family. In S. E. Rix (ed.), *The American woman: A status report 1987–88.* New York: Norton, p. 67.

Clarke-Stewart, A. (1993). *Daycare* (2nd ed.). Cambridge, MA: Harvard University Press.

Cole, P. M., & Putnam, F. W. (1992). Effect of incest on self and social functioning: A developmental psychopathology perspective. *Journal of Consulting and Clinical Psychology, 60,* 174–184.

Committee on Ways and Means, U.S. House of Representatives (1992). *Background materials and data on programs within the jurisdiction of the Committee on Ways and Means* (102nd Congress 2nd session). Washington DC: U.S. Government Printing Office.

Committee on Ways and Means, U.S. House of Representatives (1993). *Overview of entitlement programs: 1993 Greenbook.* Washington DC: U.S. Government Printing Office, p. 1110.

Conte, J. R. (1987). Child sexual abuse. In *Encyclopedia of Social Work* (Vol. 1). Springfield, MD: National Association of Social Workers, pp. 255–260.

Conte, J. R. (1995). Child sexual abuse overview. In *Encyclopedia of Social Work* (19th ed.). Washington, DC: National Association of Social Workers, pp. 402–408.

Cowan, R. S. (1983). *More work for mother.* New York: Basic Books.

Danziger, S. K., & Danziger, S. (1993). Child poverty and public policy: Toward a comprehensive anti-poverty agenda. *Daedalus, 122*(1), 57–85.

Diehm, C., & Ross, M. (1993). Battered women. In V. Cyrus (ed.), *Experiencing race, class and gender in the United States*. Mountain View, CA: Mayfield, pp. 404–406.

Duvall, E. M., & Hill, R. (1948). *Reports of the committee for the dynamics of family interaction*. Prepared at the request of the National Conference of Family Life, Washington, DC. Mimeographed.

Falicov, C. J. (1982). Mexican families. In M. McGoldrick, J. K. Pearce, & J. Giordano (eds.), *Ethnicity and family therapy*. New York: Guilford Press, pp. 134–163.

Fine, M. A. (1995). Stepparenting. In D. Levinson (ed.), *Encyclopedia of marriage and the family,* Vol. 2. New York: Simon & Schuster/Macmillan, pp. 683–686.

Garcia-Preto, N. (1982). Puerto Rican families. In M. McGoldrick, J. K. Pearce, & J. Giordano. (eds.) *Ethnicity and family therapy*. New York: Guilford Press, pp. 164–186.

Germain, C. B. (1991). *Human behavior in the social environment*. New York: Columbia University Press.

Ghali, S. B. (1982, January). Understanding Puerto Rican traditions. *Social Work, 21,* 98–102.

Gigy, L., & Kelly, J. B. (1992). Reasons for divorce: Perspectives of divorcing men and women. *Journal of Divorce and Remarriage, 18,* 169–187.

Gold, R. B., & Daley, D. (1991). Public funding of contraceptive, sterilization, and abortion services, fiscal year 1990. *Family Planning Perspectives, 23*(5), 204–211.

Goodman, B. (1980). Some mothers are lesbians. W. Walsh (ed.), *Normal family processes*. New York: Guilford Press, pp. 297–330.

Goodman, M. E. (1964). *Race awareness in young children*. New York: Collier.

Gordon, W. E. (1969). Basic constructs for an integrative and generative conception of social work. In G. Hearn (ed.). *The general systems approach: Contributions toward an holistic conception of social work.* New York: Council on Social Work Education, pp. 5–12.

Gray, J. D., & Silver, R. C. (1990). Opposite sides of the same coin: Former spouses' divergent perspectives in coping with their divorce. *Journal of Personality and Social Psychology, 59,* 1180–1191.

Guralnick, M. J., & Groom, J. M. (1988). Friendships of preschool children in mainstreamed playgroups. *Developmental Psychology, 24,* 595–604.

Hartman, A. (1981). Family: A central focus for practice. *Social Work, 26,* 7–13.

Hill, R., & Rogers, R. H. (1964). The developmental approach. In H. T. Christensen (ed.), *Handbook of marriage and family*. Chicago: Rand McNally.

Ho, M. K. (1987). Family therapy with Asian Pacific Americans. In M. K. Ho (ed.), *Family therapy with ethnic minorities*. Beverly Hills, CA: Sage, pp. 24–38.

Houseknecht, S. K., & Macke, A. S. (1981). Combining marriage and career. The marital adjustment of professional women. *Journal of Marriage and the Family, 43,* 651–661.

Isisaka, H. A., & Takagi, C. Y. (1982). Social work with Asian and Pacific Americans. In J. W. Green (ed.), *Cultural awareness in the human services*. Englewood Cliffs, NJ: Prentice Hall, p. 50.

Jones, R. M. (1995, July). The price of welfare dependency: Children pay. *Social Work, 40*(3), 496–505.

Kinard, E. M. (1987). Child abuse and neglect. *Encyclopedia of Social Work* (Vol. 1). Springfield, MD: National Association of Social Workers, pp. 223–231.

Kitano, H. H. L., & Kikumura, A. (1977). The Japanese American family. In C. H. Mindel & R. W. Habenstein (eds.), *Ethnic families in America*. New York: Elsevier Scientific, pp. 41–60.

Lincoln, C. E., & Mamiya, L. H. (1990). *The black church in the African American experience*. Durham, NC: Duke University Press.

Longres, J. F. (1990). *Human behavior in the social environment*. Itasca, IL: Peacock.

Love, H. (1973). *The mentally retarded child and his family*. Springfield, IL: Thomas.

Madden, N. A., & Slavin, R. E. (1983). Mainstreaming students with mild handicaps: Academic and social outcomes. *Review of Educational Research, 53,* 519–569.

Martin, E., & Martin, J. (1978). *The black extended family*. Chicago: University of Chicago Press.

Mead, M., & Hayman, K. (1965). *Family*. New York: Macmillan.

Meade, R. (1971). *Assessment of personal motivations for child bearing: Proceedings of Conference on Psychological Measurement in Family Planning and Population Policy*. Berkeley: University of California Press.

Meyer, C. H. (1990, April 11). *Can social work keep up with the changing family?* Monograph. The fifth annual Robert O'Leary memorial lecture, Columbus: The Ohio State University College of Social Work, pp. 1–24.

Minuchin, S. (1974). *Families and family therapy*. Cambridge, MA: Harvard University Press.

Mizio, E. (1974, February). Impact of external systems on the Puerto Rican family. *Social Casework, 55,* 76–83.

Moore, K. A., Blumenthal, C., Sugland, B. W., Hyatt, B., Snyder, N. O., & Morrison, D. R. (1994). State variations in rates of adolescent pregnancy and childbearing. Final report to the Charles Stewart Mott Foundation, Washington, DC: *Child Trends*.

Moore, K. A., & Burt, M. R. (1982). *Private crisis, public cost: Policy perspectives on teenage childbearing*. Washington DC: Urban Institute Press.

Moskas, C. (1993, April 30). Homosexual bashing. *Virginian-Pilot and Ledger-Star,* p. A4.

Motenko, A. K., & Greenberg, S. (1995, May). Reframing dependence in old age: A positive transition for families. *Social Work, 40*(3), 382–390.

Neugarten, B. L., & Weinstein, K. K. (1964). The changing American grandparent. *Journal of Marriage and Family, 26*(2).

Okun, B. F., & Rappaport, L. J. (1980). Working with families: An introduction to family therapy. Boston, MA: Duxbury Press.

Parsons, T. (1964). *The social system*. New York: Free Press.

Patterson, C. J. (1992). Children of lesbian and gay parents. *Child Development, 63,* 1025–1042.

Patterson, C. J., Kupersmidt, J. B., & Vaden, N. A. (1990). Income level, gender, and ethnicity and household composition as prediction of children's school-based competence. *Child Development, 61,* 485–494.

Peplau, L. A. (1991). Lesbian and gay relationships. In J. C. Gonsiorek & J. D.

Weinrich (eds.), *Homosexuality: Research implications for public policy*. Newbury Park, CA: Sage, pp. 177–196.

Pillari, V. (1991). *Scapegoating in families: Intergenerational patterns of physical and emotional abuse*. New York: Brunner/Mazel.

Plotnick, R. D. (1987). Income distribution. In *Encyclopedia of Social Work* (18th ed.). Silver Spring, MD: National Association of Social Workers, pp. 882–883.

Plotnick, R. D. (1995). Income distribution. In *Encyclopedia of Social Work* (19th ed.). Washington, DC: National Association of Social Workers, pp. 1439–1447.

Price, J. A. (1977). North American Indian families. In C. H. Mindel & R. W. Habenstein, (eds.), *Ethnic families in America*. New York: Elsevier, pp. 248–270.

Price, J. A. (1981). North American Indian families: Patterns and variations. In C. H. Mindel & R. W. Habenstein (eds.), *Ethnic Families in America* (2nd ed.). New York: Elsevier, p. 265.

Queralt, M. (1984, March–April). Understanding Cuban immigrants: A cultural perspective. *Social Work, 29,* 115–121.

Rapp, R. (1982). Family and class in contemporary America: Notes toward an understanding of ideology. In B. Thorne (ed.) with M. Yalom, *Rethinking family: Some feminine questions*. New York: Longman.

Rubin, L. B. (1984). *Intimate strangers: Men and women together*. New York: Harper & Row.

Ryan, A. S. (1992). Asian-American women: A historical and cultural perspective. In A. Weick & S. T. Vandiver, (eds.), *Women, power and change*. Washington, DC: National Association of Social Workers, pp. 78–88.

Santiago, A. M. (1992). Patterns of Puerto Rican segregation and mobility. *Hispanic Journal of Behavioral Sciences, 14*(1), 107–133.

Sawhill, I. V. (1992). Poverty in the U.S.: Trends, sources and policy implications. *Social Insurance Update,* No. 25, pp. 1–4.

Scanzoni, J. (1982). *Sexual bargaining: Power politics in the American marriage* (2nd ed.). Chicago: University of Chicago Press, p. 48.

Schultz, R., & Decker, S. (1985). Long-term adjustments to physical disability: The role of social support, perceived control, and self-blame. *Journal of Personality and Social Psychology, 48,* 1162–1172.

Scott, S., & Eisenberg, M. (1993). Child care research: Issues, perspectives and results. *Annual Review of Psychology, 44,* 613–644.

Shon, S. P., & Ja, D. Y. (1996). Asian families. In M. McGoldrick, J. K. Pearce, & J. Giordiano (eds.), *Ethnicity and family therapy*. New York: Guilford Press.

Sidel, R. (1993). Who are the poor? V. Cyrus (ed.), *Experiencing race, class and gender in the United States*. Mountain View, CA: Mayfield Press, pp. 111–114.

Song, Y. I. (1993). Asian American women's experience in the crossfire of cultural conflict. Y. I. Song & E. C. Kim (eds.), *American mosaic*. Englewood Cliffs, NJ: Prentice Hall, pp. 186–203.

Song, Y. I., & Kim, E. C. (1993). Introduction, *American mosaic: Selected readings on Americans*. Englewood Cliffs, NJ: Prentice Hall, pp. xiii–xv.

Stack, C. B. (1974). *All our kin: Strategies for survival in a black community*. New York: Harper & Row.

Stack, C. B. (1983). Sex roles and survival strategies in an urban black community. In H. R. Clark & C. Clark (eds.), *Social interaction: Readings in sociology*. New York: St. Martin's Press.

Star, B. (1987). Domestic violence. *Encyclopedia of Social Work* (18th ed., Vol. 1). Silver Spring, MD: National Association of Social Workers, pp. 463–476.

Sugland, B. W., Moore, K. A., & Blumenthal, C. (1994). State family planning services delivery administrators' perspectives on service delivery options for family planning services. Washington, DC: *Child Trends*.

Tidwell, B. J. (1997). *The black report*. New York: Data Deeds, L. LP & University Press of Americas.

Tienda, M. (1989). Puerto Ricans and the underclass debate. *Annals of the American Academy of Political and Social Sciences, 501,* 105–119.

Timberlake, E. (1980). The value of grandchildren to grandmothers. *Journal of Gerontological Social Work, 3,* 63–76.

Timberlake, E. M., & Chipungu, S. S. (1992, May). Grandmotherhood: Contemporary meaning among African American middle class grandmothers. *Social Work, 37,* 216–222.

U.S. Bureau of the Census. Poverty in the United States, 1995. *Current Population Reports*. P60-194. Washington, DC: U.S. Government Printing Office.

U.S. Bureau of the Census. (1992a). The black population in the United States: March 1991. *Current Population Reports,* P20–464. Washington, DC: U.S. Government Printing Office.

U.S. Bureau of the Census. (1989a). *Current Population Reports* (Series P-25, Nos. 1045 and 1057. Washington, D.C: U.S. Government Printing Office.

U.S. Bureau of the Census. (1989b). *Current Population Reports* (Series P-60, No. 161). Washington, DC: U.S. Government Printing Office.

U.S. Bureau of the Census. (1991a). The Hispanic population in the United States: March, 1990. *Current Population Reports,* P20, No. 449. Washington, DC: U.S. Government Printing Office.

U.S. Bureau of the Census. (1991b). *Percentage of people age 65+ who are poor and near poor, 1990*. Washington, DC: U.S. Government Printing Office.

U.S. Bureau of the Census. (1993). *Statistical abstract of the United States: 1993*. (113th ed.), Austin, TX: Reference Press, p. 63.

U.S. Bureau of the Census. (1988). *Statistical abstract of the United States: 1987*. Washington, DC: U.S. Government Printing Office.

U.S. Bureau of the Census. (1992b). *Statistical abstract of the United States*. Washington, DC: U.S. Government Printing Office.

Visher, L., & Visher, V. (1988). *Step-families and divided loyalties*. New York: Brunner/Mazel.

Wald, E. (1981). *The remarried family: Challenge and promise*. New York: Family Service Association of America.

Walsh, F. (1980). The family in later life. In E. A. Carter & M. McGoldrick (eds.), *The family life cycle: A framework for family therapy*. New York: Gardner Press, pp. 197–220.

Wright, J. W. (1993). *The Universal Almanac*. Kansas City, MO: Andrews and McMeel.

Yarrow, A. L. (1987, January 12). Divorce at a young age: The troubled twenties. *New York Times,* p. 719.

Zaretsky, E. (1973). *Capitalism: The family and personal life*. New York: Harper Colophon, pp. 56–66.

Zick, C. D., & Smith, K. R. (1991). Patterns of economic change surrounding the death of a spouse. *Journal of Gerontology, 46,* S310–S320.

3

What Are Groups?

People become members of groups either because they chose to, or because they are members of a natural group. For example, a person could choose to be a member of any specific university, depending on his or her needs, interests, aspirations, and commitments. This university system would then be a group of choice. We are also born into natural groups, for example, by being male or female, or by belonging to a particular ethnic or racial group. In Chapter 5 we also discuss ethnic and racial groups as communities.

All groups have effects on people and influence them in ways that may take us by surprise—for example, when people become members of cults. It can be amazing to hear about everything members of a group will accept and adapt to, in order to fit in, satisfying the need to belong. Or, they may be so taken in by a group leader that they are willing to listen to and perform whatever is required. In the small Branch Davidian cult in Waco, Texas, David Koresh called himself God or the Messiah and then slept with and/or married eight to ten women from the group and fathered a number of children. As the members are inducted into the ways of the group by a charismatic leader, everything becomes acceptable.

Like communities and organizations, groups are evolving systems. They create an atmosphere and a social, psychological, and physical culture that influence the development of the members (Shulman, 1982). Individuals are affected by their social environment and conform to group norms because they feel a need to belong. For example, Corky is a member of a religious group that meets three days a week. Her manner of dress symbolizes that she belongs to this group. In addition, Corky does religious missionary work, which satisfies a group expectation and gives her status and identity as a member of the group.

In this chapter we look at social groups, beginning with group membership, social structure, and formed and natural groups. We discuss group membership, stages of group development, norms, cohesion, goals, leadership, types of groups, and implications for social-work practice. We also consider attitudes—how they are formed and maintained, and how they can be changed by the group.

Social groups arise when a person develops a continuing relationship with one or more others. A group is a social system, made up of two or more people who are psychologically related and who may depend on each other to fulfill certain needs and goals. Like other living systems, groups are goal oriented (Miller, 1978). Sometimes people join groups that already exist; sometimes they organize new groups. Northen (1988) notes that, besides the family,

> People belong to many other types of groups, during their life span. Early in his (her) development, a child participates in many informal play and fellowship dyads and larger groups; these affiliations change as he (or she) grows older and assumes new roles. People spend many years of their lives in formal and informal educational groups. Many join groups of a supportive,

> self-help, developmental or therapeutic nature. Many adults are members of committees and organizations that further their interests or make contributions to the community. (pp. 40–41)

Anderson and Carter (1990) note that everyone belongs to several social groups, which offer the person the chance to satisfy a range of human needs. Some of these needs are a need to belong and be accepted, a need to be validated through feedback processes, a need to share common experiences, and an opportunity to work with others on common tasks. The term *group* includes those patterns of associations in which people engage most of their "selves" on a day-to-day basis.

INTRODUCTION TO GROUPS

We belong to a number of groups, some intentionally and others because we just happened to be there. Some are formed, or formal, groups, and others are informal. Examples of formal groups are college, school, and recreational clubs. In this chapter we focus on small groups, group boundaries, and concrete membership in groups. Such groups, which are made up of people with whom one visits frequently and has face-to-face encounters, are called *interactional* groups (Blumberg, Hare, Kent, & Davis, 1983).

When you are building new friendships with a group of people, you are working in an interactional group, and you have become interdependent with others. In groups you cannot be "just yourself," because you also must consider the needs of other members. This interdependence can be viewed as an "exchange"; you give up some personal autonomy in return for the actual or potential advantages of group membership.

One advantage of being a member of a group is having people to talk to and share things with. Other benefits are practical and task oriented, such as being able to get together to work on a school project, to play tennis, and to participate in discussions about various issues. People who have affection and respect for each other and have similar attitudes toward life or have common goals and interests make up a large number of interactional groups (Blumberg et al., 1983).

SOCIAL STRUCTURE OF GROUPS

A group consists of two or more people interacting in such a manner that each influences and is influenced by every other. Groups typically form when two or more people feel that the pleasure of each other's company would be more rewarding than being socially isolated (Shaw, 1981).

Informal groups have no stated set of regulations that govern members' behavior. They do have informal rules based on members' needs and cultural expectations of how people should behave in different social situations. For instance, at a party, if a person is too noisy or is assaultive he or she could be asked to leave.

At times groups begin as dyads. When two people are attracted to each other, they may feel no initial need to discuss rules of interaction, because there is no conflict. However, when differences emerge, the dyad may not last very long, even though it may have begun as an exciting relationship. In a dyad, when there are differences each person must compromise and adjust to the other's needs and feelings. No group can survive unless there is at least a certain level of consensus on what members can and cannot do (Hewstone, 1988). If there is no minimum agreement, the group may never get off the ground.

Formed and Natural Groups

As noted earlier, there are basically two kinds of groups: formed (formal) and natural. Formed groups are established either by individuals or by an organization such as a social agency, a school, or a company. The group members convene for a particular purpose. Such groups may be committees, teams, classes, clubs, or therapy groups.

Group membership may be voluntary or involuntary. A person may choose to join a committee or take a class. However, sometimes membership and participation are mandatory. For example, members of counseling groups in prisons are generally required to attend meetings. If they do not, the consequences may include loss of visitation or other privileges. Patients in a rehabilitation center for alcoholics may be required to attend group meetings every day.

Although we will focus on formed groups, remember that skills and concepts concerning formal groups also apply to natural groups. Natural groups begin in a spontaneous manner, with people coming together on the basis of informal attraction, common backgrounds, shared interests, location, and so on. Natural groups include peer groups, street gangs, and cliques. They also include friendship groups such as may develop in hospitals and nursing homes or other residential settings where people live together for a while. For example, when an elderly man had a paralytic stroke he was admitted into a rehabilitation hospital, where he progressively became more functional. There were other people like him, and he enjoyed their company. It became an informal ritual for the men to meet daily in their wheelchairs and discuss their progress. They also discussed their families and their marriages, and who was the most caring of their relatives, and so on. As they became better, they chatted while eating and missed each other's company when they were not together. Finally, when one was well enough to leave, they exchanged addresses and hoped to be in touch with each other and get together at a nearby restaurant for the fun of chatting, laughing, and being together.

Group Membership

People join groups for a variety of reasons. They may wish to participate in the activity being conducted, and they may like the group members. Another reason for joining groups is to satisfy needs that lie outside the group. Some businesspeople joined a very exclusive and expensive social club frequented by wealthy people who soon became their customers. Mentioning the name of the club was a name-dropping technique that lent them prestige.

People often belong to several groups simultaneously. In a single day, June participates in a faculty journal club, lunches with friends from law school, conducts a seminar on family violence, and attends a PTA meeting in the evening. People may even join groups with conflicting norms or values. For example, a person is not usually a member of both a traditional orthodox Catholic church and also a member of Planned Parenthood. Yet someone who engages in sleazy business practices may be an outstanding member of a church on Sundays. A minister may sexually abuse congregants, yet be an active member of the civil rights groups in town.

Factors that attract or repel people from particular groups are highly individual, depending on the person and on the group. What attracts one person to a group, including prestige, size, and so forth, may turn another person off. A group that Jane sees as prestigious, John may see as snobbish. Some people like small groups because they want intimacy and involvement; others prefer larger groups oriented toward goals rather than relationships.

The group may offer the individual different types of prestige: the prestige of the group itself, and the prestige or standing of the individual within the group. For example, belonging to a particular golf or country club may offer prestige to some people, and they may join to make the "right" friends and "move" in the right circles. And individuals are sometimes attracted to a group because they themselves are given authority in the group. In another group they might have lower status. Those who maintain high positions and high prestige in a group work to maintain this status.

When group members are more cooperative, an atmosphere of care and nurturing is developed. A cooperative setting is more helpful for members than a competitive setting. The degree of intimacy among the group members increases when they interact. Heightened interaction among members may increase the group's attractiveness, as may participating or enjoying each other's company and making good friends with each other. If group members are bored or do not care about each other, the group becomes less attractive.

For example, Katie has worked for a large company for eight years. It is one of the best things that has happened to her. Working with her colleagues is fun, and she has learned to get involved in all the extracurricular activities. She married a co-worker and is very happy; some members of her department have become her best friends.

The size of the group also affects group members. In a small group, it is easier to have personal relationships than in a larger group. As a group increases its membership, interests become more heterogeneous. Feelings toward each other become less personal, formal goals may take precedence, and intimacy and personal involvement may decline. In large groups, a few members often dominate the discussion, and the rest of the group membership may feel less satisfied and may interact less (Levine & Moreland, 1990).

Factors that decrease the attractiveness of groups and cause members to leave include constant disagreement on how to solve group problems, unreasonable or excessive demands on one person, and members who dominate discussions or behave in unpleasant ways. Another factor that may reduce group participation is time. The group may meet at an inconvenient time, or someone may not be able to take on another commitment. And whenever outsiders negatively evaluate the group, members may fall away.

Groups also become more attractive when their position is improved with reference to other groups. People are more likely to join groups that are successful or prestigious (Doreian, 1986).

Ayanna joins a group organized to raise needed funds for the homeless. But a great deal of time is spent on backbiting and other dynamics that hurt group members. The longer Ayanna participates in this group, the less enthusiastic she becomes. Finally, she decides to leave.

Sometimes the interests of a group member change significantly from those of the group, so he or she leaves. Separation may be amicable but necessary, in the best interests of both parties. And sometimes people leave groups and join others, because a second group may be better able to satisfy and fulfill their needs.

Stages of Group Development

Group development is not a straight-line progression from beginning to end but rather shows both positive movement in relationships and setbacks from time to time. In every group, the group dynamics follow complex, interacting internal forces as the group works to achieve goals (Reid, 1991).

The process of group development is complex and represents a pattern of change that can be compared to human life-span development, when growth and development take place from conception and infancy to old age and death. Conception and pregnancy may be viewed as analogous to the pregroup planning and organizing phases; birth is like the first meeting. Just as facing death can arouse denial, rage, and anger, so may the termination of a group. Like individuals, groups do not always move in an orderly fashion but may revert to earlier stages or die when there are problems. A group's life span and development are influenced both by internal forces and by external environment. All successfully functioning groups require a reasonable fit between the level of group development and the members' social and emotional capacities.

In every group there are beginning, middle, and end stages. Different thinkers and group leaders have classified group development into different stages. W. Schutz (1973) writes about three stages in group development: inclusion, control, and affection. Mahler (1969) describes five stages: formation, involvement, transition, working, and ending. Gazda's (1989) four stages are similar to Mahler's: exploration, transition, action, and termination. Hansen, Warner, and Smith (1980) discuss initiation of the group, conflict, confrontation, and development of cohesiveness, productivity, and termination. Yalom (1985) identifies three stages: The initial stage is characterized by orientation, hesitant or ambivalent participation, and the search for meaning; the second, by conflict, dominance, and rebellion; and the third, the cohesion stage, by an increase of morale, trust, and self-disclosure. Corey (1977) has developed a four-stage analysis of group development: orientation, transition, working, and consolidation.

All these formulations present similar pictures of the way groups begin, develop, and end. The description of group development by Garland, Jones, and Kolodny (1965) is especially relevant to groups organized and led by social workers. In the first "preaffiliation" stage, the potential members are ambivalent toward each other. Group members work to maintain some degree of emotional distance from one another, because they do not know each other well and are cautious. They engage in what is called approach-avoidance behavior; tentativeness toward group involvement is reflected in their fluctuating willingness to interact with others and assume responsibility for group programs. Members show a great deal of hesitancy to participate, as they are preoccupied with their own problems and feel uneasiness and apprehension in the initial encounters with the group (Hepworth & Larsen, 1990). But members are also attracted to the group, which is why they joined. They have had rewarding experiences with groups, and hope this group can offer similar rewards. The group leader plays a vital role "by allowing and supporting distance, gently inviting trust, facilitating exploration of the physical and psychological milieu, by providing activities if necessary and initiating group structure" (Garland & Frey, 1973, p. 3).

As the group members become more comfortable, they begin to risk expressing honest feelings or showing some gesture of trust. All the different members can enhance their own experiences by creating a trusting atmosphere. For example, Andrew, an older member in a support group begins to discuss his fears in the group session. He fears that he might be overlooked or excluded from activities because he is older, and he adds that he does not wish to be treated as a parent figure. Other members express empathy with him and praise Andrew for being willing to share his fears and his mistrust. This also helps other group members to loosen up, and they begin to talk about their own fears and inadequacies in the group. Soon all the group members find out that everyone has fears and discomfort in the beginning session of the group.

In the initial meetings of the group, the members decide how much they wish to talk about themselves. Sometimes members are led to believe that the more they disclose, the better off they will be. However, this is not always true. Although self-disclosure is important, it is not healthy to reveal great secrets in group meetings because the person may wrongly believe that sharing such secrets will improve their position. The most useful type of self-disclosure usually happens in an unrehearsed manner. Such disclosures express concern and a certain degree of risk. It is useful when a member shares that he or she is shy, quiet, and afraid to speak up in the group. This gives the other members a frame of reference for more accurately understanding him or her.

All group members should be encouraged to participate in group activities and not merely observe. Although people can learn by observing interactions, such learning is limited. When they do not contribute, others will never get to know them. In turn, they may feel cheated and angry at being the object of others' misjudgments. Group members should pay attention to consistent feedback. If different group members offer the same type of feedback to a member, that member should be able to use it for his or her own benefit.

In the initial session, group members tend to be vague and tentative about what they hope to get from a group experience. Members may ask, "What are we supposed to be doing here?" or "Why don't we get down to business?" and so forth. A certain degree of conflict and lack of direction is to be expected at this stage. As Corey and Corey (1992) comment, the members may have an inner dialogue that says, "I'll take a chance and say what I am thinking, and then I'll see how the leader and others in the group will respond. If they are willing to listen to what I don't like, then perhaps I can trust them with some deeper feelings." Opening dialogues help members clarify the milieu and atmosphere of a group.

In any opening session, members should be able to clarify their personal goals. In every therapy group, there are general goals for the group and personal goals for each member, such as "I want to get in touch with my feelings" and "I want to work on my anger."

The type of structure a group should have depends on what the group members need, such as the need to take on responsibilities. The leader's theoretical orientation and the membership population help determine the amount and type of structuring employed.

The second stage, dominated by power and control issues, commences when the characteristics of the group begin to develop. Patterns of communication, alliances, and subgroups emerge, as do roles and responsibilities. The group members go through a transition as they struggle to belong. They endure the ambiguity and turmoil of change from a nonintimate to an intimate system of relationships while they try to establish a frame of reference wherein new situations become understandable and predictable (Hepworth & Larsen, 1990). Norms and methods for handling group tasks develop, and membership questions arise. To protect themselves, group members seek power and control. During this period, the group leader is viewed as the person with the greatest amount of power and influence, which is aimed at giving or withholding emotional rewards. At this point in the transitional stage, certain basic issues need to be resolved. These include limits of power for the group leader. That is, to what extent will the leader use his or her power to develop leadership within the group? Formal leadership is related to one's official role or position in the group (for example, chairperson or group worker), and informal leadership emerges from the interplay of personalities in the group. This distinction is discussed more fully later in this chapter.

In the second stage, members may feel anxious because they fear looking foolish, being rejected, and not knowing what is expected. There is a great deal of testing as group members establish norms for the power and authority of the group and the group leader. Participants are torn between wanting to stay safe and wanting to risk getting involved. No group effortlessly begins intensive work; leadership is required. The leader should not chastise a reluctant group member but rather explore why he or she is resistant. In some cases the resistance may reflect on the leader's own lack of competence or lack of genuine concern. The leader should respect the members' resistance. Otherwise, the leader is not really respecting the members themselves (Corey & Corey, 1992).

To test the group leader, sometimes members will rebel. During this struggle, the group leader should seek to help the members understand the nature of the power struggle. There may be problem behaviors, and difficult group members may block the establishment of a cohesive and productive group. Two opposite qualities in group members may also create problems: Some members are silent or do not participate at all. Either these members may go unnoticed, or they may be resented. Other people loudly monopolize the discussion and activities of the group. These members use others' opening statements to tell detailed stories of their own lives or problems, revealing self-centeredness. Others ask too many questions, at inappropriate times, so that group meetings become unproductive. Still others jump to give advice. This can become disruptive because other members are not given a chance to think through their own issues. A related tactic is "band-aiding." A group member may use this behavior inappropriately to soothe wounds and lessen pain and also keep people cheerful. Here is an example of band-aiding.

Fred has finally been able to feel his own sadness over the distance he created between himself and his daughters and sons. Sobbing, he talks about how he wants to be a better father. However, before he can complete his cathartic crying, Bill, another group member, puts his hands on Fred's shoulders and tries to reassure him that he has not been such a bad father, because he is still supporting his kids. Bill wants to make Fred feel better so that Bill himself can feel better.

In many situations people want to protect others because they wish to shield them from the intensity of their own pain, and fail to observe the therapeutic effect feeling pain may have. There is a great difference between genuine concern and band-aiding. In real caring, the interest of people who are feeling the pain takes precedence over the feelings of others.

Other problem situations may arise around hostile or dependent members, those who act superior, those who intellectualize every situation, and those who emotionalize everything by talking about "getting in touch with your feelings." The group leader should learn about these patterns of behavior and be ready to deal with them, to help both individual and group to move forward. These situations are opportunities to observe and deal with client problems.

The group leader should give emotional support when group members feel uncertain and are not sure about what direction the group is taking. The group should establish norms or rules of behavior to resolve the uncertainty. To function effectively, the members need confidence and trust in the leader and need to maintain a certain degree of shared power and control. Trust helps group members make a commitment to the group.

In the third stage, intimacy develops, and the group begins to resemble a family. Sibling rivalry crops up, and the group leader is sometimes referred to as a parent. In this stage, the members move from mistrust to trust, the struggle for power is worked through, and members begin to work on their own issues. Some group members begin to disclose themselves in significant and appropriate ways. Others still hold back, fearing rejection or misunderstanding. If the group process is effective, most of the remaining participants will risk the process of self-disclosure to find out about themselves. The group becomes cohesive as group members work together and develop bonds. Members make themselves known to others, by sharing their own pain, allowing themselves to care, initiating meaningful work, and giving meaningful feedback to others. Whenever members avoid discussing crucial matters, there is a chance that the group may fragment. Cohesion is enhanced when both painful and joyous experiences are shared—preferably with a large dose of humor.

For example, let us look at a therapeutic group where career women meet to work through their stress. Candy endlessly complains about how her husband and her children take advantage of her. She complains that her life would be better if they were different. Other group members challenge her and help her see that if she focuses on blaming others and trying to get them to be different she will continue to be powerless. The only person she can change is herself. She may need to say no more often, face the consequences of not being what her family was used to. Candy is becoming more comfortable with the idea that her family members need not like her all the time, and she is paving the road to better understanding of roles and rules in the family.

Confrontation is also allowed in group sessions. Constructive confrontation is a basic part of the productive group. Sensitive confrontation ultimately helps people develop to their fullest capacity and apply confrontation to problems they need to deal with in facing their everyday life.

For example, Julie is helpful by nature. In the group she complains that she is always tired and drained. She says everyone in her life is too demanding. But her behavior in the group is that of a helper. If anyone needs anything, she is there at their call, ready to help. She is always attentive to others and rarely asks for anything for herself. One day she complains that she is not getting anything out of the group for herself and wants to leave. The group leader confronts her: "Many times in the group sessions I have seen you do what you say you do at home. I see you being very helpful to others, and yet you hardly do or ask anything for yourself. I am not surprised by your desire not to come back. In reality you have created the same environment in here as the one at home. I am glad you are finally able to discuss it, and I want you to continue to talk about it until your issues are worked out for you. . . . Quitting the group would only be a copout."

Often group members' ability to change their interpersonal styles depends on their willingness to give and take. Offered sensitively, the observations and reactions of other members can have a great impact. The manner in which interpersonal feedback takes place helps members learn that they are, to a large extent, responsible for creating favorable and unfavorable outcomes and for changing the style in which they relate to others (Rothke, 1986).

During the third stage of group development, there is a great deal of cohesiveness, which is the result of the group members' willingness to let others know them in meaningful ways. The group has moved to a state of intimacy. Conflicts in the group seem to fade, personal involvements among members intensify, and there is a growing recognition of the significance of the group's experience. Members experience an increase in morale and "we-ness" and a deepening commitment to the group's purpose and heightened motivation to carry out plans and tasks to support their group's objectives (Hepworth & Larsen, 1990). This is particularly true when they have faced the conflicts of the earlier stages and have developed trust that allows a "working-through" process. At this stage of group development, feelings are more openly discussed, and personal growth and change are more likely to take place. In this third phase, members feel free to examine and make special efforts to change personal attitudes, look at problems they have, and also work through some of their own concerns.

The differentiation stage can be compared to the well-functioning family where children have successfully reached healthy and well-adjusted adulthood, where they are mutually supportive of each other, and are rational and objective in their behaviors. By this time the group is a well-functioning unit where trust and lack of trust are openly expressed. Goals are specific, cohesion is high, and emotional bonds have developed among different members. Conflict among members or with the leader is recognized, discussed, and often resolved. Members take responsibility for their actions, and feedback among group members is exchanged freely and accepted without defensiveness. When confrontation takes place, the confronter shares his or her reactions, and this is accepted as a challenge to examine behavior, not as an uncaring attack. Group members use each other as resources, and members feel powerful and share this power with one another. There is a growing awareness of the group process; members know what makes the group productive or nonproductive. Diversity is respected, and there is respect for individual and cultural differences. Group members work on their issues diligently and follow group rules and norms (Corey & Corey, 1992).

The final stage of group development is separation or termination. After the purposes of the group have been fulfilled and the members have learned new behavior patterns, they reach out for other social experiences. This stage is also referred to as the *consolidation period,* when members begin to consolidate their own learning. The intensity of the work tapers off, and participants are reluctant to bring up new business to explore. Members begin to separate, loosening the intense bonds often established with other members of the group and with the leader, to search for new resources and ties in order to satisfy needs (Hepworth & Larsen, 1990).

This is a difficult time, as group members say goodbye. A number of important factors come into play. Both members and leader need to deal with the separation. The leader may need to deal with feelings of sadness and help others to do the same. Unfinished business between members or with reference to group goals must be wound up. In the final sessions, the group leader should encourage a review of what members have learned in the sessions that they can carry forward into the real world.

Members also review what they liked and did not like about the group, and turning points they took in the group. Giving and receiving feedback becomes especially important in the final sessions. What the members learned and did not learn becomes a matter of discussion to help members resolve their own issues, if possible. The final feedback must be constructive and conclusive—stated in such a manner that the individual is not left hanging loose. Members are encouraged to think of ways by which they can keep their new skills or decisions alive after the group dissolves.

Termination is not easy. Members may not want to move on. Some members may regress in behavior, to prolong the safety of the group. Some members become very upset when the group dissolves, and may psychologically deny that the end is near.

It is very common for group leaders to plan a smooth transition and to be disappointed when this does not happen. Group endings depend on individual behavior styles when they separate from each other. An awareness of behavior styles is helpful to the social worker in charge. At times talk about follow-up meetings and plans for accountability is helpful, so that the members will be encouraged to carry out their plans for change (Corey, 1990).

Although we have focused on the stages of group development for therapy groups, keep in mind that there are many different kinds of groups, with different dynamic patterns. Sometimes termination is a happy event, as when a friend gets out of the army, or out of prison, or graduates from school.

THE CONCEPT OF GROUP NORMS

Group norms are the implicit expectations and beliefs shared by members concerning how they or others should behave in given circumstances. Norms are regulatory mechanisms that give groups stability and predictability and also give group members information about what they can and cannot expect from others (Hepworth & Larsen, 1990). Newcomb (1981) notes that the ability to predict the behavior of people and objects seems to be intrinsically rewarding. An important aspect of belonging to a group is that each member can to some degree predict what the other members are likely to think and do in most situations. This is why rules are specified in terms of average or normal behavior of each member and what role(s) each member should play (Levine & Moreland, 1990). However, Asch (1987) comments that no group member fits all the norms exactly, and also most groups accept some deviation as long as it is not "too abnormal." The system is maintained by norms, by shared beliefs about what is desirable and what is not (Garwin & Seabury, 1984).

Norms emerge from interaction of group members or from the broader environment. They may be strongly and overtly stated and enforced, or they may be implicit—but no less powerful. A norm communicates a particular group's own way of doing things. Norms may involve arriving on time, sitting in a particular pattern, speaking in particular sequences, interrupting other members, following the lead of prestigious members, sharing a certain amount of information, and so on. Norms reveal the group's ways of doing things and influence and control members' behavior. Norms also reveal what is highly valued by the group, what is considered good, true, or beautiful, and notions about how members should control each other's behavior so that these values are manifested in them and the group notes that manifestation (Henry, 1981).

To learn about group norms, observe groups in action. Toseland and Rivas (1984, p. 67) point out that when we watch the behaviors of people in groups, "soon it becomes clear that sanctions and social disapproval result from certain behavior and that praise and social approval result from other behaviors." Once members are aware what is approved and what is not, they begin to accept the norms and function accordingly.

At a group level, norms are largely shared ideas about what members should do and feel, how these norms should be enforced, and how sanctions should be applied when behavior does not coincide with the norms (Northen, 1988; Ephross & Vassil, 1988). Group norms function to regulate the performance of the group as an organized unit and keep it on course. Norms vary from those held at a formally stated level to those that are practiced informally and at an unconscious level. At every level of behavior, implicit and explicit standards have important implications for the feelings and behaviors of group members.

Formal Norms

Napier and Gershenfeld (1993) classify norms into formal, explicitly stated, implicit, and unconscious. By-laws and codes of conduct are formal norms. They are written, formal statements that are to be taken literally as group rules and then enforced by organizational sanctions to ensure compliance. In reality, however, things often happen differently. For example, when wealthy teenagers break laws, they may get away with their behavior, whereas teenagers from visible minorities may receive disproportionately harsh treatment by police or in the courts.

It is important to distinguish between norms that actually influence people's behavior in a group and formal rules that may or may not be enforced. People who are new and unfamiliar with a group or organization may pick up a copy of its bylaws or constitution and believe that what is written reflects how the group actually functions. These people are likely to be confused or disappointed when official pronouncements conflict with practice.

Explicit Norms

Explicit norms do not appear in formal written form. However, they are explicit and clearly understood by all because they are communicated either verbally or by example. When a person is hired, he may be told, "Everyone gets here by 9 A.M." (the explicitly stated norm being that you're late if you arrive thereafter). The new employee may notice that all men in the office are wearing suits and ties, and women are dressed in formal skirts and jackets and present themselves in a businesslike fashion. So the new employee quickly understands the explicit norm that he too will be expected to wear a suit and tie to work.

Implicit Norms

Within every group, implicit norms influence behavior. Implicit norms result from preconceived ideas about what should take place in a group. For example, members of a therapy group may assume that every thought or feeling must be verbalized, with no room for tact or privacy. Or the implicit norm may be that unless the group leader specifies that members must self-disclose, all members can maintain a certain degree of privacy—not all information about a person need be shared.

Implicit norms are created by imitating a leader's model. If a leader uses bad or abrasive language, then members may begin to use such language as well. Implicit permission has been given to do so, even if the leader did not expressly encourage such behavior. Another example: When a boss asks for a report, it is implicitly understood that the report need not be submitted until a couple of days have passed. And although members may not be assigned seats at committee meetings, it is implicitly understood that the chairperson generally sits at the end of a long table or the center of a room, and the vice chairperson sits to the right of the chairperson.

Often norms become explicit only when they are violated. For example, Reverend Smith frequently preaches about justice and equality for all under God and asks his congregation to live according to these principles. Yet when he joins a picket line to protest the firing of a lesbian teacher whose professionalism is not questioned, he is rebuked by his congregation for going beyond his position. He did not understand that the norms allow him to preach about morality but that action on social issues is reserved for others. The norm of the congregation is invisible until it is violated.

Unconscious Norms

Some norms are called *unconscious* norms; they exist outside our direct awareness. An example is the sexual discrimination evident in the business world, the professions, and in government. Why do we have a "glass ceiling" that makes it much harder for women to get to the highest levels of leadership? Until the recent gender revolution, *both* men and women were more comfortable with having men in charge and women as helpers. Much of this discrimination was unconscious. Today, there is more social awareness of such norms, and in some workplaces a special effort is made to correct these biased norms.

Group Conformity and Identity

The process by which a group pressures members to conform to certain norms of behavior is sometimes referred to as social control. When the norms and goals of the group accord with a person's preference, it is easy for that person to conform. However, if the person finds that his or her behavior is not in accordance with group norms, he or she can resort to four different ways of dealing with the situation: conform, change the norms, remain deviant, or leave the group. What makes group members conform to norms, and why would a person want to conform to group norms? If a group member wants to continue to be a member of a group, then he or she must conform to the regulations of the group. A person who wants to continue as a member is more likely to be influenced by other members of the group and to avoid certain types of sanctioned behavior. Members quickly realize when sanctions are applied to certain types of behavior, and usually try to adapt, to avoid disapproval or punishment. If a person wants to stay in the group, he or she will seek to demonstrate loyalty to the group and conformity to its rules (Gould, 1986). For example, if a management trainee in a corporation wants a promotion, he or she is unlikely to challenge the company's leadership or its policies. As the management trainee works together with others in the group, his or her identification with the group and its norms increases.

Sanctions

A sanction is a consequence, usually a punishment, for breaking group norms. (Oddly enough, a sanction can also be defined as a reward.) For example, when group members became distracted by a political event and began to arrive late for office meetings at an advertising company, a simple sanction was created for those who came late: They would not be allowed to participate in the coffee break. As most important work was done during the break and networking was an effective, informal way to function, group members immediately began to arrive on time. Sanctions in groups are powerful regulators; Lieberman (1980, p. 501) remarks that "ordinarily, sanctions do not need to be exerted frequently or vigorously; rather, the anticipation of sanctions is often seen as being as effective in controlling deviant behavior as is actual application."

In groups, sanctions are expected. Norms exist for specific purposes and if members value these purposes, those who deviate can expect sanctions. For example, Tony is a very talented violin player, and is one of the best singers in his performing group. However, he is often absent, as he is distracted and careless. The sanction for Tony could include fines, negative comments, sarcasm, ridicule, and finally even exclusion from the group. Sanctions help make members follow the rules.

Norms provide stability and predictability in groups. However, groups also need to grow and change to achieve their objectives and meet members' needs. Sometimes established norms may need to be discarded or modified, and nonconformity encouraged, because it may be more helpful to the group than sticking with old, established ways of doing things.

GROUP COHESION

When the group is cohesive, the group members feel their needs are being met and the group is one in which people wish to be members. The more cohesive a group is, the more likely it is that the members conform to group norms and the greater the pressure is on members to conform to such norms (Janis & Mann, 1977). A cohesive work group can be very productive, because management and the line workers, or different group members and the leader, understand each other well.

How does group cohesion develop? As Corey and Corey (1992) indicate, usually when a group begins to develop people do not yet know each other well enough to have a strong sense of group belonging. They may feel a bit awkward in this period of becoming acquainted. Although members talk to each other, they are still usually presenting their public self rather than the private self. Genuine cohesion is achieved as groups struggle with conflict, share pain, and commit to taking significant risks. This process lays the foundation of cohesion.

Northen (1988) notes that cohesiveness is enhanced as the members develop affective ties with each other. Cartwright and Zander (1960) conceptualize cohesion as the sum of attraction forces of the group—attraction of members to the group itself, and to what the group does. Cohesion is also related to the culture of the group—that is, to the outward manifestation of the group's uniqueness, which both gives an indication of cohesiveness among the group members and attracts other people to the group.

Newcomb describes cohesiveness as the psychological glue that holds group members together. The more cohesive a group becomes, the longer it will last and the more resistant it will become to external pressures (Levine & Moreland, 1990; Newcomb, 1981). According to Gregory (1986), members of an established group often adopt their own "group jargon" or unusual patterns of speech. This jargon is not only a "badge of group membership" but also it tends to increase group cohesiveness, because outsiders often cannot understand what members of the group are talking about.

How can cohesiveness be developed? The first steps are cooperation, attendance, and punctuality. The group members must be willing to show up for the meetings and be punctual. The group members should view the group as comfortable. Cohesiveness is encouraged by willingness to listen to and accept others, and to express reactions to and perceptions of others in group interactions. Genuine cohesiveness is not a fixed condition but rather an ongoing process of solidarity developed through the risks members take with each other. As Jeffrey commented, "The group session was not as good today as it usually is; there was something in the air, mostly discomfort for young men like me to open and talk about our divorce and conflicts that led to it. . . . I am sure it will get better by next week . . . we (group members) always work well together."

According to Corey and Corey (1992), group cohesion can be developed, maintained, and increased in a number of ways, as follows. When the leader demonstrates trust in the group, that contributes to a group climate characterized by respect for the opinions and feelings of different members. Members should also be encouraged to openly express feelings that concern the degree of trust they feel in the group. Sharing concerns and opinions and reservations about the group can begin to build trust and cohesiveness.

When group members begin to share meaningful aspects of their work or themselves based on the goals of the group, and when they take risks in discussions, they should be offered sincere support and recognition. These attitudes create a sense of closeness. When Sheila shared about her problems in her workplace, she found genuine support from the group members, and this led her to feel positive and also caring toward other group members.

Cohesion is also encouraged by setting clear goals. The group goals and individual goals can be jointly determined by the members and the leader. When a group does not have clear goals, and members have differing expectations, animosity may build up, leading to fragmentation and resentment. For example, students may meet to write evaluations of their programs and their professors. If the goal is to provide objective, useful comments, that helps reduce any individual agendas or vendettas. However, if members do not share the group goal or are distracted by other concerns, the purpose is defeated and no true cohesiveness can develop.

Cohesion is increased in a group by inviting all members to become active participants. In every group a few members are passive or withdrawn, and they should be invited to express their feelings. The group needs to be aware why some members prefer to be silent. When asked to do so in a group, Amanda said, "I am very attentive to all that goes on, but I am not very talkative and like to be accepted that way." This clear statement sets the stage for other members in the group to accept Amanda as she presents herself.

A group becomes more cooperative when group members are encouraged to participate in member-to-member and whole-group interactions. In this atmosphere group members share and search for ways to involve as many members as possible. When group members begin to care for each other, group cohesiveness builds.

Conflicts are part of any group situation. When conflicts appear, it is important that group members recognize the sources of conflict and deal with them openly. Groups can be strengthened by conflict as they seek to work through differences honestly.

Group attractiveness and cohesion are closely interrelated. If the group deals with matters that interest members, they feel respected, and if the atmosphere is supportive, the chance of this group being attractive is very high. Group members should be encouraged to reveal their own ideas, feelings, and reactions within a group. When there is honest exchange between people, a sense of group belonging develops.

Sookja, a young immigrant woman, is a member of a church group. She is very bright, but has had difficulty expressing herself in English and at first hardly ever spoke. She has been in schools where her communication was sharply judged by others; she sensed her own "foreignness" and learned not to participate. However, in this church group she is asked for her opinions and treated with respect for her contributions. As she becomes more comfortable, she starts to contribute her considerable talents to the choir and the drama group. At one point, she expresses how she has always felt left out in other groups. This is accepted by other members of the group with understanding, so she goes on to talk about her initial fears of being a member of this church group.

Yalom (1985) indicates that cohesion is a strong determinant of a positive group outcome. The leader can help the group become cohesive by focusing on common themes that link group members together. In Sookja's church group, for example, several women are immigrants, and the leader helps bring them together to lead a workshop on family roots and traditions, which the whole group enjoys a lot.

GROUP GOALS

Levine and Moreland (1990) note that achieving clarity about the purpose of the group provides a framework for observation, assessment, and action. It also provides a foundation on which group members can develop bonds and the means for attaining common objectives. When the purposes of a group are clarified, they provide a base on which specific goals and objectives can be constructed. The overall purpose of a social work group is to work at goals that have been established by and reflect the perspective of the agency, the client, and the social worker. Clients should be helped to clarify the purpose of the group, their expectations, and their own needs and objectives for the group. The social worker's expectations of the group as a whole and of the different members are also important, as well as what will be attended to and how interventions will be directed. Finally, the agency or the organization's rationale for using groups as an intervention treatment method is also a defining goal. These sources or levels of goals quickly become apparent when a group is organized through an agency (Hartford, 1972; Schopler & Galinsky, 1995).

According to Egan (1976), there are two types of goals: general group goals and group-process goals. General goals in a group vary from group to group, depending on the purpose of the group. An example of a general goal is that a university will accept students of all races and genders. A general goal of an agency is to provide services for the well-being of clients of all races and genders.

Group-process goals include self-exploration, staying in the present, making oneself known to others, taking risks, challenging oneself and others, giving and receiving feedback, listening to others, dealing with conflicts, deciding on what to work on, acting on new insights, and applying new behavior in and out of the group (Corey, 1990). For example, a group of clients who suffer from manic depression discuss some of their unwanted and unacceptable behaviors. One client, John, begins to explore what circumstances in his life made him misbehave in ways that he never would have done if he had not been depressed. This self-exploration is useful, but the leader may ask him to stay in the present.

An overall group goal should be established and communicated to the members before the first session. The social worker then works with group members to formulate specific goals at both individual and group levels. Individual goals reveal the hopes, expectations, and objectives of members as they enter the group. An individual goal could be for a member to identify his or her own self-defeating patterns and to replace them with more functional behaviors. Group goals are the "emergent product of the interaction of all participants together, the organizer and the members, as they express their ideas and feelings about the reasons for existence of the group and its anticipated outcomes. Group goals include rationale, expectations and objectives toward which the group put its collective efforts" (Hartford, 1972, p. 139). A group goal includes enhancing problem-solving and decision-making skills in both individual and group contexts and also applying them to specific problems that the group or a member are working on. For example, the group goal may be to help group members become self-assertive but also to work on specific problems in the group, such as being cooperative, or to achieve goals without losing self-worth or being overly hostile.

Group goals provide the mobilizing, energy-generating momentum for what a group is supposed to do. Schopler and Galinsky (1995) specified that "for a group to be effective, there must be sufficient consensus on which goals the group will pursue. Sufficient consensus means that the group has enough support for particular goals to mobilize members. . . . Sufficient consensus exists when a majority of the members of the group system agree on goals and priorities." Sometimes goals flow directly from target problems; here the "opposite" of a problem defines the goal—unemployment defines a goal of employment, dependence defines a goal of independence (Maple, 1977). Goals at this level of generality are not especially useful, so the worker must help the group members make their goals more concrete (Schmidt, 1969). A concrete goal consists of a *behavior* (not a thought) that the person will try to achieve, and a criterion for acceptable performance. For example, Jill wishes to lose 5 pounds in a month and sets a concrete goal of losing 1¼ pounds in a week. She eats a good, balanced diet and does not starve herself but to her excitement she finds herself steadily moving toward her goal.

After people have set goals, the leader and the group members next contract for the specific objectives—actions, activities, and responsibilities—that each party will take on to achieve the goals. Goals are general, long-term concepts; objectives are more specific and short term. Objectives are the building blocks of goals and represent immediate steps that can be used to achieve long-range circumstances (Garwin & Seabury, 1984). Every time a person makes a choice, he or she ranks and places value on objectives. For instance, when a group of single fathers met, the first priority they discussed was how and where to find baby-sitters for their children. This was an important beginning aspect of their initial work with being fathers without partners and as their roles stated, before they could make a commitment to their own work on themselves and their roles as single fathers, they needed someone to help them take care of their kids.

Beside working through goals, the group leader must bring hidden agendas of individual members into the open when they are functioning at cross-purposes to the needs and goals of the group. Some members may wish to be the center of attention, for example. Others may wish to sabotage intimacy because they are afraid of getting too close to others.

Goals can be classified in many different ways: informal and formal, implicit and explicit. Formal goals are stated. Formal goals entail certain objectives of the group as a whole. How well formal goals are carried out depends heavily on the informal goals. Any movement in any group setting takes place with reference to goals, and this rule affects informal dynamics as well. A formal goal in a study group meeting, for example, is to get a particular course outline completed within a semester. The chair has the goal of creating a conducive positive atmosphere so that all members can communicate easily with each other. In other words, the informal goal in the group is for members to become friendly and comfortable with each other. This leads to the achievement of the formal goal—getting a course outline covered constructively with the least amount of friction and controversy.

Goals can also be classified as operational and nonoperational. Nonoperational goals are broad and general, such as "enhancing self-esteem." Within the framework of these nonoperational goals, a group needs to develop operational goals to direct action. For example, the self-esteem goal might lead to the introduction of activities in which the members can experience success.

Every operational goal creates a number of differing roles, norms, and leadership patterns for the group. Movement with reference to reaching goals can be understood on both implicit and explicit levels. Particularly when there is work to be accomplished, in setting up, say, a budget for a community mental-health center, two types of agendas may run simultaneously: the surface agenda and a hidden agenda, where people enact their own plans. In the example, the surface or explicit agenda is the preparation of a budget. The implicit agenda of the administration may be to enhance trust and cohesiveness in the staff by engaging them in problem solving and decision making for the entire agency. A truly hidden agenda might involve the desire of an individual or subgroup to sabotage the process because of resentment against the administration.

For group meetings to be successful, the members should have clear, personal objectives that are identical to or compatible with the group's objectives. Thus a major task in therapy groups is to establish and proceed toward both group and individual goals. General group goals include creating a climate of trust and acceptance and also promoting self-disclosure in significant ways and encouraging group members. If this goal is not achieved, then conflict and confusion may ensue.

LEADERSHIP

There are different types of leaders for different types of groups, and leaders can obtain their positions in different ways. They can be appointed or selected by some higher authority, by succession, by election, by consensus, or by seizing control. Once the position is attained, leaders have a certain degree of authority and influence in the group. A position of leadership carries certain expectations that influence how the person behaves and how the members of the group respond. Before proceeding further, let's distinguish between *leader* and *leadership*. Leadership behavior is distinguished from leader position; leadership by anyone influences the group regardless of the person's position. A leader can be described as a person in a position of authority who is given the right to make certain decisions for the group, such as a teacher in the classroom, or the social worker in a therapy group. It can also be said that anyone who influences the group exhibits leadership qualities.

An effective leader working with social-work groups should have certain important characteristics: courage, honesty, creativity, self-knowledge, empathy, and being action oriented and enthusiastic (Reid, 1991). Like the people he or she is working with, the group leader is seeking wholeness and integration within his or her own life and is also willing to live the way he or she encourages group members to live. The worker is committed to the lifelong goal of becoming a fully functioning human being. The leadership position produces expectations in people of how someone in that position should behave. People hold the leader to higher expectations than other individuals.

Again, leadership behavior is distinguished from leader position, and may be exhibited by any member of the group. For example, let's say a formal leader is conducting a meeting. A well-respected member of the group, Andy, walks in and the group begins to focus on him and listen and respond to him alone. All the participants turn their full attention to Andy, and different members in the group are reassured that he is in the group, because he has established his position as a decent and caring member of the group.

Leadership entails power. Power sometimes suggests visions of manipulation, control, personal feelings of powerlessness, or an omnipotent Big Brother. Therefore, before proceeding further, let us distinguish between influence and power. Influence is the capacity of the person to produce effects on others by intangible or indirect means. Power is the ability or capacity to achieve something, the possession of control or command over others. Napier and Gershenfeld (1993) identify five different components of power: referent power, legitimate power, expert power, reward power, and coercive power. Let's discuss each in turn.

Referent Power

Referent power may be described as the type of influence we do not think of as power. We may dress according to a particular person's style, or we may espouse an argument because we first heard it from a brilliant intellectual with whom we identify. We may be influenced by a person's high status, intelligence, competence, personal style, or charisma. In these situations the person holds referent power over us, and we identify with or refer to them in certain ways. They influence us without our feelings ever being seen.

Legitimate Power

Legitimate power is power considered properly or rightfully exercised by virtue of laws, traditions, or common practices that are universally or nearly universally accepted. For example, we accept the authority of the student who represents us at the student council, or the professor who supervises our work because we accept the system that led to that person's appointment or election.

Expert Power

Closely connected to legitimate power is expert power, the influence of a leader by virtue of specialized knowledge or skills, relevant to the group's needs. For example, when we call a TV repairperson, we do so because we believe he or she has expert power for repairing the TV. A social worker conducting a treatment group may be viewed as having expert power both in conducting groups and in helping people cope with problems of living.

Reward Power

Reward power is the ability to influence group members to behave in a certain way, by providing special incentives such as money, privileges, or special recognition. In a residential treatment center, a child might be given an extra home visit because of how well he has behaved during the preceding week. In a social-work group, a nod, a smile, and verbal approval may be very meaningful rewards in some situations.

Coercive Power

Coercive power is the ability to enforce certain behavioral requirements by using or threatening negative consequences for noncompliance. For example, a new employee may be reprimanded (and warned of termination) for not following the group norms. This type of power can be useful in deterring violations of group norms, but it is relatively ineffective in enhancing group cohesion and positive identification with group goals. A group of people cannot be threatened or mistreated and asked to follow group goals, because resentment and anger may rule the group.

STYLES OF LEADERSHIP

Every leader wants to be effective and also liked. This is a dilemma that every leader faces. How can a leader lead a group in such a way as to be effective and liked?

In a classic research study, White and Lippitt (1968) investigated the following questions: What difference do styles of leadership have on the group? Is the group more productive if the leader is autocratic, democratic, or laissez-faire? Does this create a difference in the social climate? Which is the best form of leadership? There are different types of groups, and all groups need different types of leadership.

An *autocratic* leader is directive, supervises the activities of other members, and takes ultimate responsibility for decision making. An autocratic leader in a workplace decides whom to employ without consulting other subordinates.

A *laissez-faire* leader may be viewed as incompetent and lacking in leadership qualities. He or she may be operating under a philosophy calling for giving the workers a "free rein" and or "He who rules least, rules best." What kind of supervision is appropriate under what circumstances—when should we allow "free rein," and when should we hold the reins tightly? Jon, for example, ran his business in a laissez-faire manner. He allowed his manager to make all his major decisions, and all the other subordinates were allowed to make decisions they thought would be useful to the company. When it was time for a final evaluation, it became clear that Jon had made some terrible mistakes. The company ran out of funds and was taken over by another, larger company. Jon now finds himself an employee of the company he originally owned but mismanaged through his laissez-faire attitude. His biggest mistake was probably not knowing what was going on in the company.

A *democratic* leader is usually well liked. This leader shares all his decisions with others regardless of consequences. Yet it is difficult to say that a democracy is totally free; it may actually be in the middle between autocratic and laissez-faire. In one university department, everything was student governed. All important decisions were made by the students. However, when the students decided to dispense with grades and final exams, the board of trustees took control of the program and instituted more formal procedures.

"Democratic," "autocratic," and "laissez-faire" are simplistic labels applied to complex role relationships. People do not face a choice of one specific form of leadership, but must decide which combination of styles will help the group survive and also reach their goals. Leadership strategies include both leader-centered and group-centered patterns. They are as follows:

1. At one end of the continuum, the leader decides and announces decisions.
2. The leader announces his or her decisions and also "sells" them to the group.
3. The leader puts out his or her ideas and invites suggestions and comments before making decisions, retaining the power to use or disregard any ideas presented.
4. The leader can present the issues but not his or her ideas and invites ideas and alternatives from others. He or she also presents the group with different alternatives and choices among the same.
5. The leader can also state limits within which the decisions must be made, such as "Customers expect to be serviced every day of the year," leaving the members to work out the implementation. In this case, the employees prepared a vacation schedule that assured both that they could get their vacation and that the clients were serviced.
6. At the other end of the continuum, objectives and a plan of action are decided, with the leader having no more authority than any other member of a group.

Leadership is closely related to followership. An act of leadership involves acceptance of influence by others, and this can theoretically be provided by any member. Finally, an effective leader can behave comfortably over the whole continuum. The leader adapts his or her behaviors to the requirements of members, the problem at hand, and other factors in the situation. A good leader is also flexible and can adapt his or her approach to help the group move toward its goals.

No one style of leadership is "best" for all situations. At times groups want a close, warm relationship with the group leader and with each other. At other times they may prefer a more formal relationship. Some groups may need alternatives to reach decisions, whereas others may need a firm direction from the person in charge. The role of the leader involves boundary setting and autonomy and also an awareness of differentiation, hierarchy, and role keeping. For example, Joshua is a staff supervisor in a social agency. He cares about all the members of his unit, but some are closer to him than others. When he is dealing with agency business, Joshua draws a clear boundary between his role and the role of the direct service staff. He can use the differentiation in roles and his position in the hierarchy to maintain congenial working relationships and high-quality service most of the time. In behavioral terms, Joshua *adapts,* which implies an outcome at a given point in time, an adjustment that is a state of relatedness, between a person and his or her surroundings. He *socializes,* behavior that is based on social interaction, by which individuals develop their human potential and learn the patterns of the subculture, in this case, the agency business. He also *communicates,* which involves talking and listening together, which increases the person's interpersonal skills and creates more meaningful relations with others and the group leader. He exercises *social control,* a process by which members of a culture encourage conformity to cultural norms. And he moderates *social conflict,* in which members of an agency may compete for the valued resources that are available. In this case, Joshua can keep in mind the resources and the agency divisions with its employees, while he is working with them. When a new leader comes into the picture, group members "test" the leader to find out about his or her ability to communicate, adapt, and socialize. The group functions more effectively when the role of leader is respected (unless the leader is dysfunctional).

In social-work group settings, the role of the leader is fairly democratic. The function of the leader is to challenge what is right for the clients, not to persuade them to do what he or she thinks is right. The leader's personal values and life experiences are a fundamental part of who he or she is. But a leader need not express what he or she feels when values are in conflict during a session. However, in certain group situations some clients become dependent on the leader's suggestions. Needy and dependent members may feel pressure to please the leader and assume the leader's values automatically (Corey & Corey, 1992). The leader must help clients make their own decisions congruent with their own values, *most of the time.* However, there are important exceptions. First, some people are not capable of deciding what is in their own best interest, such as children, the mentally ill, the mentally retarded, the infirm elderly, and so on. Second, there are those whose behavior and values are in conflict with the norms or mores of society, and hurt other people, such as child or spouse abusers, alcoholics, and other addicts and criminals. In these situations the social worker takes on a protective or social control function that may be viewed as violating the principle of client self-determination. In groups set up for abusive husbands, delinquent teens, drunk drivers, prison inmates, and so on, the goal is to help members change their values and lifestyles in a more socially acceptable direction.

Take, for example, Nora, who is struggling with the decision about whether or not to file for divorce. She tells the group she is not sure if she wants to risk loneliness, and she fears if she does not divorce she will remain stuck in an unhappy marriage. Your own values may come into play as you relate to her. However, it is one thing to challenge Nora to look at all her alternatives before she makes a decision and to use the group to explore her feelings and alternatives. It is quite a different matter to persuade her to do what you think "should" be done. In therapeutic or social-work groups, the basic function of the leader is to help group members find answers that are reasonable and congruent with their own lives and values. The leader's role is to provide a context in which members can examine proposed solutions that are in their best interests (Corey, Corey, & Callahan, 1990).

TYPES OF CLIENT GROUPS

Many different types of groups are started for the purpose of helping people deal with their issues and their problems and that are simultaneously intertwined with growth and development objectives. A number of factors influence how these groups can operate, including purposes and objectives as defined by workers, the needs of potential group members, and the goals and resources of the sponsoring agencies.

Corey and Corey (1987) identify four different types of helping groups: counseling, personal growth, structured, and self-help groups. Other classifications of groups are mutual sharing, educational, discussion, task, growth, therapy, and family groups. Toseland and Rivas (1984) have identified four categories of treatment groups: educational, growth, remedial, and socialization.

Social-work practitioners are often asked to provide information on topics such as divorce, schizophrenia, depression, human development, and child guidance. These are structured educational groups, designed to provide information and answer questions on a specialized topic.

Some self-help groups allow people with a common interest or problem to create a supportive network for themselves without professional leadership. There are also remedial groups. For example, such groups may be held for men and women who have difficulty managing their anger and who beat up their spouses, hospitalized patients who suffer from depression, or young people in a drug rehabilitation center who are addicted to crack and cocaine.

The remedial group has three categories: supportive treatment, interpersonal growth, and intrapsychic growth. When people in a group are grieving the loss of a loved one, the purpose of the group is to be supportive and empathetic. In interpersonal groups, members could be siblings or marital partners, where the purpose is to help them develop better interpersonal relationships with each other so that they can move to a better understanding in their relationships. When the group members meet to improve their own self-esteem, they begin to look at and work on some of their own issues that have held them back from growth. These groups aim at helping clients develop insight and growth, and also change their relationships. Let's look at the different groups that Reid (1991) discusses.

Growth groups include helping a person focus and go through the normal developmental stages. In these groups the person is interested in becoming more aware of him- or herself. For example, a marathon encounter group might be held for college students where they learn rules, regulations, and expectations at the college they are entering. New students can ask questions and discuss their issues in this encounter. Another example is a values-clarification group for children, where they are taught to be kind and considerate, honest and truthful. Such a group develops the distinction between what is acceptable and right and what is socially not acceptable and wrong. Another kind of group may clarify mutual expectations. For example, a group of community leaders may join together to have a question-and-answer encounter about different issues within the community, in order to work at understanding the expectations of the community.

Mutual groups are made up of individuals who share a problem or an issue. People with similar problems get together to work on their own problems, which are basically the same as the rest of the group. This may include people who are recently divorced, a group of men or women who have a spouse in prison, children of divorced parents, and mentally or physically challenged college students who have difficulty with their studies. When group members have similar problems, each person's discussion of his or her issues can provide support, insight, and so forth into their own problems and help them understand that everyone in the group is in much the same boat.

Task groups are found in residential settings such as psychiatric hospitals where there are social-action groups and governments run by patients. For example, in the Menninger Clinic patients play an active role: Patients represent a number of planning activities, such as addressing patient–staff problems, discussing the amount of food needed in the wards, weekend activities, and organized activities such as interest groups and going to movies and field trips. The staff sees this type of government as a vehicle to help patients learn skills, enhance their self-esteem, gain prestige, and find legitimate new roles (Harlow, 1961; Reid, 1968).

The functions of social-work groups are varied. They aim to help individuals with their interpersonal relations and also their relationships with the environment. The group is a means to individual or group change, not an end in itself. The challenge within the social-work profession is to continue the tradition of using groups for environmental change and personal development, and to include treatment of psychosocial dysfunction (Brown, 1991). As Tropp (1969) indicates, "group-oriented efforts revolve around common concerns or common life situations." The creative use of activity is another important aspect of group work. For some kinds of groups, especially children, planning activities or a program is the most effective way to fulfill the group's purpose. Activities can also be used spontaneously to fill individual and group needs (Middleman, 1983).

Klein (1972) and Reid (1991) discuss various objectives of group work. *Rehabilitation* involves restoring someone to a previous capacity or level by helping and working with the group members with reference to their feelings, behavior, and social functioning. It may also mean changing underlying attitudes or values. *Habilitation* involves growth and development rather than treatment: for example, services may be provided to mentally challenged (disabled) people who did not learn basic skills of daily living when they were young. *Correction* is the process of helping people who are legal offenders or violators. *Socialization* groups help people learn what to expect socially and how to get along with others. *Prevention* anticipates difficulties before they occur and provides what people need to develop well. *Social action* is the process of joining with others to combat social problems by promoting changes in laws or social policies. Social-action efforts also help people learn to lead, follow, take part in decision making, and assume responsibility for themselves and for the larger society. *Problem solving* involves using groups to accomplish tasks, make decisions, and solve problems. *Value clarification* is the process of helping individuals develop viable social values that are relevant to living in society.

We need, further, to distinguish between self-help groups and therapy groups. Both self-help and therapy groups, of course, emphasize expressing and sharing emotions. This focus is grounded on the assumption that some people bottle up their feelings and therefore develop maladaptive attitudes and behaviors; when feelings are expressed, behavior improves. Self-help groups are also called support groups, because these groups tend to emphasize member autonomy and internal group resources (Katz, 1981), as do therapy groups. In many self-help groups, the goal is to help members help themselves (Riordan & Beggs, 1988). However, although there is a certain degree of similarity between self-help and therapy groups, there are also certain crucial differences. One basic difference involves goals: Self-help groups take as their central issue a single topic such as addiction, cancer, or obesity. Therapy groups have more global goals, such as reducing stress and improving mental health and interpersonal functioning (Riordan & Beggs, 1987). Both types of groups offer support, reduce stress, and aim for behavioral change. Self-help groups emphasize inspiration, persuasion, and support, whereas therapy groups employ self-understanding, behavioral reinforcement, and member feedback (Lakin, 1985).

A further difference involves the type of leadership involved in each type of group. Self-help groups are usually led by people who are struggling with the same issues as other members of the group. Usually the leaders are not professionals, unless the members employ such a person to monitor their behaviors. In such groups leadership emerges, rather than one person being designated as leader (Riordan & Beggs, 1987; Barker, 1991).

Counseling, therapy, and self-help groups are good microcosms of society. In therapy groups, the members reflect the members' real social environment. The therapeutic factor that is important in such groups is that the participants in the group process work with each other because they confront interpersonal conflicts in their own lives. The interactions among group members are viewed as an important factor in change. The group becomes a means of helping people modify their beliefs, attitudes, and feelings about themselves.

More than other groups, self-help groups stress a common identity based on common life situations. Because there are a myriad of unmet needs in our society, self-help groups are necessarily diverse. In addition, the structure and size of these groups range from small local groups that meet in individual members' homes, to national organizations that consist of thousands of members. These members share common characteristics, including limited reliance on professional, mutual sharing, support, advice giving, and pooling of group resources (Newsome & Newsome, 1983). Reissman (1982) notes that the characteristics of informality, antiexpertism, experiential wisdom, shared leadership, and a strong ideology create a self-help ethos (spirit or style). Riordan and Beggs (1987, 1988) maintain that practitioners in the field must be aware of differences between self-help groups so they can assess the potential benefits of each type for different clients. They suggest that self-help groups have been a valuable help for thousands of people, but are not appropriate for everyone. Self-help groups do not replace therapy groups, because different benefits are provided by these two different groups (Riordan & Beggs, 1987, 1988; Barker, 1991).

WORKING IN A MULTICULTURAL CONTEXT

America is becoming a more and more multicultural society. In working with different types of helping groups, it is imperative that the worker understand and work well with cultural differences. Pedersen (1988) defines race as a shared genetic history of people, including physical features. Ethnicity is a shared sociocultural heritage of religion, history, or common ancestry. A minority group can be a majority in a set where power is exercised by a dominant few, or a minority may be women, who are a numerical majority in any society. Note that minorities from other countries may not be a minority in their own native land, but may be in American society—and the same might be said of white American males in another country.

Pedersen comments that all counseling should be considered multicultural counseling, because it is necessary and important to understand both individual and group differences in making accurate interpretations of behavior. Different cultures often interpret the same behavior in different ways. Belonging to a specific culture influences but does not totally determine how a person thinks, feels, and perceives.

Research shows that mental-health and social services are not used effectively for all cultural groups (Chu & Sue, 1984; Mokuau, 1985, 1987; Pedersen, 1985, 1988). There are a number of reasons for this. Helpers may be insensitive to the culture, cultural values may inhibit the use of services, and in some cultures informal helping processes are used more often than formal ones. Often the extended family becomes the source of family helping. Underuse of services may also be caused by language difficulties, stigma and shame, geographic or community inaccessibility, and conflicts between clients' value systems and values underlying contemporary Western therapeutic approaches (Mokuau, 1985).

It is important to keep in mind that when we speak of different cultures in America, we are speaking of different *subcultures*. There is a dominant American culture. The overwhelming majority of us speak the same language, go to the same schools, watch the same TV shows, shop in the same stores, drive the same cars, and so on. Members of a racial or ethnic minority are also members of the dominant culture, with the added burden or privilege of trying to integrate elements of their cultural heritage and elements of the dominant culture within a coherent world view. In many cases, the cultural heritage is itself diverse, reflecting several different ethnic groups. Another complication or variation is that within cultural minorities, different individuals attach different significance to their cultural roots (Queralt, 1996). One Mexican-American may be very active in Hispanic cultural and political organizations. Another may not even speak Spanish.

All counseling should take into consideration individual differences related to person, problem, and situation, including clients' or members' backgrounds, values, and lifestyles. Special attention should be paid to members of minority groups.

If you are involved in working with culturally diverse populations, you will need to modify your strategies to meet unique needs of different members. Although it is impossible to have a thorough understanding of different cultures, it is not unrealistic to expect a social worker to have a comprehensive grasp of general principles for working effectively with cultural diversity. People should not think that their culture is superior and impose their standards on other people. If you do not understand a specific culture, it is best to be open-minded and learn from the clients about their culture. Such openness goes a long way in building the trust that is necessary to bridge differences.

When working with different cultural groups, avoid making rigid and stereotyped generalizations about individuals within a particular social and cultural group. For example, Asian Americans are sometimes classified as one group, but in actuality they are members of many different ethnic groups and have diverse cultural experiences (Chu & Sue, 1984). A stereotypical way of viewing them, for example, would be to see Asian-Americans as being emotionally reserved or nonverbal. Effective work with clients means being able to challenge stereotypes about particular groups and to modify them to fit clients.

In a similar manner we can look at different cultures and ways of behavior that may or may not be stereotypes. Some practitioners use the label *resistant* when clients from some cultures do not participate as readily as others do. However, it could be the worker or the agency that is resisting the idea that established policies or practices need to be modified to be more responsive to the needs of a culturally diverse population, rather than clients being resistant to receiving help. Some social workers also think in "cultural encapsulation" terms—that is, they place culture in a capsule or can see it only in one way. They have cultural tunnel vision (Wren, 1985). Culturally blind workers may evade reality and depend entirely on their own stereotypes in working with clients and decide what is good for others based on their own value system. For example, Sampson (1988) comments that self-contained individualism helps sustain the core values and institutions that represent the United States as it is today. In this country, freedom, responsibility, and achievement are all assumed to help sustain and attain individualism. Yet clients from non-Euro-American cultures value interdependence equally highly, and value social consciousness and welfare of the group rather than just their own welfare.

There are certain advantages of group work with ethnic clients (Chu & Sue, 1984). Group members may gain strength and power through collective feedback. In working with groups, cross-cultural universality should be emphasized. Clients thus learn they are not alone in their struggles, and they understand that all people undergo psychological pain.

Some disadvantages of working with groups in certain cultural backgrounds are that they may be reluctant to disclose personal material or share family conflicts in front of others (Ho, 1984). They may believe it is shameful to talk about such difficulties in front of others. Rather than receive such help from professionals, they may turn to extended family.

As a group worker, you may want to help a client more intensively, but given the cultural background of the client you may not be sure if the client would use such services. There may be conflicts between members' values. Also, talking about intimate family relationships may make some groups very uncomfortable, just as touching and physical contact may be misunderstood. In many cultures, displaying physical affection is done privately rather than publicly (Chu & Sue, 1984). Members may be offended by the spontaneous touching that often occurs in groups.

Another important factor that needs to be remembered is that confrontation is an important aspect of group work. Although confrontation is therapeutic, it is easily misunderstood. Whenever a client is requested to explore a situation deeply, the intervention needs to be well timed and appropriate. In some cultures, confrontation is considered harsh, attacking, hostile, uncaring, and harmful to people. And in fact confronting clients quickly and directly *can* often be counterproductive, especially with certain cultural groups (Ho, 1984). If the clients feel rejected or angry, such feelings may add to their reluctance and resistance in participating in the therapy sessions. For example, quiet clients may be listening and waiting to be called on to talk. Some clients may be unwilling to talk about their families. Some clients may be influenced by taboos of discussing their families in front of others. If the group leader is respectful and is aware of the client's world, he or she will be patient and help such clients speak when appropriate. When clients feel respected, there is a greater chance that they will begin to challenge their own hesitation in communicating.

Multicultural group counseling, particularly with disadvantaged minority groups, demands adequate preparation in screening and selecting clients and orienting them to group procedures (Corey, 1990). This type of preparation is necessary because many behaviors in a group may be different from what people are accustomed to in everyday lives. For example, one culture may value indirect communication. Such people discuss their feelings indirectly and are taught to mask their feelings. They find it difficult to become a member of a group and abide by norms of being open, honest, and direct. Depending on a person's cultural background, some of what is expected in a group may be greatly demanding and may go against the grain of one's own culture. The prospective group members should identify what they consider important for them to work through in the group.

Sue (1978, 1981) identifies the following characteristics as necessary for working effectively with different cultures.

Group workers should develop an awareness of both their own values and the values of others. The basic concepts and philosophy of helping remain the same for many peoples, but workers should understand the sociopolitical forces that influence the attitudes of minorities and other, different groups. Social workers should be able to share without being critical of another group, and they should be exposed to different belief systems, attitudes, ideas, and skills that enable them to develop therapeutic relationships with diverse clients.

When the worker does not know enough, it is best to allow clients to teach him or her about their culture. It is also important to assess the amount of acculturation that has taken place. In how many cultures has a client lived? People always have allegiance to their own culture but may find certain characteristics of the new culture attractive; they may experience conflicts in integrating two cultures. All these core struggles can be productively explored in the context of a helping or accepting group.

Multicultural counseling situations are very diverse. The worker must be flexible and be willing to modify strategies to fit needs and situations of individuals. Practitioners who respect clients are also willing to be aware of the client's hesitation, and are not too quick to misinterpret behaviors. Instead, they wait patiently to enter the world of the clients, and are open to their feelings and struggles, which are similar to those of clients belonging to the majority culture.

IMPLICATIONS FOR SOCIAL-WORK PRACTICE

When beginning work with a group, it is important to discuss who you are in terms of your credentials and strengths as well as skills, to establish your authority. When working on a task or skill in establishing a deadline or reaching a goal, the group members should be helped to remain task oriented. Working with tasks offers order and safety, but in any formal group another set of forces works for greater intimacy and personalizing of behaviors as well as greater authenticity. In a group where trust is built around performance, people can be vulnerable and willing to risk. Formal and intimate personal relations can be combined, but this can complicate relationships. Intimate personal relations may constitute unnecessary risks for some participants. In a task-oriented group, efficiency may be reduced and overall problems may increase.

Members behave differently, depending on whether a group has created a cooperative or a competitive atmosphere. In a cooperative atmosphere, the group creates personal goals for members that are perceived as being compatible, identical, or complementary with the group goal. A good example of a cooperative group is a basketball team, where the goal of each member is to win. In a cooperative group, members coordinate to achieve the goals of the group. The rewards to members are based on quantity and quality of group performance rather than individual performance. In contrast, in a competitive group the members see their personal goals as being incompatible, different, and conflicting with others' goals. Often competition in a group among its own members encourages rejection of differences of opinion, divergent thinking, and cultural and individual differences. A competitive atmosphere reduces the problem-solving effectiveness of different members (Johnson & Johnson, 1995). The social worker needs to be aware of both individual and group goals and the atmosphere that has been created in the groups.

In all types of groups, human emotions may not be expressed directly but they have a powerful influence on the way the group functions. These feelings can be brought into play by weaving the interpersonal issues into the task to be performed. Exactly how a group weaves interpersonal factors into its development can be understood by following a typical social-work group from its inception and through various stages of growth.

A group goes through various stages of development, as discussed earlier. The initial stage includes identifying and setting goals in the group. Like a baby, a group begins at conception, not at birth. The planning that takes place before the first meeting is a crucial aspect of the group's development. The second stage involves the transition stage, where the leader's reactions to resistance and problem solving become an important aspect of the group's work. At this stage leaders recognize difficult behaviors by different members of the group, and find effective ways to lead. The working stage of the group includes addressing all problem situations. When the tasks or goals have been reached or when the time is ready for closure, the group ends. The social worker needs to be aware of and work through these stages with clients.

Social-work groups can be either voluntary or involuntary. In involuntary groups, the worker must begin by stating goals and giving factual information. In both voluntary and involuntary groups, the worker should create an atmosphere that is nonthreatening and where members feel accepted and safe to communicate feelings. The worker must convey to members that he or she is knowledgeable and understanding. The tone of the worker should show that he or she cares and understands. A worker should view all members as equals and should use a "shared vocabulary" with the members. This does not mean using slang or mimicking their speech patterns; rather, it means communicating clearly and respectfully. Attempting to imitate the group members' speech would likely be viewed as phony and patronizing. The worker should explain the basic ground rules and let the group members know what needs to be kept confidential, depending on the group. For instance, in an incest victim group, the worker might say, "What is said in the group, remains in the group."

The worker, with the group members participating actively, can explore problems and facilitate the group process by examining the extent of the problems, how long they have existed, and so on. Workers should convey empathy and encourage group members to do so also. When a worker believes that a client has touched on an important aspect of concern, he or she should be encouraged to talk. A competent worker will also look out for nonverbal cues to identify a sensitive area, such as when a client displays anxiety with a changing tone of voice, fidgeting, yawning, or stiff posture. The worker and group members should explore alternatives to problems by asking something such as, "How do you think you can resolve the problem?"

A group member's right to self-determination should be respected by the social worker. The worker also needs to remember that the purpose of group work and the group process is to help clients function effectively *by* themselves, *for* themselves. When an individual makes a decision that might hurt the person or the group, action should be discouraged, and if possible, prevented. When a group member chooses an alternative, he or she should clearly understand what tasks need to be carried out and how to accomplish the tasks and who will do them. Whenever a group member lacks confidence, it is best to role-play a task before actually attempting to do it. When group members meet commitments, the group leader should reward them verbally or in other ways.

Ending a group process may offer a great deal of potential for additional gains. Group members now feel a sense of urgency, realizing that little time is left. This can lead to expression of very sensitive and personal concerns.

If group members have become close to each other, they will experience a number of emotions. They may try to prolong the group by presenting and dealing with additional problems. Some group members may feel guilty because they believe they failed to take certain steps that could have benefited themselves or others. If members left prematurely, others may feel that the group let them down, and they may need to discuss this. The concluding sessions may bring in strong emotions that must be ventilated and worked through. Eventually members will go through the stages of grieving and let go of the group situation.

The ending phase should offer the members and the group leader enough time to sort out their feelings and use the ending productively. Members should be ready to test their new skills and do things independently. The worker must acknowledge their independence and make positive comments about the group. The ending of the group is a transition back to the real world. The most important factor is to help group members develop a game plan so that the transition enables them to reach higher goals.

At the final session, the group members can discuss what they got out of the group, the merits and limitations of the group, and suggestions for improvement in future groups. Finally, it is important for the worker to understand that we are capable of helping some people but not all. When a client's needs are not being met, it is important to openly acknowledge this fact and consider what other resources or approaches might be more useful.

SUMMARY

All people belong to groups. Social groups begin when a person gets into a continuing relationship of one kind or another with one or more people. People belong to different types of groups. Groups form when two or more people sense and experience the pleasure of each other's company. These are called informal groups. There are two kinds of groups, natural and formed. In a formed (formal) group, people convene for a particular purpose. These groups may be committees, teams, classes, clubs, or therapy groups. Group membership can be voluntary or involuntary. Natural groups begin in a spontaneous manner; people come together with common backgrounds and shared interests. No forced external issues are bringing such people together.

People join groups for a variety of reasons, including prestige, size, and so forth. Smaller groups help create personal relationships better than do larger groups. Unattractive groups have unreasonable demands, members who dominate discussions or display unpleasant behaviors, and negative competition.

The initial stage of group development is characterized by orientation and by hesitant or ambivalent participation. The second stage develops power, control, and patterns of communication, alliances, and subgroups. Group members feel some anxiety in this stage. In the third stage, intimacy develops among group members. The development of cohesiveness results in group members being willing to let others know them in meaningful ways. The final stage of group development is separation or termination. Group members now spend time reviewing their own group experiences. Termination is often not easily achieved.

Group norms are implicit expectations and beliefs shared by members concerning how they or others should behave under given circumstances. Norms can be classified as formal, explicitly stated, implicit, or unconscious. The process by which a group pressures group members to conform to certain types of behavior is sometimes referred to as *social control*. When a member wishes to continue as a group member, he or she must conform to the same regulations as others in the group. Sanctions are used to regulate group behaviors. The anticipation of sanctions is effective in controlling deviant behaviors. When the group is more cohesive, members would conform to group norms and the greater the pressure would be to do the same.

Group goals provide clarity about the purpose of the group and a framework for observation, assessment, and action. Group goals can be classified as informal, formal, implicit, and explicit. There are also operational and nonoperational goals.

Leadership positions in groups can be obtained through appointment or selection by some higher authority, by election, by consensus, or by seizing control. The effective leader has certain important characteristics, such as courage, honesty, creativity, self-knowledge, empathy, and being action oriented and enthusiastic. Types of power include referent power, legitimate power, expert power, reward power, and coercive power. Styles of leadership include autocratic, laissez-faire, and democratic.

Client groups include self-help groups, remedial groups, growth groups, encounter groups, mutual groups, and task groups. The functions of social-work groups are varied. They aim at helping individuals in their interpersonal relationships. Rehabilitation involves restoring a person to a previous capacity or level with reference to their feelings, behavior, and social functioning. Habilitation encourages growth and development. There is a great deal of difference between self-help groups and therapy groups. Self-help groups emphasize member autonomy and internal resources. More than most other groups, they stress a common identity. Therapy groups, which function with a leader, help people modify their beliefs, attitudes, and feelings about themselves.

America is a multicultural society, and it is imperative that the worker understand and work well with cultural differences. To offer multicultural counseling, it is necessary to understand both individual and group differences in making accurate interpretations of behaviors. To work effectively with different subcultures in the United States, group members should develop an awareness of their own values and the values of others who are different. They should understand the sociopolitical forces that influence the attitudes of minorities and women. When the worker does not know enough, it is best to allow the client to teach him or her about their culture. Multicultural counseling is very diverse, and the worker should be flexible and be willing to modify strategies to fit the needs and situations of individuals within a group.

SUGGESTED READINGS

Bankston III, C. L., & Caldas, S. J. (1996, April–June). Adolescents and deviance in a Vietnamese American community: A theoretical synthesis. *Deviant Behavior, 17*(2), 159–181.

Chiu, R. K., & Kosinski, F. A. (1995, September). Chinese cultural collectives and work-related stress: Implications for employment counselors. *Journal of Employment Counseling, 32*(3), 98–110.

Gunther, A. C. (1992, Summer). Biased press or biased public? Attitudes toward media coverage of social groups. *Public Opinion Quarterly, 56*(2), 147–167.

Katz, J. (1995, Summer). Reconstructing masculinity in the locker room: The mentors in violence prevention project. Special issue: Violence and youth. *Harvard Educational Review, 65*(2), 163–174.

Noran, A. R. (1995). Literature search on the wives of firefighters. *Employee-Assistance Quarterly, 10*(3), 65–79.

Peat, B. J., & Winfres, L. T. (1992, June). Reducing the intrainstitutional effects of "prisonization": A study of a therapeutic community for drug-using inmates. Annual meeting of the American Society of Criminology (1990, Baltimore, Maryland). *Criminal Justice Behavior, 19*(2), 206–225.

SUGGESTED VIDEOTAPES

Alternatives to violence: Losing it. (1995). Orange County Human Relations Department. Concept Media, P.O. Box 19542, Irvine, CA 92713. 19 minutes.

Brain waves: Case studies in diversity (Module III). Cultural and ethnic identity; communication issues. (1994). BNA Communications Inc., 9439 Key West Ave., Rockville, MD 20850. 9 minutes.

The communication process. (1995). Rancho Santiago College. Concept Media, P.O. Box 19542, Irvine, CA 92713. 14 minutes.

Front of the class: Learning to lead. (1996). Media Partners. Advantage Media Inc., 2226 Devonshire St., Chatsworth, CA 91311. 24 minutes.

Invisible rules: Men, women and teams. (1996). Corvision. 34 minutes.

With fingers of love: Development of the economic civil rights movement. (1994). University of Alabama. Films for the Humanities and Sciences, 11 Perrine Rd., Monmouth Junction, NJ 08852. 27 minutes.

REFERENCES

Anderson, R. E., & Carter, I. (1990). *Human behavior in the social environment* (2nd ed.). Chicago: Aldine.

Asch, S. E. (1987). *Social psychology*. Oxford: Oxford University Press.

Barker, R. L. (1991). *The social work dictionary* (2nd ed.). Silver Spring, MD: National Association of Social Workers.

Blumberg, H. H., Hare, A. P., Kent, V., & Davis, M. E. (eds.). (1983). *Small groups and social interaction* (Vol. 1). Chicester, England: Wiley.

Brown, L. N. (1991). *Groups for growth and change*. New York: Longman.

Cartwright, D., & Zander, A. (eds.). (1960). *Group dynamics, research and theory* (2nd ed.). Evanston, IL: Row Peterson.

Chu, J., & Sue, S. (1984). Asian/Pacific American and group practice. In L. E. Davis (ed.), *Ethnicity in social group work practice*. New York: Haworth, pp. 23–35.

Corey, G. (1990). *Theory and practice of group counseling* (and *Manual*). (3rd ed.). Pacific Grove, CA: Brooks/Cole.

Corey, M. S., & Corey, G. (1977). *Group process and practice*. Belmont, CA: Wadsworth.

Corey, M., & Corey, G. (1987). *Group process and practice* (3rd ed.). Pacific Grove, CA: Brooks/Cole, chaps. 3–7.

Corey, M. S., & Corey, G. (1992). *Group process and practice* (4th ed.). Pacific Grove, CA: Brooks/Cole.

Corey, G., Corey, M., & Callahan, P. (1990). Role of group leaders' values in group counseling. *Journal for Specialists in Group Work, 15*(2), 68–74.

Doreian, P. (1986). Measuring relative standing in small groups and bounded social networks. *Social Psychology Quarterly, 49*, 246–259.

Egan, G. (1976). *Interpersonal living: A skills/contract approach to human-relations training in groups*. Pacific Grove, CA: Brooks/Cole.

Ephross, P. H., & Vassil, T. V. (1988). *Groups that work: Structure and process*. New York: Columbia University Press.

Garland, J. A., & Frey, L. A. (1973). Application of stages for group development to groups in psychiatric settings. In S. Bernstein (ed.), *Further explorations in group work*. Boston: Milford Press, pp. 1–33.

Garland, J. A., Jones, H., & Kolodny, R. (1965). A model for stage development in social work groups. In S. Bernstein (ed.), *Explorations in group work*. Boston: Milford Press.

Garwin, C. D., & Seabury, B. A. (1984). *Interpersonal practice in social work: Processes and procedures*. Englewood Cliffs, NJ: Prentice Hall.

Gazda, M. (1989). *Group counseling: A developmental approach* (4th ed.). Boston: Allyn and Bacon.

Gould, J. L. (1986). The biology of learning. *Annual Review of Psychology, 27*, 163–192.

Hansen, J. C., Warner, R. W., & Smith, E. M. (1980). *Group counseling: Therapy and process* (2nd ed.). Chicago: Rand McNally.

Harlow, M. (1961). Group work in a psychiatric hospital. In R. Felix (ed.), *Mental health and social welfare*. New York: Columbia University Press, pp. 152–174.

Hartford, M. E. (1972). *Groups in social work*. New York: Columbia University Press.

Henry, S. (1981). *Group skills in social work. A four-dimensional approach*. Itasca, IL: Peacock.

Hepworth, D. H., & Larsen, J. A. (1990). *Direct social work practice. Theory and skills* (3rd ed.). Belmont, CA: Wadsworth.

Hewstone, M. (1988). *Introduction to social psychology and European perspective*. London: Basil Blackwell.

Ho, M. K. (1984). Social group work with Asian/Pacific Americans. In L. E. Davis (ed.), *Ethnicity in social group work practice*. New York: Haworth Press, pp. 49–61.

Janis, I., & Mann, L. (1977). *Decision making: A psychosocial analysis of conflict, choice and commitment*. New York: Free Press.

Johnson, D. W., & Johnson, F. P. (1995). *Joining together* (5th ed.). Englewood Cliffs, NJ: Prentice Hall.

Katz, A. H. (1981). Self help and mutual aid: An emerging social movement. *American Review of Sociology, 7,* 129–155.

Klein, A. (1972). *Effective group work: An introduction to principle and method*. New York: Association Press.

Lakin, M. (1985). *The helping group: Therapeutic principles and issues*. Reading, MA: Addison-Wesley.

Levine, B. (1979). *Group psychotherapy*. Englewood Cliffs, NJ: Prentice Hall.

Levine, J. M., & Moreland, R. L. (1990). Progress in small group research. *Annual Review of Psychology, 41,* 585–634.

Lieberman, M. (1980). Group methods. In F. Kanfer & A. Goldstein (eds.), *Helping people change*. New York: Pergamon Press, pp. 470–536.

Mahler, C. A. (1969). *Group counseling in schools*. Boston: Houghton Mifflin.

Maple, F. (1977). *Shared decision making*. Beverly Hills, CA: Sage.

Middleman, R. R. (ed.). (1983). Activities and action in group work. *Social Work with Groups, 6*(1).

Miller, J. G. (1978). *Living systems*. New York: McGraw-Hill.

Mokuau, N. (1988). Counseling Pacific Islander Americans. In P. Pedersen (ed.), *Handbook of cross-cultural counseling and therapy*. Westport, CT: Greenwood Press, pp. 147–155.

Mokuau, N. (1987). Social workers' perceptions of counseling effectiveness for Asian American clients. *Journal of National Association of Social Workers, 32*(4), 331–335.

Napier, R. W., & Gershenfeld, M. K. (1993). *Groups: Theory and experience*. Boston: Houghton Mifflin.

Newcomb, T. M. (1981). Heiderian balance as a group phenomenon. *Journal of Personality and Social Psychology, 40,* 862–867.

Newsome, B. L., & Newsome, M. (1983, Summer). Self-help in the United States: Social policy options. In *Special Issue on the Privatization of Social Work: The New Nonfederalism, 16*(2), 19–23.

Northen, H. (1988). *Social work with groups* (2nd ed.). New York: Columbia University Press.

Pedersen, P. (1985). *Handbook of cross-cultural counseling and therapy*. Westport, CT: Greenwood Press.

Pedersen, P. (1988). *A handbook for developing multicultural awareness*. Alexandria, VA: American Association for Counseling and Development, pp. 49–61.

Queralt, M. (1996). *The social environment and human behavior*. Boston: Allyn and Bacon.

Reid, K. (1968, January). Social group work enhancing milieu therapy. *Hospital and Community Psychiatry, 9*(1), 26–29.

Reid, K. E. (1991). *Social work practice with groups.* Pacific Grove, CA: Brooks/Cole.

Reissman, F. (1982). The self-help ethos. *Social Policy, 13*(1).

Riordan, R. J., & Beggs, M. S. (1987). Counselors and self help groups. *Journal of Counseling and Development, 65*(8), 427–429.

Riordan, R. J., & Beggs, M. S. (1988). Some critical differences between self help and therapy groups. *Journal of Specialists in Group Work, 3*(1), 24–29.

Rothke, S. (1986). The role of interpersonal feedback in group psychotherapy. *International Journal of Group Psychotherapy, 36*(2), 225–240.

Sampson, E. E. (1988). The debate on individualism: Indigenous psychologies of the individual and their role in personal and societal functioning. *American Psychologist, 43*(1), 15–22.

Schmidt, J. T. (1969, January). The use of purpose in casework practice. *Social Work, 14,* 74–84.

Schopler, J. H., & Galinsky, M. J. (1995). Group practice overview. In R. L. Edwards (ed.), *Encyclopedia of social work,* Vol. 2. Washington, DC: National Association of Social Workers, pp. 1129–1142.

Shaw, M. (1981). *Group dynamics: The psychology of small group behavior* (3rd ed.). New York: McGraw-Hill.

Shulman, L. (1982). *The skills of helping individuals and groups* (2nd ed). Itasca, IL: Peacock.

Sue, D. W. (1978). Eliminating cultural oppression in counseling: Toward a general theory. *Journal of Counseling Psychology, 25,* 419–428.

Sue, D. W. (1981). *Counseling the culturally different: Theory and practice.* New York: Wiley.

Toseland, R., & Rivas, R. (1984). *An introduction to group work practice.* New York: Macmillan.

Tropp, E. (1969). *A humanistic foundation for group work practice.* New York: Selected Academic Readings.

White, R., & Lippitt, R. (1968). Leader behavior and member reaction in three social climates. In D. Cartwright & A. Zander (eds.), *Group dynamics.* New York: Harper & Row.

Wren, C. G. (1985). Afterword: The culturally encapsulated counselor revisited. In P. Pedersen, *Handbook of cross-cultural counseling and therapy.* Westport, CN: Greenwood Press, pp. 323–329.

Yalom, I. D. (1985). *The theory and practice of group psychotherapy* (3rd ed.). New York: Basic Books.

Organizations

Every social worker is part of an organization. The organization may be small or large, formal or informal, and every member who works in it needs to fit into it. When there is no "goodness of fit" between an organization and its members, either the members must leave or the organization may become dysfunctional. No matter how you approach an organization, whether you wish to work in it, study it, consult for it, or use it in the interest of another organization, you need to understand what you are dealing with.

The purpose of this chapter is to help students develop a perspective on organizations. Perspectives depend on who is studying an organization. For example, an economist looks at an organization from the viewpoint of finances, whereas the political scientist may see it from the viewpoint of political parties, or which party has the most power and control in the legislature. In this book the viewpoint is that of a social worker: how to understand social-welfare organizations, how to become a part of one, and how to change one if you need to.

The conceptual framework used throughout this book is the ecosystems framework. It highlights the social, psychological, and physical aspects of organizations to provide a clear and holistic understanding for social-work practitioners, administrators, and social-policy makers. Taking a broad perspective illuminates the universal aspects of human organizational behavior, and helps prevent stereotyping, which simply means people are viewed and understood from the point of view of their uniqueness in background and contributions (Norton, 1993). As Shriver (1995) notes, organizations shape our daily lives and behavior. There are many types of organizations, such as social-welfare agencies, hospitals, schools, offices, and clubs. Virtually all aspects of living are intertwined with and influenced by organizations. For example, most of us are born in hospitals, which are organizations of doctors, nurses, social workers, and other helping professionals, as well as physical buildings.

When Amanda goes into premature labor, she is rushed to a hospital for the birth. She and her husband Ron enter the hospital, and Ron quickly completes the paperwork to admit her. A team of nurses takes her away to her room, and Ron follows. He is given instructions about what to do. Amanda's doctor predicts a difficult birth.

Amanda has a daughter by a caesarean section. When Amanda recovers, her husband shows her the baby, Violet, and then leaves the baby in a nursery where nurses keep an eye on all the premature babies. Violet is already a member of a small organization, the nursery, beside belonging to a large one, the hospital. Violet is fed at regular intervals and changed when she cries, but more often at a particular time. Violet continues to be a member of the nursery until she is out of danger and ready to go home. Violet is a member of a larger organization, the hospital, which influences her physical, mental, and emotional well-being.

Organizations, like all systems, change. For example, employee assistance programs (EAPs) have been broadening their scope to view the whole organization as the client. Romanelli (1991) indicates that most EAPs focus on the problems of individuals, but many are beginning to address the rapidly changing human and social issues of the environments in which the whole organization operates. Thus practice is being refocused to include the organization as the client. For instance, when a minority employee is mistreated in terms of salary, profit sharing, or subtle discrimination, the whole organization needs to be reeducated so that such discrimination does not continue. In this case the idea of change is continuous. Here the organization itself has become the client that needs assistance in dealing with human issues.

This chapter focuses on the meaning, goals, and leadership functions of social-welfare organizations.

THE MEANING OF A SOCIAL-WELFARE ORGANIZATION

Social-welfare organizations are formal organizations legitimized by the state to deliver personal social services and other benefits and goods to citizens, participate in deviance control on behalf of the state (Kamerman, 1983; Austin & Hasenfeld, 1985), and promote the public interest or common welfare (Bellah, Madsen, Sullivan, Swidler, & Tipton, 1985). Social-welfare organizations may also be described as public, private, or quasi-public, intrinsically embedded in the social, physical, and cultural environments of the area. They may be either for profit or not for profit and may cater to a large variety of clients. They are dynamic arenas where social policy and the recipients of social benefits meet in a formal setting—the agency (Lipsky, 1980; Prottas, 1979). Such agencies are often value based and value driven (Files, 1981; Martin, 1984). These values are based on the rules and regulations of the agency, plus the informal agency cultural values.

Social-welfare organizations are further classified as nonprofit or profit organizations. For example, some nonprofit government organizations process food-stamp applications and also investigate child-abuse cases. Some not-for-profit organizations address family problems, children's problems such as bedwetting, phobias, and abusive situations such as battery of wives. They may also lobby legislators for better laws. For-profit organizations provide personal social services to different types of clients, such as detoxification support, and also diverse levels of social services, some of them similar to nonprofits but also much more diverse. For example, a person can get help for working on self-esteem, assertiveness, and more serious problems such as alcoholic rehabilitation, drug-dependency programs, and so forth. The cost may be paid by a client, employer, or insurer, or by social-welfare organizations.

Social-welfare organizations are rarely organized around technical/productive goals and tend to be more humane in many symbolic ways (Lipsky, 1980; Imershein, Frumkin, Chackerian, & Martin, 1983). For example, in a social-welfare organization rules of payment for treatment may be relaxed for a specific client who is undergoing an economic hardship. The client's fees may be reduced or spread out for a longer period of time, which symbolizes humane treatment. Because most social-welfare organizations are bureaucracies, people often complain about their inefficiency and insensitivity to people. (This can be more true of public-welfare agencies than of private and profit agencies.) It may be difficult to combine efficiency with client needs, particularly if success is measured in numbers rather than in quality of services. However, private nonprofit organizations may not be bound by national or state nondiscrimination law, and therefore may be freer to discriminate. Because they are usually local in nature, they may exhibit provincialism. For-profit agencies may operate with the bottom line being profit, rather than service, and may sacrifice client needs for money. Social-welfare organizations face many contradictory expectations from clients, from other agencies, and from their own board of directors. To be effective, social-welfare organizations must function well within the social context of which they are a part (Patti, 1985).

All social-work agencies structure themselves in some form of bureaucracy. The bureaucratic character of modern organizations reflects urbanization and industrialization. A formal definition states that an organization is a collection of people engaged in specialized and interdependent activity to accomplish a goal or a mission. Large and complex bureaucracies are specialized and highly interdependent. A large bureaucratic organization has an elaborate administrative apparatus. The bureaucratic division of labor permits efficiency and creates interdependency and a demand for mechanisms to coordinate different and interdependent tasks. The roles of different members are determined by job description, so that a bureaucracy can adapt by making personnel changes. Of course, people may not work to accomplish some formal, intangible goal but rather to earn a living. Organizational character is affected by questions of control, motivation, and supervisory style (Gortner, Mahler, & Nicholson, 1989). Bureaucratic organizational structure and characteristics are discussed further in a later section of this chapter.

Social workers need to know how to make organizations work and how change will affect clients, practice, policy, and programs. When social workers know how organizations work, they can help their clients negotiate productively. By learning how their own organization functions, they can help organizations become more responsive to the needs of the people being served (Germain, 1991).

Social-work organizations must function within community context to fill client needs. For example, Andrea, now 15, was pregnant and received counseling from a family-service agency at minimal cost. However, when she left after the birth, no follow-up work was done to note how she is functioning in her role as a new mother. By program development and advocacy work, the social-work agency staff has been able to create another type of service in which the new single mother and her child receive more services from the agency until the child is two years old. With program planning advocacy and fund-raising, therefore, the agency managed to provide more services to young teen mothers and their offspring.

SOCIAL-WELFARE ORGANIZATIONS AS OPEN SYSTEMS

Social-welfare organizations can be viewed in terms of their dependency on environment, enforced openness, mapping of the environment, and filtering (Martin & O'Connor, 1989). Although many social-welfare organizations are formal, they depend on their environments for support. American support for social welfare organizations is ambivalent at best. (Most societies have philosophies that explain or justify social inequity; the U.S. tradition is rooted in European Calvinism, which said that prosperity is a sign of God's approval.) Often an individual's situation is considered to be that person's fault; the feeling is that any person who "really tries" will make it in society. With the exception of a few benefits such as Medicare and Social Security, there is not much support for welfare. Thus, social-welfare organizations in the United States depend on social support, and outside forces can influence an agency in terms of goals, priorities, and practices. The type of political government in power has a tremendous influence. Funds for social-welfare organizations usually come from resource controllers in the environment rather than from customers or recipients of services; thus agency priorities are determined externally. Social-welfare organizations therefore devote a great deal of time, energy, and effort to relating to the social environment. The organization's very legitimacy, its ability to hire staff, lease office space, and purchase supplies—all depend on the external social environment.

Because social-welfare organizations do not have tight control over their settings, they function in *enforced openness*. Many social-welfare organizational administrators spend most of their time on fund-raising and recordkeeping. No social-welfare organization can turn its back on the environment (Meyer & Scott, 1983), which provides its legitimacy. *The quality of the relationship to the outside affects organizational well-being more than does its achievement of its official goals* (Meyer & Rowan, 1977).

Because social-welfare organizations are open systems, they are interdependent with their environment. The term *mapping* describes an agency's efforts to learn about, understand, and mirror the environment (Martin & O'Connor, 1989). Their dependency on the environment for legitimacy, funds, clients, staff, goodwill, and so forth requires social-welfare organizations to map—study, monitor, and learn about—the characteristics and development of the environment. Some social-welfare organizations employ lobbyists, liaison staff, researchers, and public-relations experts for these purposes. In smaller agencies, the director acts as public-relations and liaison officer. In large state agencies, staff is employed full time for this purpose.

Social-welfare organizations use *filtering* to differentiate between eligible and ineligible clients. In filtering, boundaries are created to allow selective inputs and outputs. Filtering is also used with employees and resources. These procedures may close or partially close a system to certain clientele. For example, when a particular type of service is subtly disapproved of by members of the community, that disapproval filters through to the attention of the agency rather quickly. When a social-welfare agency opened its doors to help homeless people in the fairly affluent area where the agency was located, the local community protested by not attending agency-sponsored programs and meetings. The agency administrators also were made aware of the disapproval through the grapevine and as they watched funders and powerful members of the community boycott the fund-raising meetings. When this information filtered in to the agency head, the program was reevaluated, with one eye toward gaining the involvement and support of the informal community leaders. Filtering is prevalent in other agencies as well, but may become more apparent in a social-welfare organization because those settings are more formalized in terms of filtering, which is explicit and written down.

An ecosystems understanding of organizational behavior is very valuable to social agencies. Lewis, Lewis, and Souflee, Jr., (1993) state that administrators who view their organizations from an ecosystems perspective also tend to see the organization more as a process than as a structure. They are aware that structural changes both affect and are affected by changes in all the different components of the organization. They know that the goals and activities they choose will be affected by environmental factors that may be beyond their control. When human-service professionals develop structures, they need to keep in mind relationships between the agency and other systems, as well as those within the agency. A major strength in using the systems approach is to encourage human-service professionals to think of themselves as part of a network that as a totality can also serve the individual client in a coordinated manner. Moreover, seeing yourself as part of a larger ecosystem can help you stay afloat and continue to help people even when your particular agency is in trouble.

GOALS OF ORGANIZATIONS

There has been much criticism of human-service organizations for discrepancies between stated goals and actual performance. For example, some public schools are under attack for failing to educate children properly. Welfare agencies are accused of perpetuating poverty and dependency and not helping people become self-sufficient, contributing members of society (Mandell, 1971). And some studies of human service organizations suggest that these organizations are established not to meet their purported goals but to fulfill hidden agendas. Piven and Cloward (1971) argue, for example, that the real purpose of public welfare is to regulate the flow of unskilled labor in and out of the labor market, depending on fluctuations in the business cycle. These conflicts about goals become apparent when people disagree over human-welfare values. For example, when the goals of a psychiatric hospital emphasize short-term care and community-based rehabilitation for its patients, the hospital adopts certain values about human welfare: that the mentally ill should become an integral part of the community as much as possible, and that mental illness should be viewed as a situational problem rather than a serious form of deviance.

Many social groups in the community uphold opposing values and beliefs about the mentally ill, as presented by people's overt behaviors. For example, why has Grand Central Station in New York City become an eyesore for many commuters and other travelers? Because many mentally ill patients hang out there who have been released from hospitals, often owing to lack of funds and failure to develop new policies and programs for the mentally ill. In many cases, families do not help their mentally ill relatives. Such people end up homeless, and congregate where they can find food and a place to sleep. One such place is Grand Central Station. The homeless pile up on the benches, sometimes one person over another, to keep warm. Commuters pass by as if nothing is wrong, because when a problem stares at you and you cannot do anything about it, you may just accept it. The city of New York has instituted several measures to offer services to this population. Steps have been taken to keep the homeless out of the station, out of commuters' sight. From an organizational perspective, you can see that human-service goals have here been changed or short-circuited for funding reasons. Human-service organizations are often pressured to adopt goals that satisfy the interests of diverse social groups, and therefore may pursue multiple and even conflicting goals. For example, correctional settings operate under simultaneous goals of keeping offenders in custody as well as rehabilitating them.

Although we are highlighting human-service organizations, these issues are also experienced in industrial and commercial organizations where social workers find jobs. In industrial organizations such as auto factories and concrete-mix companies, for example, the primary function is productivity. The welfare of employees is taken care of by a small unit of personnel—for instance, social workers—as the managers see fit. Commercial organizations such as telephone companies with over a thousand employees may use social workers as part of their personnel welfare plan.

Organizations are human systems. Effective functioning depends on motivating people (Gortner, Mahler, & Nicholson, 1989). Bernard Berelson and Gary Steiner (1964, p. 240) offer a definition: "A motive is an inner state that energizes, activates, or moves (hence motivation), and that directs or channels behavior toward goals." Any organization that provides goals, incentives, or rewards to motivate people focuses on the needs of the individual. Needs are internal—for example, the need for food when a person is hungry. Incentives or goals are external or environment based. Money, or financial incentive, is the most important motivator in the life of employees.

To meet goals, no good administrator works alone. No manager can singlehandedly maintain a high level of organizational functioning and thereby achieve organizational goals—the energies and actions of others must be directed into the right channels. Because administrators delegate work to others, the administrator must understand their motivations and needs (Gartner, Mahler, & Nicholson, 1989). Goals guide motivation efforts in an organization.

Official and Operative Goals

At a general level, organizations have goals that fulfill basic societal functions. For example, Parsons (1957, p. 108) defines the official goals of a mental hospital as being able "to cope with the consequences for the individual patient and for the patients as a social group, of a condition of mental illness." He notes that official goals can be classified as a set of social responsibilities such as custody, protection, socialization, and therapy. The existence of this organization is justified only to the degree that it articulates societal goals, values, and norms. Operative goals in a mental hospital may include protecting the community and ensuring continued employment for all staff.

As Perrow (1961, p. 856) defines them, "Official goals are the general purposes of the organization as put forth in the charter, annual reports, public statements by key officials and other authoritative pronouncements. . . . Operative goals designate the ends sought through the actual operating policies of the organization: They tell us what the organization actually is trying to do, regardless of what the official goals say are the aims." The relationship between official and operative goals is of major importance to social-policy analysts and to human-service practitioners. Official goals often reflect complex legislative processes and have important consequences for the future of organizations. Human-service organizations represent social-welfare legislation and policies. Directives aimed at implementing these policies become the official goals of an organization (Hasenfeld, 1983). The gap that is almost always present between official and operative goals can be used to critically assess the effectiveness of the policy or legislation. Operative goals reveal an organization's actual commitment to resources. The allocation of money in terms of goals shows how a particular organization functions. For example, say a mental hospital commits most of its money, personnel, and time to hiring a large number of attendants for taking care of patients' physical well-being—that is, giving medicines. This leaves very little money to allot to psychotherapy. Therefore, it can be deduced that the operative goals of the hospital are custody and control of patients. For example, Alan, 19, was abused as a child and has come to a mental hospital through the state. He has lived in the mental facility for five years, and the only treatment he has received is medication. He is allowed to walk around the hospital grounds, he is considered harmless, but whenever he is not well medicated he begins to act out. The hospital's response is to administer more medication.

Alan does not have any family visiting him, and he functions minimally with medication. The hospital considers this acceptable because custodial care is one of its operative goals and part of its treatment plans.

Defining Organizational Goals

Organizational goals are separate from individual goals, yet individuals make up organizations and create the organization's personality. For example, a local agency is well known for treating its employees with consideration and flexibility. People who work here are easy-going, friendly, and more helpful than those in other organizations. Hence this agency reflects a positive culture and personality. In a human-service organization the administrator needs to ensure that the interests and necessities of the immediate community are satisfied by the agency's goals. All the service needs of the community often cannot be fulfilled in any one agency. The funding provided by interest groups dictates what issues the agency will address. Not all issues can be addressed, so they must be ranked. And because board members have different interests, setting priorities can become complex.

In human-service organizations, multiple goals are usually assigned by various publics. To fulfill demands with the available resources, the organization may develop multiple goals. The organization must set priorities based on these goals, depending on the needs of the organization.

Achieving specific, stable goals is another problem. For example, the agency needs to distinguish between means and ends. What may be seen as an end at one level of the organization (achieving punctuality) may be seen as a means at another level (getting caseloads handled). Such a distinction must be made to avoid misjudgments and misplaced internal emphasis. Conflict is reduced by making goals very specific.

After goals have been specified, they must be stabilized. In other words, goals must be pegged to time frames and schedules for implementation. Goals may be broken down into short- and long-term goals.

Organizational goals are also multidimensional and rather unstable, depending on needs and changes in the environment. Despite the demand for specificity, they are often indeterminate (Hannan & Freeman, 1977). Yet clear goals are a great aid to the organization—as well as to the individual. Mento, Steel, and Karren (1987) and Tubbs (1986) state that specific and challenging work goals are a powerful work motivator. Research shows that having specific goals such as "I will complete three cases today" leads to greater productivity than a generalized goal such as "I will do all I can do today."

Mohr (1973) classifies goals in human-service organizations as either transitive or reflexive. Transitive goals reflect commitment of resources to certain programs, whereas reflexive goals reflect resource commitments to the personal needs and interests of members. Transitive goals refer to providing services to certain groups of people in the environment, such as providing shelters and other services for runaway children or victims of domestic violence. In terms of reflexive goals, White (1974) says that inducements in an agency should be sufficient to evoke adequate contributions from all members of the organizational coalition. Every organization should establish targets and procedures for internal allocation of resources, to motivate members.

Effects of Goals on Service Delivery

In human-service organizations, goal commitments guide the formulation of programs and services. The manner in which resources are used reflects goals and activities in every unit of the organization. For example, in a nursing home for the elderly, when the primary goal is seen as custodial, minimal resources may be set aside for social rehabilitation. In another situation, a health-care system committed to serving low-income families may find itself unable to reach them. Such a system needs to develop other programs to fill the goal of reaching such clients.

At times organizational goals must change to meet the demands of changing times. For instance, during the 1980s, the National Association of Social Workers (NASW) responded to political changes by becoming politically active. Political involvement of both the national organization and NASW chapters increased. Chapters now inform members about political action needed to support social-services legislation, encouraging lobbying, and organizing members to support political candidates running for office.

Goals are also used to measure accountability. Accountability gives an organization credibility and legitimacy. The goals become the criteria by which an organization is evaluated. Organizations structure their units and service delivery patterns to follow the evaluative criteria required by monitoring and legitimizing groups. For example, Blau (1955) found that success in a public employment-placement agency was structured in terms of job placement. Jobs were the criterion for agency effectiveness.

Unfortunately, too often organizations evaluate themselves on the basis of services rendered, rather than goals achieved. They track and report on numbers of clients, numbers of interviews, or fees collected, instead of treatment or service outcomes. Such organizations need to rephrase evaluations in terms of goals.

To reach goals, agencies need objectives. Objectives are the most concrete translation of goals. They are specific, measurable, and set within a time frame. An example of an objective might be "Introduce a family-therapy training program for at least five staff members by January 1." Such an objective can be achieved. (However, it remains to be seen whether staff members with such training will produce better results in treating families in which family violence in one form or another is the presenting problem. This is a more complex question, requiring an operational definition of "better results.")

THE NATURE OF ORGANIZATIONS

Organization involves how social controls order and organize the conduct of individuals under varying circumstances, how social relations are structured, and how shared goals and beliefs unite the members and guide their behavior.

The broad structure of an organization shows *roughly* how different units relate to each other; as the saying goes, "The whole is greater than the sum of its parts" (Blau & Scott, 1961). The fact that an organization has been formally established does not mean that all activities of its members conform to the official blueprint. Within every formal organization, there is also an informal organization. Different groups in the organization develop their own practices, values, norms, and social relations as the members live and work together—sometimes in harmony, sometimes in conflict. Each organization is thus an ecosystem.

Often large organizations represent a pyramid structure with a large number of employees who are line workers at the bottom, followed by supervisors, department heads, and directors.

Moreover, organizations fit into a larger ecosystem. No organization operates in a vacuum. It affects both its employees and the environment in which it exists, and vice versa. Furthermore, organizations are formed to pursue certain goals, but they also engage in activities that may or may not be related to achieving those goals. For example, some colleges are known as "party schools," suggesting that, for many students, social and recreational activities take precedence over the pursuit of knowledge. Students who are in "party schools" are often from a middle- or upper-class environment, where the ecological culture accepts these ways of behavior in such an environment.

Environmental Factors

Organizations must carry on transactions with their environment to survive and to grow. Environmental conditions contribute to what goes on within an organization, the form it takes, and the consequences of its actions. Input from the environment is returned to it, and the output is consumed, used, and evaluated in the environment. As Brager and Holloway (1978) note, systems theory suggests that when environmental factors essential to the organization's functioning are stable, organizational programs and policies tend to persist over time. When environmental factors shift, the organization may or may not adjust to the external force that places pressure on it. Organizations are in a constant state of flux, which may or may not be adaptive to external forces; however, the *degree* of their vulnerability to danger may be over- or underestimated. Its adjusting or not adjusting may not be the primary issue; other issues, such as degree of adjustment, *over time,* and the capacity of the organization to draw on its internal resources, all affect the continued viability of the organization. Hence each interaction that takes place between an organization and its environment represents a real or potential internal change.

Not-for-profit human-service organizations depend on donors and/or government subsidies for survival. Human-service organizations are influenced by the norms and sociocultural characteristics of the local community and depend on the community for legitimatization. Sometimes, therefore, the agency may not be able to fulfill the needs of the community. A funding agency may not be willing to continue to support an agency program for various reasons, in which case the agency must change or reevaluate its goals and the types of services it offers to the community.

Brager and Holloway (1978) identify two environmental factors that influence an organization's development. First, situational demands generated by different types of technologies impact an organization's structure. For instance, given increased use of computers in all areas of human life, the organization must adjust its structure and processes accordingly. Second, the rate of change in the environment may be considered a barometer of potential innovation within the organization. Thus, increased turbulence in the outer world can spur greater internal change.

According to Wamsley and Zald (1973), Gummer (1990), Farrell and Petersen (1982), and Vredenburgh and Maurer (1984), a wide variety of economic and political factors affect agencies. Following Brager and Holloway (1978), we will confine our discussion of these economic factors to funding and technology. Our discussion of political forces focuses on the value systems and on powerful interests that shape the conditions of the agency's existence.

Economic Factors

Three economic factors affect agencies: the shifting availability of funds, the characteristics of the funded agency, and the dependency of the organization on the funding agency (Brager & Holloway, 1978). Fligstein (1991) reviewed national trends in corporate giving to human-services agencies, examined how corporations make funding decisions, and reported on philanthropic giving among 29 companies in Cambridge, Massachusetts. The study found that most corporations make funding decisions informally rather than formally; many rely on tradition, social contacts, and intuition to guide allocations. This informality in turn affects the planning and development of human-service organizations.

Changing economic conditions often do not affect all parts of an organization equally. During economic distress, an organization may cut back or eliminate those individuals and programs that are less important to overall goals. This is the organization's response to environmental financial factors, and it affects the organization and its staff. Quite often morale is low among new and lower-down-the-ladder employees.

Fluctuating availability of funds When the funding of an organization is stable, agency programs and policies flourish. However, when the funding is not stable or is decreasing, the organization becomes vulnerable to all types of morale and management problems. Employees and clientele conflict over who gets the most money. When the pool of funds is expanding, more positive changes occur in an organization, but when funding is scarce or decreases, changes are more negative. Sometimes, however, an agency with stable funding becomes complacent and does not seek to improve services, and sometimes an agency with declining funds becomes more innovative and flexible.

When funds diminish or dry up in an agency, economic distress affects employees' morale and the quality and quantity of services to clients. There may be reductions or freezing of salaries, retrenchment of staff, expanded workloads, and longer waiting lists. Reduced funding encourages consolidation and coordination of services to conserve funds.

Funding constriction also may lead to a search for funding in other areas, and may require modification of the agency's programs to accommodate new sponsors. Changes also occur in terms of clearer accountability and the mechanisms of evaluating an agency. For example, when one family-service agency faced funding cuts, it took a keener look at its employees and wasteful practices. Some hours were cut from workloads, and some positions were made volunteer jobs. Some staff were laid off; others let go. Counseling programs were made short term, and group work replaced most one-to-one therapy. Some resource orientation sessions were cut, and a resource booklet was published for clients.

Fund-raisers were put on commission or percentage, and donations of materials were solicited. The agency moved rapidly toward short-term services, although originally it had catered to clients on a long-term basis. During lean times when resources contract, demand expands, and the call for efficient management is made with great fervor (Lewis, 1975).

When the economic atmosphere is favorable, innovative or expanded services may be developed. Administrators always welcome more funding. This allows the agency to expand and to create new programs providing additional resources in the struggle to deal with environmental uncertainty. During this time organizational purposes become more pliable as administrators seek to offer more varied services. For instance, if an agency's main focus is individual and family treatment, it can use increased funding to move toward community education or other types of outreach programs.

For example, Jim, the chief executive of a family-service agency, found that money was available for extra activities, so he began a program for single mothers that included help in developing parenting skills, budget planning, and family management.

Characteristics of funded agencies Money is an important environmental input. It gives funders a high degree of power to influence and command agency decision making. How do organizations get funded, and where do they get funds? A key factor is whether the agency is part of government (public) or nongovernmental (private).

Historically, innovation has been seen as a function of private agencies, because public agencies may need to avoid controversy (Brager & Holloway, 1978). This does not mean that private agencies do not face pressure; it simply means that the type of pressure faced is different, although the effects may be the same. In 1968 Warren and Hyman surveyed 35 instances of planned change in agencies, and found that change seemed to have happened consensually in private agencies, but was filled with conflict in public agencies. The situation remains the same in the 1990s. Private agencies may be more flexible than public ones in shaping program goals and meeting mandates.

Most private agencies today get public funding in the form of purchase-of-service contracts or grants. Public agencies, however, must follow legislation, which often leaves little room for deviation even when outside funds are available to support growth and change. For example, a public-welfare agency that provides protective services to children and refers abusive parents for help may have money available for innovative services such as offering parents home-service helpers when the parents need "time out" from their children. But this money may not be used because there is a great deal of controversy over how much a public agency should do for "irresponsible" or "crazy" or "bad" parents.

Dependency of agencies on funders The degree of dependency on funders varies from agency to agency. Some agencies are completely dependent on a main funding source for their survival, while others depend on a number of funding agencies and thus face a different set of problems. Those agencies with more stable funding are less prone to modify organizational goals under outside pressure. Agencies that do not have a secure funding base must interact more with the environment and are more subject to outside influences.

In social-welfare agencies, resource development is a social-work skill. But systematic learning of specific skills with reference to specific issues is rarely taught and must be picked up by trial and error. For example, while working with Tina, a brain-damaged child, a social worker finds that many such children and parents need help. Would the provision of a unique program for providing homemaker services to needy families of such children be useful? How would an organization find funding for such a program? Dependence on funding that fluctuates according to the political climate affects services offered to people. Sometimes programs may be eliminated, diminishing the overall well-being of clients as well as of the providing agency. When dependency increases, it is harder to accomplish required tasks, and this may affect the funding sources' attitudes.

An agency's dependence on (or independence from) funding sources is closely related to how money is raised and allocated. Endowments are a chief example of a funding pattern that can insulate an organization from environmental stimuli. For instance, an Ivy League university usually has enough endowments to let it function with relative insulation from environmental change stimuli.

When funding becomes difficult, agencies—often in desperation—may become innovative and look for purchase-of-service contracts. Public agencies sometimes buy services for their clients from private agencies. Such contracts can be renegotiated, but case-by-case accountability in such situations is difficult to supervise. Purchase-of-service contracts provide a large portion of the budget for some agencies and do not receive the wide-ranging surveillance that is ordinarily necessary when there is significant financial support.

When funding is dispersed, agency independence increases. Because the agency is less dependent on one source, it is freer to avoid the restrictions that a single giver could impose. Categorical grants mandate legal constraints and policy controls, but by their very nature prevent the use of resources to address problems other than the category funded. It should be added that the relationship between a funder and the agency is often ambiguous. Sometimes mutual dependence exists between agency and funder. Ideally, a positive or productive program is satisfying to both. The funder may become involved in the progress of the agency program because it adds to the funder's own credibility. Usually a great deal of physical distance separates the two, however, and distance makes the funder less attentive to problems of program operation.

Outside pressure from a funder is not always negative. At times, outside pressure is what an agency needs to update its program and improve the quality of service. Moreover, accountability *can* be maintained under purchase-of-service contracts. A representative of the agency paying the bills can receive periodic reports, review records, and interview clients to monitor services and outcomes.

The business community has traditionally helped social agencies through its support of United Way, but more recently, many corporations have purchased social-work services from agencies (Family and Children's Services of Buffalo, New York, for example) for their employee assistance programs.

Another important source of income is fees for services rendered, paid either by clients directly or by managed care companies or other third-party payments that cover mental-health services as part of health insurance. Such services must usually be provided by certificated or licensed personnel. For this reason, more and more agencies are making a state license or certification a condition of employment for social workers.

Technology Technology is an important environmental factor that shapes organizational structure and process and provides impetus for internal organizational change. *Technology* is defined as procedures, methodologies, and inventions that help an organization reach its goals. For example, foster care, case management, and crisis intervention can be viewed as technologies, as they are designed to bring about changes in behavior. Brager and Holloway call them *social technology*. Whatever is newly discovered or invented and is directly related to people's problems can impact human services. For example, if an AIDS vaccine is discovered, the types of services offered to AIDS patients will change. Also, social-service organizations set up specifically to care for AIDS victims might have to find new rationales for existence, or dismantle. Other examples of technology affecting social services are automatic data-processing systems and the use of computers for diagnosis and treatment. Although use of computers has been progressive and positive, in some instances data have been misused. In New York, private practitioners have claimed that managed care has violated client confidentiality by allowing staff in managed-care offices easy access to data on clients. In many instances, office staff let the clients become aware that the staff had private, confidential information on them. This caused a great deal of discomfort and mistrust (*New York Times,* October 24, 1994).

Human-service organizations tend to be quite vulnerable to power arrangements and prevailing social values in a community. Agencies developed through public action must address some significant social problem, which may vary from dealing with drug addicts, to teenage pregnancy, to whatever happens to be on the social-value agenda. Thus, human-service agencies are vulnerable to program fads and fashions. They may start a new program in response to public concern but give it up when the public, politicians, and media shift attention elsewhere. Often such programs mushroom throughout the country and are contagious, but the excitement turns to disillusionment when there is no follow-through. For example, sometimes much funding for the mentally retarded is available. But when the political climate changes and the funding dies out, the agency is left with a group of frustrated workers and dissatisfied clientele until this arena of help (due to lack of funds) is closed down. This creates problems for the mentally retarded and their relatives, as well as unemployment problems for the staff.

Political Forces

In any community ecosystem, there are close relationships among economic, technological, and political factors. The political atmosphere influences how agencies are used. Systems of values, beliefs, and rituals may benefit some groups and harm others. For example, more help may be offered to substance abusers than to homeless people, because people unfortunately continue to blame victims. The Judeo-Christian work ethic suggests that if you work hard enough, you can "make it"—but the reality is that people lose jobs, which leads to other problems, like not being able to pay rent and buy basic necessities such as food. However, our society has often lumped all homeless people as lazy and unwilling to work. Although this may be true of a few, this is not true in general of all homeless people, and the judgmental attitude of the general public is not founded on reality.

Any organizational setting has superordinates, users, and providers. The superordinates have the responsibility of overseeing the organizational functioning. These people directly or indirectly pay for the legitimacy of services. In a public agency the superordinates could be a complex hierarchy of authority figures; in private agencies, a board of directors. In reality the money for the agency often comes from the public, either the taxpayers or the community. So when anything goes wrong in an agency, the public becomes conscious that money was misused or mishandled and gets involved. The users are the clients, and they are also the taxpayers and therefore affect the manner in which an agency functions. If an agency caters to poor clients, it is run in a particular fashion; when it has a middle-class clientele, it is organized and functions differently. Frequently the clients are satisfied receivers of services. However, if one or a number of middle-class clients who are taxpayers are seriously dissatisfied and aggressively gather an oppositional group to represent dissatisfaction with services, this may catch the attention of people in power or/and create consumer activism. For example, an agency catering to AIDS patients may shut down services due to lack of support from the funding agencies. A burst of public reaction may immediately follow. An opposition group may form and move aggressively toward collecting funds so that services for AIDS patients can resume.

Whether an agency receives or does not receive enough attention could still affect change and stability at the agency. Depending on whether this attention is needed, it affects the functioning of the agency accordingly. Too much attention from the environment entails constant vigilance, whereas very little attention could mean that the agency has power and control to do what it wants.

Social-work models use integrative and segmentalist actions to solve problems and change. An integrative approach emphasizes wholeness, eagerness to combine problems with new ideas, and also a positive view of change as an opportunity to test limits in a system (Kanter, 1983). Thus racial discrimination, teen pregnancy, substandard housing, unemployment, and crime might be seen as aspects of the same problem. This integrative action approach is consistent with open-systems theory, which emphasizes wholeness, interdependence, and potential for change. Segmentalism compartmentalizes actions, events, and problems and isolates system elements from each other. Similarly, some minority groups/organizations isolate themselves by choice from other organizations in society, including the majority. When taken to the extreme, they run the risk of aggravating their already-existing race-induced isolation. Kanter contends that problems are best approached by breaking them down into small parts and assigning each part to logically appropriate subunits. In contrast, integrative organizations view aggregate subproblems as parts of larger problems and thus create a unity that provides more insight.

Ethnicity- and Race-Based Organizations

It is important to understand how racial and ethnic organizations maintain a sense of continuity and provide caring and nurturing for their members. Rubin and Rubin (1992) report that different types of such organizations have been developed in different areas. A few are ethnicity- or race-based and aimed at helping members of their own community to move forward in life, to have a place to go to, and to work through their own issues. For example, the members of the Renegades Housing Movement in Spanish Harlem provide their own labor ("sweat equity") to improve local housing conditions. They repair and turn over buildings to a housing cooperative that neighborhood people can join. Seed money was first provided by nonprofit sponsors of cooperatives; later funds were provided by Housing and Urban Development (HUD). Another example is the Mid Bronx Desperados (MBD). This organization developed out of a local initiative support corporation guarantee, to involve MBD in a neighborhood crime-prevention program, to reduce crime, and to increase positive publicity for the community-development organization (Rubin & Rubin, 1992). These goals are slowly being achieved. Finally, Lincoln and Mamiya (1990) point out that the

African-American church acts as a formal and an informal organization for religion-oriented African Americans.

The National Congress for Community Economic Development (NCCED) points out that 2000 or so community-development organizations are run by different ethnic groups with the specific purpose of helping and empowering their own members. Some reasons for the success of these organizations are as follows:

- Grassroots organizations understand their communities.
- They meet needs and offer opportunities and resources.
- They operate with a clear mission and a comprehensive, strategic approach to community revitalization. They are involved in a long-term process, with each project building on the last and toward the next.
- They forge partnerships with local developers, lenders, businesses, foundations, religious institutions, other nonprofit organizations, and government at all levels.
- They have the political and technical skills and tenacity to pull together a complex array of resources needed to get projects done.
- Also, these organizations achieve success because they have integrated a developmental ideology with managerial skills (NCCED, 1989, pp. 3–4).

Often ethnic groups begin participatory development through small projects where a small, single group with limited resources can achieve and let those successes generate more funding, members, hope, and projects. "Chicanos Por La Causa (CPLC) began as an advocacy and protest group . . . by some young men and women of Mexican descent. . . . As it expanded from advocacy to housing development and services, CPLC enlarged its range of operations . . . to build an emergency medical clinic. . . . A dramatic shift, both financially and programmatically, took place . . . [that] enabled Chicanos Por La Causa to become designated as a statewide, nonprofit community development corporation" (Task Force, 1987, pp. 19–21). Bootstrapping works because ethnic groups create pride through successful projects, which increases people's willingness to participate in future projects.

Thus racial and ethnic groups develop organizations to benefit their people. This is also true of Asian cultures. Diverse groups such as Koreans and Filipinos open their own cultural centers for promoting their culture and for people to experience a sense of belonging. Such groups can help offset experiences of prejudice and discrimination from other groups in society.

Arab Americans have been victims of prejudice because others do not understand their culture and religion, and because of conflicts in the Middle East. In areas where Arab populations are higher, such as in Michigan, they have developed their own groups. Arabs rarely seek help outside their own group. They have a traditional social-service agency called ACCESS (Arab Community and Concern for Education and Social Services). This small community service agency in Detroit helps Arabs with family problems, acculturating to the United States, and learning English. The employees are all Arab Americans and speak Arabic, to keep the organization focused on Arab family and culture.

Ethnicity-based community organizations grow out of people's desire to work together to combat shared problems; the participants must share knowledge to make projects work. Such organizations often manage social and economic programs and solve problems that handicap poor and disempowered members (Rubin & Rubin, 1992). They may offer shelter to battered women, comfort to the dying, and raise community consciousness about the ethnic group. It is essential for social workers to become aware of such natural support networks and the comfort and protection they offer to their own people. Social workers can use them for working with diverse groups of people. They can also offer sensitivity and awareness training to help organizations increase awareness of ways to support diversity in the workforce. And multicultural participation councils can help manage diversity.

Organizational Models and Effectiveness

How effective a social-welfare organization is depends on the model that is used to evaluate its programs. The following classification of organizational models is based on Cameron's (1984) approach. These models are used to assess organizational effectiveness, especially in social-welfare organizations.

The goal model In the goal model, effectiveness is evaluated in terms of how well the organization or the program fulfills its *official* goals. When goals are clear, consensual, time bound, and measurable (Cameron, 1984), the goal model helps encourage accountability in social work. Problems may arise because of lack of consensus on goals and also because of an inability to measure goal accomplishment. For example, when people are the "products," it is impossible to tell how many people have benefited on a long-term basis, unless there is a clear way to measure real benefit. So the goal model requires clear goals and clear measurement of progress.

The system-resource model The system-resource model measures how well the organization obtains resources, particularly for organizations where survival is problematic and popular support is minimal (Thurston, 1987). Some agencies have closed, and others function with minimum staff as budget cuts occur and priorities change. Obtaining resources for an agency is a legitimate organizational-performance criterion. In this model, the emphasis is on organizational well-being based on inputs rather than on output or service effectiveness. It can be combined with other criteria to evaluate the whole agency.

The multiple-constituencies model The multiple-constituencies model can be used to identify competing groups of people and agencies that have invested in, and who therefore can place demands on and expect results from, the organization (Martin & O'Connor, 1992). Social-work organizations must at least minimally meet the demands of strategic constituencies. Constituencies are groups being served by the social-work organization. A multiple-constituency model is externally and internally oriented, because members of the constituency can be within the organizational system and also outside of it. In social-work agencies, the constituency could be the community at large, or the staff in the agency that forms the constituency. Depending on the constituency and its needs, the agency must meet demands accordingly.

The legitimacy model The legitimacy model draws attention to how the agency is perceived and how it interacts with other people and organizations in the environment. Legitimacy involves people conforming or seeming to conform to institutionalized principles, rules, and standards. In the legitimacy model, organizational effectiveness is evaluated on the basis of legitimacy conferred by the institutionalized environment (Meyer & Rowan, 1977; Cameron, 1984).

If, for example, the outside environment needs a program to combat drug abuse, the agency may start such a program. The environment thus defines the agency program as rational and legitimate. Such structures encourage the development of specific roles and programs within an agency (Meyer, Scott, & Deal, 1981, p. 152). For example, an agency may have a drug counselor, a drug-program director, and a special fundraiser. The legitimacy model is useful for understanding organizational evolution, change, and survival strategies (Cameron, 1984). An agency that seeks to survive, seeks legitimate programs and funds from outside. In such a model, organizational effectiveness is externally oriented (Martin & O'Connor, 1992).

Each of these models has merit, and they are not mutually exclusive.

The Bureaucratic Environment

As used by an average person, the term *bureaucracy* is almost a dirty word. It usually suggests rigid rules and regulations and a hierarchy of offices, the director's office being bigger and more luxurious than the rest. The person second in command may have a slighter smaller one, and so forth. Having a window with a view on the topmost floor of a skyscraper in New York City means you have made it. Bureaucracy also connotes narrow specializations of personnel, numerous channels of approval, and considerable resistance to change.

Every organization of any significant size is bureaucratized to some degree. Despite the negative connotation, hierarchy is important in organizations. It sets legitimate rights to use power to hire, give orders, fire, evaluate, and reward people. Usually people at the upper level give orders to people at a lower level. Some people see this as a threat to equality (Rothschild-Whitt & Whitt, 1986). Hierarchy is an efficient way of organizing collective efforts by a large group of people (Tannenbaum, Kevcic, Rosner, Vianello, & Wieser, 1974), but it can foster in employees learned helplessness and an inability to act independently. Organizational power can be used to split, control, exploit, and dominate employees (Ferguson, 1984). Many social agencies today, however, are more likely to allow such things as professional autonomy and shared decision making than in the past.

Differentiation and Integration

Agencies are both differentiated and integrated. Differentiation concerns the division of labor, and independence, and the emergence of new parts and activities. Integration, in contrast, is a progression toward wholeness, interdependence, and systematization. In highly differentiated agencies, the different elements operate independently and change affects only isolated parts. In integrated systems, a change in one part of the system affects others and differentiation is a consequence of learning. Thus agencies must first be integrated before they can become differentiated. As Martin and O'Connor (1992) indicate, most social-work organizations are highly differentiated. In addition to their primary activities, agencies carry on fiscal management, housekeeping and building maintenance, and secretarial and clerical activity. These services are an important part of an organization's functioning and its formal structure. Differentiation includes the way that various members of the organization function within their work roles. System managers dream of self-maintaining systems, but that is an impossible ideal, because so many varying, and sometimes conflicting, activities, goals, rules, and constituents impact organizations.

COMMUNICATION PROCESSES IN ORGANIZATIONS

Communication processes are closely interwoven with organizational structure. At the interpersonal level, communication is a transactional process that provides accurate information and crucial emotional overtones to other people. In a complex organization, a large number of people must be reached and documentation is important. Chester Barnard, an early theorist and accomplished manager, noted that "in any exhaustive theory of organization, communication would occupy a central place, because structure and information are exchanged between a giver and a taker for the purpose of conveying meanings" (1938, p. 8). Communication involves both sender and receiver, and their reciprocal effects on each other.

Communication can be classified as instrumental, expressive, consummatory, and incidental. *Instrumental communication* is purposeful or goal directed. The sender's intent is to affect the person who receives it, and this effect may include knowledge, attitudes, and behavior. Instrumental communication can be explained as the transmission of cognitive information, such as "I think we should plan this way." *Expressive communication* is the transmission of normative and affective information; for example, "I feel we should follow certain rules with reference to dress code." *Consummatory communication* arises from an emotional state of the sender such as enthusiasm, fear, or uncertainty about a situation and so forth; for example, "I am afraid our plans for a new program for children will become a disaster, because we do not have the money for it." Finally, *incidental communication* gives information to the sender without his or her being aware of it. In addition, there are also formal and informal, and impersonal and personal forms. *Personal communication* is the transmission of information offered by face-to-face interaction, and *impersonal communication* is information that is transmitted by means other than face to face. Formal and informal communications are official and unofficial transmissions. The information shared between superordinates and subordinates in official capacities is called *formal;* information transmitted among peers in primary relationships is usually *informal*. Official information is presented in meetings or by people in authority, whereas exchanges during coffee breaks and lunch breaks between peers are *informal*.

The Bases of Communication Systems

Communication may be vertical or horizontal. And vertical communication can be either upward or downward. Historically, Katz and Kahn (1966) have identified five types of downward communication, including

1. *Simple and common job instruction*. The intent of such instruction is to help ensure efficient job performance. If an employee is highly trained, job instruction can be more limited and less specific, because this person enters in with appropriate job-related knowledge and attitudes.
2. *Rationale of the task* and its relationship to the goals of the organization.
3. *Information* regarding the procedures and practices within an organization. This information is offered in a straightforward and noncontroversial manner.
4. *Evaluation,* which can be described as the process where the

individual receives information regarding his or her performance in the communication system. This can become sticky if the feedback is negative.

5. *Indoctrination,* the organization's effort to enhance the employees' ideological commitment to the values, goals, and mission of the organization.

These same types of communication may be used in a first-line supervisor–worker relationship, but communication becomes more complex when focus shifts to the top executive and vice president. A great degree of dysfunction can mark hierarchy. Some problems in hierarchical communication include differences that inhibit honest communication. For example, people do not generally criticize their superiors directly. People belonging to the same status interact more with one another than with those at other levels. Approval may be sought from superiors rather than from peers in such situations. The error-correcting function of normal social interaction is lacking. Interaction among peers serves to sort out errors and provides a common denominator through the lateral interaction process. Moreover, superiors may have superior knowledge and expertise. An intellectual gap may thus exist between the superiors and the subordinates. But if the superior is chosen because of his or her administrative skills and is a generalist, subordinates who are experts may view him or her as inexpert, which limits the leader's credibility.

Upward Communication

The situation is more complex when a person communicates upward. Employees may feel threats to themselves or their work group so they are unlikely to pass to a superior information that could harm them or their peers. Also, just as communication coming down from the top is detailed and specific, the information headed upward from below is brief and summarized.

Communication in flat hierarchies, where everyone reports to one person, follows typical hierarchical arrangements; hypothetically, all people in a flat structure have equal access to the superior. However, the communication and/or conflict in a flat hierarchy may be limited by the supervisory *span of control* (number of people accountable to a specific supervisor/administrator) or by the size of the organization. Communication takes more time in a taller structure; conflict resolution and coordination are slower in a flat structure.

Upward communication provides feedback for control purposes and is necessary for organizational functioning. It also presents many different organizational dilemmas. Some of these are structural, as subordinates want to influence policy and protect themselves from action or control by superiors. Subordinates also avoid talking about what their bosses do not wish to hear (Robbins, 1989).

Horizontal Communication

Little research has been done on horizontal communication, although this is more common than vertical communication. Some minor tasks must be left to the discretion of peer groups so that counterproductive communications do not arise to fill the void. Horizontal communication also serves several additional functions, including task coordination, problem solving, information sharing, and conflict resolution (Goldhaber, 1974).

However, horizontal communication can evoke conflict. This is particularly true when subunits in an organization have different types of expertise and are competing for money, better understanding, and acceptance. It should be understood that perfect communication is impossible. Message recipients should always be aware of the biases of the message senders and develop their own counterbiases as a protective device. Failure to consider motivations for messages will invariably result in misunderstandings and unnecessary conflict in the organization.

CONFLICT IN ORGANIZATIONS

Conflict in organizations can be understood by analyzing its bases, forms, and consequences. Let's begin by discussing the three organizational bases for conflict.

1. *Functional conflict* can be induced by various systems in the organization. Every system develops its own form of values and norms and is characterized by its own dynamics. People maintain their subsystems and preserve the character of the organization by selecting, indoctrinating, training, and ensuring standards of performance. Each system develops its own distinctive norms and frames of reference and its own elements of conflict. For example, in a hospital, conflicts will periodically arise in the general governing-body meetings regarding rules, regulations, and norms. There may also be conflicts among different departments in a hospital, such as the children's department and the ear, nose, and throat departments, regarding norms and values or limited resources.

2. The second source of conflict concerns *roles and functions*. Conflict can appear as hostile rivalry or as good-natured competition. Sometimes such competition can be beneficial, and at other times, destructive, if people can no longer work together. If hostile rivalry is allowed to dominate, the goals and purposes of the organization will be neglected. For example, conflicts may arise between social workers and child-care staff in children's institutions. A social worker may want to interview a sexually abused child, with an eye to helping the whole family get financial aid; but medical staff may want to protect the patient from further stress and trauma.

3. *Hierarchical conflict* arises from intergroup struggles over organizational rewards such as prestige, status, and monetary rewards (Porter & Lawler, 1965). Because there is never total satisfaction with the reward system, subgroups may recruit lower-level personnel and try to improve their lot by joining forces against the most privileged members of the group. For instance, in one hospital the lower-ranking employees, including security guards and custodial staff, met secretly and planned a protest because they were tired of working hard and not being rewarded.

Finally, conflicts based on interpersonal dynamics are precipitated by the way people feel and behave toward each other as individuals.

Kenneth Boulding (1978) has proposed another framework for looking at conflict, based on four components of the process. First, conflict involves at least two parties, individuals, or groups. Second, the field of conflict includes those conditions of the social system considered important by the different parties. The conflict could be a struggle by both parties to gain power at the expense of the other. Working out conflict is a process, and the parties involved in the conflict seldom maintain their positions. Third, the conflict may move different ways in a situation. According to Boulding a conflict situation could lead to various conditions, including a continuation of the present situation, or one party gaining more power than the other, or losing power to another party, or both parties gaining or losing power. The intensity of participants fluctuates during conflict. Sometimes the dynamic escalates to a total destruction of the organization or project; at other times, the situation may stabilize.

The final component is the management, control, or resolution of conflict. Conflict situations are generally not discrete situations with a beginning and an end. They may seem to disappear only to resurface in times of stress such as financial difficulties or interpersonal rivalry. Conflict is often resolved by the relatively simple mechanism of one party being peaceful. When one person backs off, the other party may also back off. This may lead to an uneasy peace, or a problem may be temporarily resolved (Boulding, 1978).

Rubin and Rubin (1992) note that organizational leaders should try to channel conflicts in the organization toward productive ends. Conflict is a central feature of democratic decision making, because democratic forms of participation are designed to allow the routine expression of different interests, values, and opinions. The challenge that faces democratic organizations is how to treat such conflict as a normal part of the decision-making process by using it as a productive way to explore and select among alternatives (Drucker, 1990).

When a conflict is brewing, a skillful manager can often see it coming and explore alternatives. Conflicts over issues are an opportunity to discuss ways of improving organizational performance. Use conflict to improve the position of an organization, without letting people waste their time battling each other (Rubin & Rubin, 1992). Social-welfare organizations are suffused with conflict, because conflicting expectations arise between inside and external groups. In project implementation, for example, people quarrel over limited resources and priorities, too. They may resent others who may not be carrying their share of work. People may fight over differences in ethnic, racial, and religious backgrounds, or because they simply do not like each other. Keeping information from subordinates can also create uncertainty and jealousy among workers.

Conflicts can be reduced by structuring work flow appropriately. This can be done by not placing people in win–lose situations and by enabling both groups to be partial winners. When negotiating, the representatives should not be forced to choose between loyalty to their group and loyalty to the best interests of the organization (Sackmann, 1991). For example, if secretarial workers in an organization want increased vacation time, the professional staff may sympathize with them but may oppose them for practical reasons (Martin, 1984). Empathy is present, but there is no solution unless some kind of rotational vacation plan can be worked out. If a vacation plan is worked out, however, no compromises are needed, because staff needs and organization needs are both satisfied.

Conflicts in social-welfare organizations may take many forms, including ideological differences about the mission of the agency, interprofessional rivalries, ineffective supervision, oppressive paperwork requirements, and so forth. Supervisors may be upset about sloppy recordkeeping by employees, or workers may refuse to complete paperwork. Conflicts in agencies also arise over unfair policies. For example, work units may fight over space and other scarce resources.

Workers often would like to have more control over their work than they have (Greenberger & Strasser, 1986; Bartolke, Eschweiler, Fleschenberger, & Tannenbaum, 1982). Effective social-work organizers must develop a collective sense of commitment and ensure that interpersonal conflicts are not becoming institutionalized in the work unit, department, or program. If they do occur, the social-work organization may become divided and segmented, which reduces the capacity of the workers to learn and adapt (Kanter, 1983).

Conflict management entails reasonable workloads, both in terms of time and in terms of complexity. When social-work staff in a hospital setting take on too many responsibilities, there are simply too many activities to perform. This may make staff ineffective, because they are overwhelmed by too much work, oppressive paperwork, and turf and professional rivalries.

Conflict control requires precise job descriptions and maximum freedom to execute work (Buffum & Ritvo, 1984). An effective supervisor balances relations with subordinates between leeway and direction, freedom and guidance. A supervisor can provide constructive ways of expressing dissatisfaction to core workers in many different types of organizations (Kerr, Hill, & Broedling, 1986).

Paperwork can create serious conflicts for workers. State welfare workers may resist opening new cases because of the amount of paperwork involved, and because 50% of their time is already devoted to paperwork. The number of professional social workers at the line levels has decreased tremendously, and therefore similar reductions are needed at the supervisory and administrative levels (Frumkin, Martin, & Page, 1987).

As mentioned, rivalries can involve employees who have low status and limited opportunities to advance (Kanter, 1977). Turf guarding is the protection of one's interests and territory against presumed intruders, regardless of costs to others. Turf conflicts can also occur among professionals such as physicians, nurses, psychologists, and social workers employed in an organization, such as in a veterans' hospital, where people of different disciplines work together. Conflict may arise because social workers would like to provide individual counseling and group treatment, and so would the psychologists (O'Connor & Martin, 1992). Similarly, when an agency gets a new chief executive officer, he or she may revamp the structure and plan things differently, based on his or her life experiences, his or her lifestyle, and what works for him or her. This may create turf problems and personality conflicts among executives at different levels and among people working closely together.

For example, when Daria obtains a position as assistant director with United Way, she is very pleased with herself. Enthusiastic and bubbling with ideas, she speaks to Jill, her boss, about organizing campaigns among the Mexican-American communities. But Jill immediately becomes angry and tells Daria that is not the direction in which she wants her to move. Daria's notion of community involvement differs from "ours." Undaunted, Daria asks if the idea could be bounced off the board's long-range planning committee. Jill refuses vehemently. Daria is surprised, because when being hired she was told that she needs to do strategic program planning for the agency.

Soon Daria finds out that 90% of her time is to be spent in working with board members, who are very impressed with her. It does not take Daria long to realize that she had not recognized a number of problems when she was hired. First, although her boss has excellent political skills in the community, she has poor interpersonal skills when working with colleagues and subordinates. Also, Jill's style inside the office is autocratic. Daria comes to quickly understand the "old guard" of United Way. The board's understanding of the agency is limited to the reality that Jill creates for them. Nationally, the organization faces a great number of problems; however, in their area it is growing. So Jill calls all the shots, and any suggestions for change by Daria are rejected.

When Daria resigns, Jill asks her if she would change her mind. Daria responds by asking if she would be allowed to implement her ideas. "Well," replies Jill, "you are living in Portland, not in southern California." Daria walks away sadly. She thinks of the changes she has tried to bring about within the organization to increase flexibility and lessen control. Although Jill agrees with her verbally, she undercuts Daria by making rules of communication more rigid. Daria feels she cannot function in such a stifling environment.

LEADERSHIP IN ORGANIZATIONS

Being a leader means making effective use of influence and power. Historically, Etzioni says, the ability to lead is based on the person's qualities and ability to elicit compliance. Leadership entails influencing—that is, changing preferences—whereas exercise of power implies that the subject's own preferences are suppressed (Etzioni, 1969). Usually followers choose to go along with the wishes of a leader. The executive or supervisor must issue orders, which is the main way of directing compliance. But demanding unquestioning obedience to orders that are not approved, perhaps not even understood, is a bad policy (Follett, 1991).

To be a good leader, one must be aware of at least four variables (McGregor, 1989): (1) the characteristics of the leader; (2) the attitudes, needs, and other personal characteristics of the followers; (3) the characteristics of the organization such as its purpose, its structure, and the nature of the tasks performed; and (4) the social, economic, and political milieu. Leadership for effective performance is not a property of the individual, but a complex relationship among several variables in a system. It is not true that "the leader makes history," nor is it true that "history makes the leader." Leadership depends both on the person and on the situation. Organizational structure and policy, for example, are established by top management. Once they are established, they limit the leadership patterns that are acceptable.

Leadership can be defined as achieving objectives effectively and efficiently. Good administrators are decisive and can back up their decision with rational and logical arguments. Leaders influence the behavior of others in any group or organization, set goals, formulate paths to those goals, and create social norms in the group (Gortner, Mahler, & Nicholson, 1987).

Functions of Leadership

Leadership performs a number of functions in an organization. These critical functions fall into four categories. The first is to develop the institutional mission and role. This dynamic process is vital in this rapidly changing world. The second function or task is the institutional embodiment of purpose, which involves building policy into the structure of an agency and deciding how to achieve the ends desired. The third function is to defend the organization's integrity. In this situation, values and public relations mix. The leader of the agency represents his or her organization to the public and its own members, and seeks to make them follow rules and regulations. The final task is to bring about order in an organization whenever internal conflict threatens stability.

Components of Leadership

Leadership is what a person does to run an organization efficiently and effectively. It means being able to persuade individuals but, even more important, it requires innovativeness in ideas and decision making that move the organization forward toward achievement. This differentiates effective leadership from the mere possession of power. In the most effective organizations, leadership roles and functions are shared among various individuals, depending on current tasks and conditions. Leadership always involves a reciprocal relationship. In some situations one person may emerge as the leader; in others, someone else may lead.

Authoritarians are task oriented, to the exclusion of concern about the people who are carrying out the tasks. A supportive leader is very considerate of members' or employees' personal needs, is easy to talk to, and has an open, democratic approach to decision making. Effective leadership depends on the organization, its goals, values, traditions, size, geographic spread, frequency of meetings, members' characteristics, and so forth. The nature of the problem, in terms of complexity and requirements, also affects the exercise and effectiveness of leadership.

No single approach to leadership is always appropriate. However, the following general principles seem to hold true. Leadership is closely related to followership, so being a leader involves among other things, acceptance of influence. Although leadership can be carried out theoretically by any member, in reality a leader must reflect movement and power in a group, as well as ability and organizational status. The kinds of assumptions a person makes about others determines how he or she leads or supervises others. Becoming aware of one's own assumptions is an important aid in developing a strong personal leadership style. Effective leaders can behave comfortably in a wide range of leadership situations, adapting their behavior according to different goals. Members feel a great deal of frustration when a leader verbally states one position, but acts differently. A leader who knows him- or herself, the group, and the situation can increase his or her flexibility and effectiveness by setting and implementing goals and plans for each challenge (Napier & Gershenfeld, 1993).

Gartner, Mahler, and Nicholson (1989) identify three levels of leadership in many organizations: the executive, the manager, and the supervisor. These terms are often used interchangeably, and it can be difficult to describe their precise boundaries. However, the differences result in different roles and opportunities for leadership. These three positions are based on authority granted through the law or the formal structure of the organization. Executives take part in establishing the bureau's structure. They establish or interpret the agency's overall goals and seek to create a general atmosphere or environment that will increase the probability of these goals being achieved. Executives are expected to pay close attention to the environment so that they can take advantage of opportunities as they arise. And they are expected to protect the organization when it is attacked or endangered, and to represent it in political frays.

Supervision and management are based on authority delegated from above within the hierarchy. Managers and supervisors must interpret generalized ideas in an ever more concrete manner, and apply them to increasingly smaller units of the bureaucracy. Supervisors organize and monitor the behavior of individual employees to accomplish specific organizational objectives. Supervisors at the bottom of the leadership ladder focus on motivation, productivity, and interpersonal relations, because they work directly in delivering goods and services. A study of human service workers by Newsome and Pillari (1992) found that there is a positive correlation between quality of supervision and overall job satisfaction.

Social-Work Administration and Leadership

Leadership in social work is similar to other forms of leadership, except that the main focus is on helping people. A major responsibility for social-work leaders is to foster a sense of meaning for members and constituents. An effective leader helps members see their participation and experiences as purposeful, meaningful, and worthwhile. Smircich and Morgan (1982) and Martin and O'Connor (1992) identify several factors necessary for creating meaning and fostering service effectiveness, as follows.

Vision of purpose It is important for the leader to have a general vision of the different purposes of the organization. If he or she lacks such an overview, members' conflicting expectations and an absence of consensus may make leadership difficult and may weaken or even destroy organizational effectiveness (Liederman, 1995).

One objective of the social-work organization is service effectiveness (Patti, 1985). This goal or vision focuses attention and energy on the quality of core work activities, because most people value excellence (Peters & Waterman, 1982). When service effectiveness is the goal, the social-work director needs to understand not only the role of the direct service workers but also the role of support staff, which includes researchers, accountants, and others in the organization. The requirements for an effective administrator include a *clear* vision of purpose, personal commitment, and implementation skills. To succeed, a social-work organization should direct all its energy and resources to reach a goal. Work at all levels should be aimed at increasing service effectiveness. For example, when external constituents are asked to help reduce paperwork, as heavy paperwork prevents workers from doing their best, directors should be able to lobby resource providers to gain approval for the change.

Having a vision is a necessary but still insufficient condition for pursuing and achieving meaningful ends. If the leader has low commitment to the vision, priorities may be mixed up and little may be achieved. The leader should be able to evoke commitment from others, too.

Besides commitment and a vision, social-work directors need implementation skills. One set of skills that underlies most of the others concerns communication. Communications skills are necessary to explain and win support for the leader's efforts to work out plans through workshops, short courses, and negotiation. Decision making, planning, analysis, and supervision skills are also vital (Peters & Waterman, 1982; Ginsberg, 1995).

Positive political powers of the social-work leader Techniques for using power affirmatively include campaigning, lobbying, bargaining, negotiating, caucusing, collaborating, and winning votes (Kanter, 1983). Positive leaders sell their ideas rather than give orders. They use proactive, prosocial attempts to win others over to an idea and gain cooperation and compliance through persuasion and influence rather than through asserting power and control (Kanter, 1983; Block, 1987; Gummer & Edwards, 1995).

Social-work administrators spend their time differently from business managers. According to Files (1981), business managers spend more time on internal affairs and in motivating and supervising staff. Social-work organizers spend more time on planning and intergovernmental relations or negotiations. Because of the nature of their work, social-work directors tend to be more externally oriented and more political (Meyer & Scott, 1983). To be successful, the social-work director needs leadership skills in negotiating, bargaining, coalition building, planning, and goal setting. Social-work administrators should be entrepreneurs who test limits and who create new possibilities for organizational action. They do so by directing innovation. An effective leader has the know-how and skills to implement goals and techniques in an agency setting.

Organizational power is the capacity to mobilize people and resources to get things done (Kanter, 1983, p. 213). According to Kanter (1983), organizational power is obtained (1) from information or data (technical knowledge), expertise, and political savvy; (2) from resources such as funds, space, time, staff, and supplies; and (3) from support, which includes endorsement, approval, and legitimacy. Administrators can turn this organizational power into corporate power by (1) gaining a consensus-bound problem definition, (2) gaining support and building consensus for the perception or definition among a wide range of organizational members, and (3) mobilizing support and resources to turn hopes and desires into reality. To achieve service effectiveness, the leader's top priority should be to get members to build the consensus. Social workers have a distaste for power and political skills because they view power as control, not as influence—as domination, rather than facilitation, which is making things happen. For example, in a university an effective dean encourages students to do what they are best at doing instead of insisting that everyone do the same thing, which might curb creativity and innovation. A dean who is a facilitator encourages every student to be the best he or she can be.

CONTROL IN ORGANIZATIONS

A control system consists of the components of a social system that motivate conformity to norms. A sanction on role performance can be gratification or can be deprivation. Positive sanctions gratify, negative sanctions deprive. A norm enforcer is someone considered responsible for enforcing the norms of a system. The norm enforcer is generally a superordinate person, whereas a norm conformer is a subordinate person. Sometimes, norm enforcement may be assigned to workers who are not officially designated as superordinates.

The types of norms enforced in a system depend in part on economics and the components involved in producing the system output. The norms help the system answer questions such as, How can income be maximized and expenditures controlled to help the organization function most effectively? What is the division of labor within the organization, and what different roles are played out? How do role differentiation, specialization, fragmentation, segmentation, and fractionalization contribute to effective operation or to organizational difficulties?

Different types of controls are used to evaluate, promote, or separate personnel. One form of control is achieved by measuring work output, which is related to costs and output measures. In a social-work setting, output measures might include size of caseload, number of interviews, and—in a medical setting—number of patients discharged.

Evaluation is another form of control used to compare the program results with the intentions of the program framers, either to improve or cull the program. Program evaluation is used in public administration to achieve control and accountability. In many agencies, program evaluation is a legal requirement for professional management. Evaluations measure effort, performance, adequacy, and efficiency.

Program evaluation may serve different purposes, both the information needs of internal systems and requirements of political and legal accountability.

INTERORGANIZATIONAL DEPENDENCE

Social agencies are generally part of larger human-service systems marked by much interorganizational dependence and rivalry. Sometimes to survive or function effectively, organizations must merge with other agencies. Some mergers work, but others prove dysfunctional, either because they were not well thought out to begin with, or because new issues surface after the merger has been made.

Administrators in organizations communicate with others outside their own agencies in search of both information and support. The external and largely informal communication network has wide-reaching implications for the organization. For instance, if a bureaucrat disagrees with a policy or budgetary decision being made at a higher level, he or she may supply significant information to powerful actors outside of the agency, such as the press, legislators, and sympathetic interest groups that can influence policy (Gartner, Mahler, & Nicholson, 1989).

Links among different organizations also can take various forms. In the hierarchical model, one bureau at the top is related to the other bureaus in the pyramid through a formal chain of command. In such a situation, information from the top agency may take the form of commands, and the lower bureaus send up information and reports desired by the top agency. In such an arrangement, interagency cooperation in delivering services is bolstered by formal rules, contracts, and such.

In another pattern, a coalition network links agencies to each other with a complex set of channels. Direct channels exist between each organization, but no agency is linked directly to all others, and none has power over all others as in a formal chain of command. In coalition models, coordination is less centralized and systematic. According to Seitz (1978, pp. 95–101), mutual adjustment is reached in the following ways. First, agencies agree to accept the current balance of power and also to respect the turf of other agencies. Second, they may agree to actively coordinate their activities with other agencies and facilitate the activities of others. Third, agencies agree to create active cooperation among the agencies. A study done of client referrals in 17 communities concluded that the communication strategies such as joint programs, formal and informal communication, and advisory boards are more important than imposing environmental constraints, limiting administrative autonomy, and mandatory ties (Boje & Whetten, 1981).

Different organizations link up because their aim is to maximize gains and prevent losses. Diversity, innovation, and the need for resources prompt the establishment of joint programs. Most organizations choose partner organizations that have complementary resources but different goals. This helps avoid problems of conflict and reduced autonomy, and facilitates cooperation. Interdependent relationships let both agencies gain additional resources. Making mutual adaptations is important. When new windows are opened, new ideas can be infused into both organizations.

The term "organizational diversity" may include (1) multiple occupations and degree of complexity, (2) multiple power groups, (3) the range of actual work roles and experiences, and (4) the degree of formalization.

Interagency interdependence depends on the number of joint programs, including the number of cases (clients and patients) who are referred, exchanged, or shared; the number of personnel who are lent, borrowed, or exchanged; and the number, sources, and amounts of financial support (Hall, 1972).

Competition is not confined to economic markets and may include political parties that compete with each other and other such organizations. For example, political parties compete for votes, religious groups compete for members, and group members compete for popularity and respect within an organization. Often there is competition between organizations, and its processes may characterize entire organizations. For example, an organization with a great deal of money and efficient administration may offer better services to the community than another agency. Organizations with a long-standing positive outlook and reputation may be better accepted than new agencies that do not have a good foundation on which to build.

Some organizations compete for dominance, and others are less successful and compete for survival. The inter- and intraorganization competition for scarce resources characterizes all human society. Some new agencies may gain a niche, others lose their niches, as the whole ecosystem seeks equilibrium.

IMPLICATIONS FOR SOCIAL-WORK PRACTICE

Organizational structure follows the work roles of members, and the values of the organization. Most organizations have some hierarchy, and most social-work agencies are bureaucratic to some degree.

How successfully an organization resists change depends on the amount of power it has. Organizations by nature operate conservatively regardless of whether they are viewed as radical or reactionary by the general population (Hall, 1972).

Resistance to organizational change may also depend on the kind of change and when in the development of an organization change is proposed. Early in the evolution of an organization or service is usually the best time to initiate change. When an organization feels vulnerable, it may also be amenable to alteration. The impetus for change is often rooted in the will to survive or to maintain one's existence in a competitive market. Social work practitioners "must take responsibility for influencing change when possible and preparing for change when it is ineluctable" (Newsome, 1997). Keep in mind that organizations are always changing; the question is, How does one guide or mold change? It is useful to remember that workers and administrators may exaggerate the restrictive nature of laws and/or regulations. Interpretation within policy constraints can be a means to "push the envelope." Policy is a guide within which much is possible. Finally, change made incrementally, over time, presents less threat to organizations/services and organizational members than sudden or radical changes.

Organizational change may also arouse other difficulties. For instance, cliques or personal opinions and motivations can block or aid change. Of course, movement may be hindered without malice or intent. But attempts to bring about change due to envy and jealousy can have negative effects and eventually harm the agency.

Social organizations can be adversely affected by staff and clients. Decision makers may support or resist change proposals, depending on how they perceive the value of such proposals to them and their organizations. But focused and sustained activities of the low- and middle-echelon members can improve organizations. And staff morale can be improved by taking an active role in the organization (Resnick & Patti, 1980).

The potential change agent in an organization is a member who can bring about change from below. As Resnick (1980) indicates, this member may urge the formation of a group of staff dissatisfied with the state of affairs. This person may be a respected member who is highly regarded. Organizational change can be brought about by someone who perceives a certain problem as crucial. A person may focus on an innovation that can solve problems and may convene an action system to consider the problem and the solution. Or a change agent may organize a group of staff members who are dissatisfied with the agency functioning and with whom he or she enjoys a relatively good working relationship. This group may work on a specific problem situation or may agree that some basic innovation is necessary to bring about other kinds of changes. This pattern can create friction between staff and administration.

Social-work organizations are a paradoxical mixture of fragmented political arenas, an organized system with a number of interrelated parts that mesh and form a dynamic whole (O'Connor & Martin, 1992). As Martin (1987) indicates, in the hands of powerful constituents social-welfare organizations are powerful tools for achieving numerous ends beside their official purpose. Social-welfare organizations provide jobs to educated and middle-class citizens and also service benefits and control to clients. They also provide work for poorer and less-educated people. An example might be those that hire clients/former clients, or those that are client-operated, such as community action associations or neighborhood organizations, which by law or local policy require the majority of their staff/employees to be disadvantaged, poor people, or minorities.

Most social-welfare organizations seek to fulfill their multiple missions within conflictual and contradictory environments. They look for internal and external help in comprehending and supporting actions that need to be taken. Leadership in such endeavors is multiple, not equated solely with one person. Any social-welfare leader should be committed to implementing positive change. A social-welfare organization is a political entity as well as a legal-rational tool for achieving goals; thus it can be committed to quality and also to innovation so that it can learn, improve, and grow.

Certain modifications or innovations must take place from within. The most significant, controversial changes require outside pressure from a new administration, from the funding source, from the political power structure, and so forth.

SUMMARY

An organization in which a person functions can be described as small, large, formal, or informal. Social-welfare organizations are formal and legitimized by the state in order to deliver personal and social services and other benefits to citizens. Social-welfare organizations are rarely organized around technical-productive goals, and tend to be more humane than technical organizations in many symbolic ways. Formal organizations are collections of people who are engaged in specialized and highly interdependent activities. Social-welfare organizations are dependent on the environment, which enforces openness.

Goals of an organization include official goals as put forth in the charter, annual reports, and so forth. Operative goals designate the ends sought through the actual operating policies of the organization. Organizational goals can be classified as transitive goals, which show the commitment of resources in certain programs, whereas reflective goals show resource commitments to the personal needs and interests of members. In human-service organizations, goal commitments of an organization serve as guides to formulate programs and services. Goals change according to changing times, and can be used to measure organizational accountability.

Organizations can be described as bureaucratic and formally established for maintaining the organization as an ongoing concern as well as for coordinating the activities of its members. Two environmental factors that affect organizations are economics and technology. Economic factors include the shifting availability of funds, characteristics of the funded agency, and the dependency of the organization on a funding agency.

Technology includes procedures, methodologies, and inventions that help an organization reach its goals. Whatever is newly discovered or invented, such as computers and social technology, affects human services.

Political forces also affect how agencies can be used. Social-work agency models may be integrative or segmentalist. Integrative approaches highlight wholeness and eagerness to combine problems with new ideas and test limits in a system. Segmentalism compartmentalizes actions, events, and problems and keeps all the pieces isolated from each other.

Ethnicity- and race-based organizations are developed in order to maintain a sense of continuity and provide care and nurturing to organizational members. Ethnicity-based community organizations grow out of people's desires to work together, combat similar problems, and share enough knowledge to make projects work. Social workers need to look at natural support systems and use them for diverse groups of people. Organizations must provide training to help organizational members become aware of and support diversity.

Organizational effectiveness is based on constructive communication patterns. The goal model, the system-resource model, the multiple-constituencies model, and the legitimacy model are used to evaluate organizational effectiveness.

Every organization of any significant size is bureaucratic to some extent. Hierarchy is an efficient way of organizing collective efforts by a large group of people but can produce learned helplessness among some organizational members. Hierarchy can be used to split, control, exploit, and dominate organizational members.

Organizations are both differentiated and integrated. Differentiation involves both the division of labor and independence and the emergence of new parts and activities. Integration is a progression toward wholeness, interdependence, and systematization. In highly differentiated agencies, the different parts of the agency operate independently of each other and change may affect only isolated parts.

Communication is closely interwoven with organizational structure. Communication types include instrumental, which is purposeful and goal directed; expressive, which conveys normative information; consummatory, which reveals the emotions of a person such as enthusiasm, fear, or uncertainty; and incidental, which gives information to the sender without awareness of doing so.

Vertical communication in an organization can be upward or downward. In a hierarchical setting, it is up to the superior to decide who gets what kind of communication and how. Horizontal communication is crucial for functions such as task coordination, problem solving, information sharing, and conflict resolution.

Functional conflict may be induced by various systems in an organization. Each system develops its own distinctive norms and frames of reference, which may conflict. Conflict may also arise from the roles and functions of members within an organization, and from struggle for organizational rewards such as status and money. Conflicts are also provoked by negative interpersonal dynamics. Ineffective supervision, too much operational paperwork, and turf conflicts among professionals can also create problems in organizations. When a conflict is brewing, a skillful manager sees it coming and explores alternatives.

Being a successful leader in an organization requires effective use of influence. Good leadership depends on the characteristics of the leader; on the attitudes, needs, and other personal characteristics of followers; on the purpose, structure, and nature of tasks performed; and on the social, economic, and political milieu. The leader performs several functions within an organization, including developing the institutional mission and roles, deciding how to achieve goals, maintaining the organization's integrity and high values, and building good public relations.

Leadership includes the ability to run an organization effectively and efficiently. Authoritarian leaders are task oriented to the exclusion of concern for the people carrying out the tasks. A supportive leader is considerate of employees' needs and uses a democratic approach to decision making. Levels of leadership include executives, managers, and supervisors.

A major responsibility for the social-work leader and administrator is to foster a sense of meaning for the members and constituents. An effective administrator has a clear vision of purpose as well as personal commitment and skills to implement the vision. A positive social-work leader uses people affirmatively for campaigning, lobbying, bargaining, negotiating, caucusing, collaborating, and winning votes. Social-work administrators should be entrepreneurs who test limits and create new possibilities for organizational action. Organizational power is obtained by information or data; resources such as funds, space, time, staff, and supplies; and through support, that is, endorsement, approval, and legitimacy.

Control in organizations is used for norm enforcement. Control can be achieved via measurement of work output and via evaluation.

Organizations become interdependent because they look outside their own agencies for information and support. Organizations may link up in a hierarchical mode. The top agency sends commands, and receives from below messages that contain information and reports. In coalition models, coordination is less centralized and systematic. Different organizations link up to maximize gains and prevent losses. The success of an agency depends on the amount of power the organization has in its environment.

Organizational change is difficult for several reasons, including cliques and people's opinions and personal motivations. Organizations can be adversely affected by staff and clients, and decision makers may either support or resist change proposals. Organizations can improve through focused and sustained activities, however, and staff morale can be improved through participation in an organization's efforts to change. Organizational change can be brought about through members' involvement with issues or through a change agent, who can organize a group of staff members who are dissatisfied with the agency functioning and with whom he or she enjoys a relatively good working relationship.

All social-welfare organizations are dynamic, complex, and conflictual arenas of social interaction and exchange. They are affected by their political, institutional, and resource environments. Like all ecosystems, the ecosystem in which the social-welfare organization functions is constantly changing and seeking equilibrium. Agencies may find their niche, or consolidate and enlarge their niche, or lose their niche to another agency.

SUGGESTED READINGS

Barker, J. R., & Cheney, G. (1994, March). The concept and practices of discipline in contemporary organizational life. *Communication Monographs, 61*(1), 19–43.

Bixby, N. B. (1995). Crisis or opportunity: A healthcare social worker director's response to change. *Social Work in Health Care, 20*(4), 3–20.

Corney, R. (1995). Social work involvement in primary care settings and mental health centres: A survey in England and Wales. *Journal of Mental Health, 4*(3), 275–280.

Gutiérrez, L., Glenmaye, L., & Delois, K. (1995, March). The organizational context of empowerment practice: Implications for social work administration. *Social Work, 40*(2), 249–258.

Motenko, A. K., Allen, E. A., Angelos, P., and Block, L. (1995, July). Privatization and cutbacks: Social work and client impressions of service delivery in Massachusetts. *Social Work, 40*(4), 456–463.

Resnick, H., & Menefee, D. (1993, December). A comparative analysis of organization development and social work, with suggestions for what organization development can do for social work. Special issue: Emerging developments in action research. *Journal of Applied Behavioral Science, 29*(4), 432–445.

SUGGESTED VIDEOTAPES

Bringing out the leader in you. (1991). American Management Association. IVN Communications Inc., 2246 Camino Ramon, San Ramon, CA 94583. 23 minutes.

Credibility. (1993). CRM Films, 2215 Faraday Ave., Carlsbad, CA 92008. 85 minutes.

The Deming Library: Quality leader. (1990). CCM Productions. Kinetic Inc., 255 Delaware Ave., Buffalo, NY 14202. 29 minutes.

The goal. (1995). American Media Inc., 4900 University Ave., West Des Moines, IA 50266. 50 minutes.

Keeping teams together. (1994). American Management Association. IVN Communications Inc., 2246 Camino Ramon, San Ramon, CA 94583. 23 minutes.

What makes a team? (1994). Conought Training Ltd. AIMS Multimedia, 9710 DeSoto Ave., Chatsworth, CA 91311-4409. 32 minutes.

REFERENCES

Austin, D. M., & Hasenfeld, Y. (1985). A prefatory essay on the future administration of human services. *Journal of Applied Behavioral Sciences,* 351–354.

Barnard, C. (1938). *The functions of the executive.* Cambridge, MA: Harvard University Press.

Bartolke, K., Eschweiler, W., Fleschenberger, & Tannenbaum, A. S. (1982). Workers' participation and the distribution of control as perceived by members of ten German companies. *Administrative Science Quarterly, 27,* 380–397.

Bellah, R. N., Madsen, R., Sullivan, W. M., Swidler, A., & Tipton, S. M. (1985). *Habits of the heart.* Berkeley: University of California Press.

Berelson, B., & Steiner, G. A. (1964). *Human behavior: An inventory of scientific findings.* New York: Harcourt Brace Jovanovich.

Blau, P. M. (1955). *The dynamics of bureaucracy.* Chicago: University of Chicago Press.

Blau, P. M., & Scott, W. R. (1962). *Formal organizations.* San Francisco: Chandler.

Block, A. (1987). Empowering employees. *Training Development Journal, 41,* 34–39.

Boje, D. M., & Whetten, D. A. (1981). Effects of organizational strategies and contextual constraints on centrality and attributions of influences in interorganizational networks. *Administrative Science Quarterly, 26,* 378–395.

Boulding, K. (1978, December). Challenges to the helping professions and the response of scientific practice. *Social Service Review.*

Brager, G., & Holloway, S. (1978). *Changing human service organizations.* New York: Free Press.

Buffum, W. E., & Ritvo, R. A. (1984). Work autonomy and the community mental health professional: Guidelines for management. *Administration in Social Work, 8,* 39–54.

Cameron, K. S. (1984). The effectiveness of ineffectiveness. In B. M. Staw & L. L. Cummings (eds.), *Research in organizational behavior* (Vol. 6). Greenwich, CT: JAI Press.

Drucker, P. E. (1990). *Managing a nonprofit organization.* New York: Harper.

Etzioni, A. (1969). *Findings in modern organizations.* Englewood Cliffs, NJ: Prentice Hall.

Farrell, D., & Petersen, J. C. (1982). Patterns of political behavior in organizations. *Academy of Management Review, 7,* 403–412.

Ferguson, K. (1984). *The feminist case against bureaucracy.* Philadelphia: Temple University Press.

Files, L. (1981). The human services management task: A time allocation study. *Public Administration Review, 41,* 686–692.

Fligstein, W. (1991). The structural transformation of American industry. In W. Powell & P. DiMaggio (eds.), *The new institutionalism in organizational analysis.* Chicago: University of Chicago Press, pp. 311–336.

Follet, M. P. (1990). *Dynamic administration: The collected papers of Mary Parker Follett.* C. M. Henry & L. Urwick (eds.) , New York: Harper & Row.

Frumkin, M., Martin, P. Y., & Page, W. P. (1987). The future of large state welfare agencies. *New England Journal of Human Services, 7,* 15–23.

Gartner, H. F., Mahler, J., & Nicholson, J. B. (1989). *Organization theory.* Belmont, CA: Wadsworth.

Germain, C. B. (1991). *Human behavior in the social environment.* New York: Columbia University Press.

Ginsberg, L. (1995). Concepts of new management. In L. Ginsberg & P. R. Keys (eds.), *New management in human services.* Washington, DC: NASW Press, pp. 1–37.

Goldhaber, G. M. (1974). *Organizational communication.* Dubuque, IA: William C Brown.

Gortner, H. F., Mahler, J., & Nicholson, J. B. (1987). *Organization theory: A public perspective.* Chicago: Dorsey Press.

Greenberger, D. B., & Strasser, S. (1986). Development and application of a model of personal control in organizations. *Academy of Management Review, 11,* 164–177.

Gummer, B., & Edwards, R. (1995). The politics of human service administration. In L. Ginsberg & P. R. Keys (eds.), *New management in human services.* Washington, DC: NASW Press, pp. 57–71.

Gummer, B. (1990). *The politics of social administration: Managing organizational politics in social agencies.* Englewood Cliffs, NJ: Prentice Hall.

Gutheil, I. A. (1992, September). Considering the physical environment: An essential component of good practice. *Social Work, 37,* 391–396.

Hall, R. H. (1972). *Organizations: Structure and process.* Englewood Cliffs, NJ: Prentice Hall.

Hannan, H. T., & Freeman, J. (1977). The population ecology of organization. *American Journal of Sociology, 82,* 929–964.

Hasenfeld, Y. (1973). Organizational factors in service to groups. In P. Glasser, R. C. Sarri, & R. D. Vinter (eds.), *Individual change through groups.* New York: Free Press, pp. 307–322.

Hasenfeld, Y. (1983). *Human service organizations.* Englewood Cliffs, NJ: Prentice Hall.

Imershein, A., Frumkin, M., Chackerian, R., & Martin, P. Y. (1983). Organizational change in human services: A framework for critical analysis. *New England Journal of Human Services, 3,* 21–29.

Kamerman, S. B. (1983). The new mixed economy of welfare: Public and private. *Social Work, 28,* 5–9.

Kanter, R. M. (1977). *Men and women of the corporation.* New York: Basic Books.

Kanter, R. M. (1983). *The change masters.* New York: Simon & Schuster.

Katz, D., & Kahn, R. L. (1966). *Social psychology of organizations.* New York: Wiley, p. 111.

Kerr, S., Hill, K. D., & Broedling, L. (1986). The first-line supervisor: Phasing out or how to stay? *Academy of Management Review, 11,* 102–117.

Lewis, H. (1975, January). *Management in non-profit social service organizations.* Key address, Institute of Management and Social Work Organizations. University of Pennsylvania Press, p. 1.

Lewis, J. A., Lewis, M. D., & Souflee, E. (1991). *Management of human service organizations.* Pacific Grove, CA: Brooks/Cole.

Liederman, D. S. (1995). Challenges for leaders of national human service organizations. In L. Ginsberg & P. R. Keys (eds.), *New management in human services.* Washington, DC: NASW Press, pp. xi–xvi.

Lincoln, C. E., & Mamiya, L. H. (1990). *The Black church in the African American experience.* Durham, NC: Duke University Press.

Lipsky, M. (1980). *Street-level bureaucracy: Dilemmas of the individual in public services*. New York: Russell Sage Foundation.

Mandell, B. (1971). Welfare and totalitarianism: Part I. Theoretical issues. *Social Work, 16,* 17–26.

Martin, P. Y. (1984). Trade unions, conflict and nature of work in residential service organizations. *Organization Studies, 5,* 168–185.

Martin, P. Y. (1987). Multiple constituencies and performance in social welfare organizations. *Administration in Social Work, 11,* 223–239.

Martin, P. Y., & O'Connor, G. G. (1989). *The social environment*. New York: Longman.

McGregor, D. M. (1989). An analysis of leadership. In J. S. Ott (ed.), *Classic readings in organizational behavior*. Pacific Grove, CA: Brooks/Cole, pp. 276–282.

Mento, A. J., Steel, R. P., & Karren, R. J. (1987). A meta-analytic study of the effects of goal setting on task performance: 1966–1984. *Organizational Behavior and Human Decision Processes, 39,* 52–83.

Meyer, J. W., & Rowan, B. (1977). Institutional organizations: Formal structure as myth and ceremony. *American Journal of Sociology, 83,* 440–463.

Meyer, J. W., & Scott, W. R. (1983). *Organizational environment: Ritual and rationality*. Beverly Hills, CA: Sage, pp. 217–232.

Meyer, J. W., Scott, W. R., & Deal, T. E. (1981). Institutional and technical sources of organizational structure. In H. D. Stein (ed.), *Organizations and the human services*. Philadelphia: Temple University Press.

Mohr, L. (1973). The concept of organizational goal. *American Political Science Review, 67,* 470–481.

Napier, R. W., & Gershenfeld, M. K. (1993). *Groups: Theory and experience*. Boston: Houghton Mifflin.

Newsome, Jr., M. & Pillari, V. (1992, Spring). Job satisfaction and the worker–supervisor relationship. *The Clinical Supervisor, 9*(2), 119–129.

Newsome, Jr., M. (1997, March 6). Presidential Address, CSWE 43rd Annual Program Meeting, Chicago, IL. *Social Work Education Reporter, 45*(2), 1, 12–13.

Northern, H. (1993). *Clinical social work practice*. New York: Columbia University Press.

Parsons, T. (1957). The mental hospital as a type of organization. In *The patient and the mental hospital,* M. Greenblatt, D. J. Levinson, & R. Williams (eds.), Glencoe, IL: Free Press, pp. 108–129.

Patti, R. (1985). In search of purpose for social welfare administration. *Administration in Social Work, 9,* 1–14.

Perrow, C. (1961). The analysis of goals in complex organizations. *American Sociological Review, 26,* 856–866.

Peters, T. J., & Waterman, R. H., Jr. (1982). *In search of excellence: Lessons from America's best-run companies*. New York: Harper & Row.

Pierce, N., & Steinbach, C. F. (1992). Corporate capitalism: The rise of America's community development. In H. J. Rubin & I. S. Rubin, *Community organization and development* (2nd ed.), pp. 3–4. New York: Macmillan.

Piven, F. F., & Cloward, R. A. (1971). *Regulating the poor*. Englewood Cliffs, NJ: Prentice Hall.

Porter, L. W., & Lawler, E. E., III. (1965, January). Properties of organization structure in relation to job attitudes and behavior. *Psychological Bulletin, 64*(1), 23–51.

Prottas, J. (1979). *People processing*. Lexington, MA: Heath.

Resnick, H., & Patti, R. J. (eds.). (1980). *Change from within: Humanizing social welfare organizations*. Philadelphia: Temple University Press.

Robbins, S. P. (1989). *Organizational behavior: Concepts, controversies and applications* (4th ed.). Englewood Cliffs, NJ: Prentice Hall.

Romanelli, E. (1991). The evolution of new organizational forms. *Annual Review of Sociology, 17,* 79–103.

Rothschild-Whitt, J., & Whitt, A. (1986). *Work without bosses: Conditions and dilemmas of organizational democracy in grassroots cooperatives*. New York: Cambridge University Press.

Rubin, H. J., & Rubin, I. S. (1992) *Community organization and development* (2nd ed.). New York: Macmillan.

Sackmann, S. A. (1991). *Cultural knowledge in organizations: Exploring the collective mind*. Newbury Park, CA: Sage.

Seitz, S. T. (1978). *Bureaucracy, policy and the public*. St. Louis: Mosby.

Shriver, J. M. (1995). *Human behavior and the social environment*. Boston: Allyn and Bacon.

Smircich, L., & Morgan, G. (1982). Leadership: The management of meaning. *Journal of Applied Behavioral Science, 18,* 257–273.

Tannenbaum, A. S., Kevcic, B., Rosner, M., Vianello, M., & Wieser, G. (1974). *Hierarchy in organizations*. San Francisco: Jossey-Bass.

Task Force on Community-Based Development. (1992). Community-based development: Investing in renewal. In H. J. Rubin & I. S. Rubin, *Community organization and development* (2nd ed.), pp. 19–21. New York: Macmillan.

Thurston, M. A. (1987). *Strategies, constraints and dilemmas of women's health centers*. Unpublished doctoral dissertation. Florida State University, Tallahassee.

Tubbs, M. E. (1986). A meta-analytic examination of the empirical evidence. *Journal of Applied Psychology, 71,* 474–483.

Vredenburgh, D. J., & Maurer, L. (1984). A process framework of organization politics. *Human Relations, 37,* 47–66.

Wamsley, G., & Zald, M. N. (1973). *The political economy of public organizations*. Lexington, MA: Heath, p. 17.

Warren, R. L., & Hyman, H. H. (1968). Purposive community change in consensus and dissensus situations. In T. N. Clark (ed.), *Community structure and decision-making*. San Francisco: Chandler.

Whitten, D. A. (1978). Coping with incompatible expectations: An integrated view of role conflict. *Administrative Science Quarterly, 23,* 254–271.

White, P. E. (1974). Resources as determinants of organizational behavior. *Administrative Science Quarterly, 19,* 366–376.

5

Communities

WHAT IS A COMMUNITY?

What is a community? In its broadest sense, the term *community* refers to a number of people with common ties or interests. They may live in the same geographic area, as residents of a certain neighborhood, city, or region. They may share a common religion or ethnic heritage, as do the Jews, the Irish, and the African Americans. They may also represent a common lifestyle or shared concerns, as do members of the military, gays and lesbians, and farmers.

In our complex society, individuals are generally associated with a number of different communities. Individuals may have membership in communities that are loose and open, by virtue of living in a particular area or neighborhood, and also in communities that have rigid rules, such as the military or certain religious communities. At times a person may become a member of a community not by choice but by necessity. Let us look at the case of April.

April has moved from one state to another with her husband, Aaron, and has always had to work at fitting into different communities for the sake of her husband's professional growth. She has often felt that she does not belong to any specific community, because her husband is frequently transferred. Meeting new people and adjusting to a new community corporate culture has been hard on April, but she has made the best of it in every community they have lived in. For instance, in one community April found herself feeling crowded and suffocated, because the wives of the men in Aaron's company insisted that she and her husband join specific institutions and clubs that were "approved" by the community insiders. Although this made them uncomfortable, April and Aaron adjusted, because they didn't want to create problems in Aaron's new high-paying promotional job. Although April's husband has had problems in new communities too, it has not been as apparent, because he has been involved in the challenges of his new job.

Some of the communities they have lived in have been quite loosely knit and open. Here April and Aaron have mingled with people of different statuses, roles, and lifestyles, and have felt free to be themselves and pursue their own interests. April actually enjoys living in such a community, because she can do what she pleases in her home and with her husband. Her time is her own, and she spends most of it reading and catching up with her personal interests, which include going to a nearby club to play soccer and do aerobics. Nobody questions her about her activities, and she enjoys coming and going as she pleases. Some people are pleasant and talk to her, and others do not. She finds more people like herself in this community.

Thus April finds that there are both homogeneous and heterogeneous communities. She has also learned that communities contain people of different class, socioeconomic status, and ethnic groups. She sees that communities can contain diverse groups of people, and that organizations can perform diverse activities. In homogeneous communities, people tend to take on the characteristics of the community, whereas in heterogeneous communities they tend to be flexible and more open to differences. However, April's life reflects more of the corporate culture—the unwritten rules of her husband's company—than of the broader community culture.

The Concept of Community

As discussed, the term *community* means different things to different people in different contexts. Communities have multiple meanings, including sociopolitical connotations. Some communities may have official boundaries, such as political subdivisions, school districts, and church parishes. And some communities are based on shared interests and values. For instance, social workers call themselves a *professional community,* and a university is called a *community of scholars*. Informal and small communities may convey a mood of warmth and togetherness, or of restrictions and exclusiveness. Today, people are viewing the world as a global community or global village, because technology has made communication among countries and cultures much easier.

People who live in close physical proximity with each other may reveal locality-relevant behaviors (Warren, 1963). For example, when April lived in different communities she tried to fit into each, with its common social structure and locality-related services. In every community there is a cultural web with norms, values, knowledge, and belief systems that may or may not fit with the larger environment. Some communities lie outside the mainstream and therefore must create their own safe communal life for themselves (Germain, 1991). These include the gay and lesbian communities, which provide safe havens for their members. Moses and Hawkins (1982) comment that the gay bar is this community's major institution, where gay men can drink and eat and also sit alone or be with partners. In lesbian communities, women enjoy a strong network of mutual support and create their own personal community.

Another type of community is the religious sect, such as the Amish or the Mormons. Such groups have formal rules in terms of traditions and expectations. A group of Amish people may have rules and regulations that characterize an informal community. However, such communities are becoming more and more rare, and usually exist only in small pockets of rural areas. The Amish live in self-contained agricultural communities and limit their use of modern technology. The Mormons, in contrast, are very much a part of contemporary American society. They are concentrated in Utah, but live all over the United States, and are active in government, business, and professions. The Mormon church itself owns stock in a great many corporations and uses state-of-the-art computer technology to conduct its affairs.

Another type of community prevalent today is based on formal relations with people. Unlike earlier forms of localized community, in such communities people get together through formal institutions, including places of employment, churches, recreational centers, and other civic and professional organizations.

Sometimes people travel in order to belong to a formal professional community. They do so to get in touch with colleagues of the same occupation or religious affiliation or recreational interests. Such networks, called *vertical communities,* consist of people with similar interests, such as professionals and businesspeople. Such people may travel long distances to socialize or work with similar people in exclusive groups. In formal communities based on rules of relationship, less time is spent in the neighborhood. In *horizontal groupings,* people socialize comfortably with others in their immediate home neighborhood. Here people of different backgrounds and interests may get together to share common concerns or even arrange a block party. George, however, is a scientist who spends a great deal of time in the university laboratory. In his own—horizontal—neighborhood, he is hardly known, because he has no time for socializing. He travels and spends most of his time in a vertical community—the university—with scientists like himself.

Formal and informal communities have much in common. All have a formal social structure with defined roles and statuses. They also have informal interaction and relationship patterns, which may be even more significant. To survive, even small and informal communities must have a formal division of labor.

Panzetta (1983) notes that a local community exists in a catchment area. Its definition depends on street names, buildings, and demographic factors. We may refer to communities by indicating that people in a particular street either live well or do not. Today, such references to particular streets are becoming rare. In New York City, for example, we are aware that Park Avenue and Fifth Avenue have beautiful and expensive apartments, but for the most part we identify neighborhoods rather than individual streets as having particular demographics or social problems —that is, Greenwich Village, Harlem, Morningside Heights, South Central Los Angeles, Hollywood, and so forth. For example, one may say there is more crime in one particular part of the city than in other parts. Looking at communities from a geographical perspective reveals boundaries in terms of ingroup and outgroup communications even within a couple of streets in the community. In analyzing where a community is, demography and epidemiology provide valuable information.

How are communities created? Communities are born out of need, they evolve, and they may eventually die. They are more stable than most other social systems, frequently surviving for decades or centuries. Many communities have been destroyed, and new ones built on their foundations.

A community is a social system that has a population, shared institutions and values, and significant social transactions among individuals and institutions, which perform many functions within communities. In modern society, communities overlap and differ in amount of autonomy and in degree of psychological identity shared by people living within them. It is difficult to develop a scheme for classifying communities, because so many variables are involved. Poplin (1979) notes three important areas of difference among communities: size, nature, and social-cultural features.

Differences in communities can be seen on an urban–rural continuum. According to the U.S. Bureau of the Census (1991), the urban population consists of people who live in metropolitan areas, cities, and urbanized areas adjacent to cities with a combined population of at least 50,000, as well as those living in villages, towns, or other places with populations of 2,500 or more inhabitants. The rest of the population is considered rural. In 1990, it was found that 25% of the U.S. population was rural and spread out over 97% of the nation's land (Luloff & Swanson, 1990; U.S. Bureau of the Census, 1992). The U.S. Bureau of the Census (1992, p. 896) uses the term *metropolitan area*—or *metropolitan statistical area* (MSA) or *consolidated metropolitan statistical area* (CMSA)—to refer to a cluster of one or more central cities and surrounding suburbs with a population of more than a million inhabitants.

Metropolitan areas contain communities that include the central city, the suburban community, and the satellite city. The nature and sociocultural factors of a community can be observed by the manner in which these communities are inhabited. For instance, the sociocultural upper class can be seen in Grosse Point, Michigan. Other communities may be inhabited by bohemian, intellectual, and artistic people, as in Greenwich Village, New York. All communities—upper middle class, middle class, lower class, and people in poverty—are of concern to social workers, because each group presents problems that are uniquely its own but nevertheless require help from social workers.

To understand a community, social workers need to be able:

1. To develop a framework by means of which to organize information
2. To locate information and resources
3. To identify information that is needed in specific situations
4. To analyze the information obtained
5. To identify the linkages and relationships among subsystems in the community (Johnson, 1995)

There is a close relationship between a community and the people who live in it. Resources and both positive and negative influences are available to its people. To work within a community it is important to note the interrelationships between people and environment. The client's problems and his or her ability to function socially are affected by the community. To work within a community, the social worker must see it as a social system, as a way of functioning that has a history. A community has energy and organization, and its functioning cannot be understood apart from the environment in which it functions.

The Functions of a Community

Historically, communities fill five major functions for their members (Warren, 1963, pp. 9–11). It is important for social workers to remember these functions so that they can work effectively in these communities.

The term *production-distribution-consumption function* refers to local participation in the cycle of goods and services. Usually this function is carried out by businesses, schools, churches, social agencies, and housing systems.

Socialization is the process whereby community units influence the behavior of members. The units include the family, school, and peer groupings that transmit knowledge, social values, and behavior patterns to different members.

Social control involves enforcement of rules and acceptable standards of behavior by social pressure, and, if need be, by punishment. This function is carried out primarily by families, supplemented by police, courts, schools, churches, social agencies, and businesses.

Social participation opportunities are provided by families, religious organizations, and other informal and formal groups of many kinds. For example, the school is also a system where schoolchildren socialize and learn behavior patterns.

In communities, members are aware of common membership or association with a locality (Bernard, 1973; Naisbitt, 1982). People share enjoyment of locality, natural beauty, and athletic teams, and participate in performing art groups and community festivals. They also come together around common feelings of anger and resentment about community problems such as crime, taxes, and pollution.

Mutual support is provided by groups such as family, friends, and neighbors, as well as by close affiliations to formal systems such as health and welfare organizations. Communities are inclusive systems with many forms and varieties of social systems within their boundaries. (In comparison with other social systems that people work in, communities tend to be the most inclusive.) These formal and informal groupings include social-service networks, school systems, and families, individuals, and small groups. To be successful, a social worker must have a good understanding of how a community functions.

Communities have many diffuse goals (Gottschalk, 1978). Unlike business, school, or social-welfare organizations, communities are loosely coupled and rarely have specific goals to pursue that are endorsed by all community members.

Communities also contain families, groups of people related by blood, marriage, adoption, or consensual agreement. Families are part —perhaps the most important part—of a community. Most families function in a partnership relationship with other community institutions, sharing common values and goals. However, some families function in conflict with community standards. For example, a family that focuses on crime as a way of life may counteract the effect of a formal organization such as the police force.

Community functions are differentiated here for the purposes of study, but in reality, functions may overlap—for example, social participation and mutual aid. A person can participate in a social cause such as fund-raising for AIDS victims and at the same time meet a personal need for socializing and social networking.

How can a community function effectively? How can communities operate to achieve common goals, particularly when there are so many diffuse goals in a community? For example, a mental-health agency that uses cooperation and mutual support by offering services to the school system and the police in the neighborhood, in turn gets their understanding, empathy, and support in carrying out these services effectively.

All communities experience conflict when anything new is begun because change entails disequilibrium. Conflict can be handled on different levels of confrontation. Panzetta (1983) identifies four levels of confrontation: physical force, antiparticipant confrontation, confrontation as a franchiser, and as a consumer. Let us again look at a mental-health organization example. If members of the community believe the mental-health organization will not satisfy the needs of the community, one dramatic way by which the community can respond is through physical force. That is, let's say the community members enter the mental-health center and literally take over, forcing personnel out and then closing down the operation of the organization. Or a community may function through antiparticipation—that is, the community feels it does not need a mental-health facility and protests through hostility and nonparticipation. In this case, the mental-health setting cannot function effectively. Or the community may take over the mental-health setting and develop a special relationship with it as a franchiser. This suggests that the community has ultimate sponsorship over the mental-health organization and has power in terms of its programs, personnel, and funds. Finally, a community as a consumer can accept or reject a service that is offered to it. For example, a community may simply decline to use the mental-health services offered.

Thus social workers must manage practice and policy issues that affect their functioning within the community. We discuss more of these implications for social workers at the end of this chapter.

The Structure of a Community

All communities have a structure in which different subsystems such as neighborhoods and institutions are connected to each other. McIntyre (1986) defines these *basic elements* in communities as families, groups, facilities, neighborhoods, institutions, and organizations, as well as community-level systems of transportation, garbage removal, markets, and places of recreation. Sociological research suggests that the relationships among these elements are characterized by differentiation, centrality, and solidarity. These concepts can help explain community structure and how it functions.

Differentiation Communities are not alike. Various characteristics of communities are associated with social-structure differentiation. For example, one small community has no church and therefore no resident priest or minister. If people need spiritual guidance or counseling, they go outside their community for help. As the community grows, it may need to develop a church within its own community. Another community may not have a hospital. As this community grows, the need for a hospital may arise. Depending on the area and the population, some communities have more differentiation in the functions they perform than do other communities. Also, communities may change how much differentiation they show, as people and places change.

Centrality Centrality in a community concerns the extent to which the community functions on its own. What facilities make a community a central place for its occupants? A given community may have developed its own shopping areas as well as schools and neighborhoods. This community may have a central meeting place such as an auditorium, and may have town meetings to discuss matters that pertain to the entire community. A portion of this community may understand basic professional standards, business principles, and other secular ethics. A community may have a name that is understood both in the given community as well as in the wider region. Quite often such communities are self-sufficient, because their central functions are taken care of in the setting.

Solidarity Structural solidarity should not be understood as individual commitment or attachment to communities. Solidarity at the community level is different from the level of individuals. For instance, some of strongest commitments found in communities are seen in primitive societies, which elicit the fiercest loyalties from its members. This is also true of some religious communities. Modern communities often become alienated, disaffected, disloyal, and uncommitted. Forms of community solidarity include group-level systems of values, ethics, standards, and operational guidelines where, beside geographic boundaries, invisible boundaries allow only the norms and rules of the accepted community members to prevail.

The concepts of differentiation, centrality, and solidarity are necessary for analyzing and interpreting social change at the community level. Community features, particularly in relation to change, can be interpreted by reference to these characteristics. For example, one can say that a particular community has a good community spirit; one can also say that a community is either isolated or solid, based on its functions of centrality. The differentiation of a community usually concerns the level of economic and social development. The more complex the division of labor, the more differentiated are the social institutions in a community. An awareness of differentiation offers a basis for assessing whether a particular service institution or group would fit into a particular community. For example, a highly differentiated community might welcome highly differentiated social-welfare programs.

The Community as a System

Because today people move from area to area so freely and frequently, some have questioned whether communities exist at all. We view the community as a system, because it implies that the component units stand in some relation to one another and—as the popular expression says—the whole is greater than the sum of its parts. This may not be true of some chemical elements, but it *is* true of people. For example, a busload of club members on a Sunday outing may link up in a network of social relations, a social structure that cannot be reduced to the sum of its individual members—it takes on a "personality" of its own. A network of social relations transforms a bunch of individuals into a cohesive group with its own character and conduct (Blau & Scott, 1962). These links among people create a community system. The subsystems in a community include not only people, but also social structures—that is, government, business, schools, hospitals, and so forth. When we think of communities, therefore, we may think of small rural areas and towns. What comes to mind is a picture of a small village where everyone knows and *cares* about everybody else, and they all look out for each other. People help each other in case of necessity, and there is an attitude of common caring. Today, there are fewer intimate, caring communities than in the past, because the United States is highly industrialized. Modernization and urbanization have deeply influenced our community life. The community has been reshaped by the influence of television and other forms of instant communication, which bring into the home every type of news, including wars in far-off lands. Community life has not completely disappeared in this society, but it may not be the center of social life, at least for adults.

Communities are complex, diverse, and continually changing; hence their boundaries are difficult to identify. Communities may be organized around orderly activities and routines that different component parts engage in. For instance, members of a church may meet on particular days for worship; this is an orderly activity pattern that is followed in the community. Or community members may participate in recreation, getting together to play and watch baseball on certain days. This may become a seasonal routine in a particular community. Communities have different activities through which members affect each other and become interdependent. Relationships in communities thus take place in specific physical space and time; also, communities set boundaries for who can and cannot be an active part of the community. Viewed as loosely coupled networks of local elements, communities qualify as bona fide social systems (Martin & O'Connor, 1989).

Knowledge of Communities

When a social-work practitioner works in a community, it is important to know not only the community, but also how the community is perceived by newcomers in the area, by members of minority groups, and so forth. Different groups of people are aware of the types of help they can seek, obtain, and use from community members. For example, when they have a problem rural families may first go to clergy, family, and friends, and only then to social services (Martinez-Brawley & Blundall, 1989). In communities, social-welfare organizations provide services to meet the needs of diverse populations. For instance, home health services can be useful for the elderly. Communities, like people, differ—what is liked in one community may be disliked intensely in another. What may be useful in Nebraska may not be useful in New York City, and so forth. In communities, people may work for the success of a program, or may work against it, depending on their awareness of community services, needs, governmental structure, values, and other characteristics. Someone who wants to initiate change should therefore first analyze the existing apparatus to see if it could accommodate the change and should check to see how each existing component fits into the rest of the system.

As Zastrow (1992) indicates, social workers and others have a high stake in finding workable solutions to the increasing demands on state governments. When planning for communities, future and present needs must be taken into account. Social workers should be able to analyze the local government's structure and functions, and how state and federal government systems may affect the local government.

Interblending of Individual and Community Problems

All human beings are members of various communities. The manner in which a community responds to problems depends on how many people face such a problem and whether a community wishes to use its resources in seeking or providing a solution. For example, two decades ago, AIDS was not known and the term *homeless* referred to the deinstitutionalized. Communities made no special effort to help victims of AIDS. But today these problems are in full swing, and more and more communities are offering services, benefits, and programs for people in the community who are confronted with such serious life problems.

Until her marriage came crumbling down, Mariah lived in a well-to-do suburban neighborhood in the South. She was a high school graduate when she married. After twenty-five years, the marriage went sour.

She went through a tumultuous divorce, fell in love with and married a handsome man with expensive tastes. They traveled in style, and lived in expensive rented houses and apartments. In her fifth year of marriage, Mariah found out that he was unfaithful to her, and this led to a painful second divorce. Mariah left the marriage with little money. She was in her early fifties, and had no paid work experience. Applying for the position of a receptionist, she was turned down because of her age. Soon her money was used up for necessities, and she was left penniless. She eventually lost her rented apartment and found herself homeless. She was still too young for Social Security, and too proud to apply for public assistance. Quite often, she would sit on a bench on the roadside wearing her sunglasses and wait to pick up leftover food from some restaurant chains. Summer was bearable—she would walk to the nearby beach and sunbathe, carrying with her a small bag that held all her belongings. At the beach or in the roadside, she quickly learned to avoid looking at people or making eye contact, because her homeless situation was gnawing away at her heart and her sense of self. The important thing was that she was able to survive.

However, during last winter's cold winds and snow storms, Mariah developed a rasping, annoying cough that lingers and makes her exhausted. She has heard that her community has developed a few shelters to take care of the homeless. So far she has been too proud to set foot in any of those new places for homeless people. She has felt she could survive on her own, but as her health gives way, she walks a very long mile to the homeless shelter, where she collapses at the front door. The caregivers and most of the workers in the shelter are volunteer members of the community. In the shelter, Mariah is provided with food, clothing, shelter, and a warm bed. Mariah gratefully thanks them and slips into a deep, comfortable sleep.

Thus in this community when a homeless person such as Mariah presents herself at the shelter as a disadvantaged member of the community, she is immediately taken care of by other members of the community. Different individuals in the community interblend to serve and to be served. The shelter exists because during the recent recession homelessness was finally recognized as a national and community problem affecting increasing numbers of people.

Actually, shelters represent a very small and inadequate response to the problem of homelessness. The number of homeless people is increasing steadily; unfortunately, good statistics are not available, because there are so many "hidden" homeless people, both individuals and families. When so many people are affected, homelessness becomes an important and difficult problem for the community. Why are we able to talk about poverty in other countries and help them, while often we do not really see the same people in our own country, at our front and back doors—the invisible homeless? Every day I (Pillari) see a certain middle-income woman who has become homeless. She avoids seeking help because she is homeless; she sleeps at the beach and is up before anyone else is up, and dresses and looks as if she works. Yet the other day I saw her sitting on a park bench with her head down. I took note of her and, just once, her tired, fleeting eyes met mine for a brief moment, but she turned away. She still has not asked for help (Pillari, personal observation, 1993). How can we offer help to people when often we treat them as if their agonizing situation were their own fault, using the old, familiar, blame-the-victim syndrome? Not only the well-to-do members of the community do it—the victims do the same, blaming themselves for their devastating plight. How can we even have good statistical data when the homeless hide from us for fear of being judged? Thus we have the new American poor, and we are left with very few options except shelters, because we have not thought or planned ahead. Questions that communities need to consider include whether to develop affordable housing or to support low-income families, because everyone wishes to pursue the "American dream."

In many communities, another new and frightening problem has been mushrooming: preteen drinking. How should the community deal with it? What different activities can a community plan and carry out to help such families and their children? The community needs to raise funds and develop skills to deal with such children, their peers, and families. Lobbying for support at the political level is necessary to raise funds. Social workers may be able to help such people through counseling and positive political activities.

Another alarming problem we have been hit with is a rise in drug use among eighth graders, as seen in a study done at the University of Michigan (*The Virginian-Pilot & Ledger-Star,* April 14, 1993) by Lad Johnston, Patrick O'Malley, and Jerald Bachman. This study, based on a survey of 18,600 eighth-graders in 160 schools nationwide, reported an increase in the early use of marijuana, cocaine, crack, LSD and other hallucinogens, stimulants, and inhalants. Johnston commented in 1990 that "drugs [had been] front-page news for 10 to 20 years and then it settled into a hole"; every year, therefore, "each new wave of youngsters needs to learn about them all over again. No one is around to tell them." Ironically, Johnston notes the decline in drug use among the older teens may have contributed to the rise among younger teens. "In 1979, for example, one in every nine high school seniors smoked marijuana daily and today, one in 50 does." As a result, younger teens have a much smaller chance of "vicarious learning through observing," he said (p. A5). Communities need to provide drug-use prevention services at the schools, to help young children understand and realize the permanent harm drugs can do.

Community Studies

To understand and function effectively within a community, we need to be aware of the different elements of the community and how they interact. Community characteristics include race, ethnicity, age composition, socioeconomic status, and other population characteristics. Is the community mixed, in terms of its population, or does it have one specific ethnic group? What are the implications for such a community in a particular state? The implications for practice are different for an elderly community and for a younger one. Older people need more services for care and well-being. Younger people emphasize schools, recreation facilities, and so forth.

Another characteristic of the community is economic. How well-to-do is a particular community? What different types of employment are prevalent? Communities are often defined by the types of jobs available. For example, communities that focus on rural jobs differ from communities that employ lower-level factory workers; and a community that has both small and big firms and employs highly qualified executives, such as Stamford, Connecticut, is economically better off than many other communities. Also, what are the different types of large companies and industries that provide jobs for local people? The various sources of income affect a community.

The unemployment rate also reveals much about a community. The kinds of people who are unemployed reflect on the community. Does this community have a large number of unemployed Euro-Americans, or Chicanos, or African Americans? In some pockets of a community, unemployment may be higher. Such pockets reflect on the larger community of which they are a part, and indicate changes that need to be made in such communities.

One must also consider the median family income of the community. Having many wealthy families in the community may skew the average income, and thus the community may overlook urgent issues of the less prosperous people. The socioeconomic character of a community is determined largely by the housing patterns, the cost of residential property, and the condition of housing (brand-new homes or old, established, and well-maintained homes, or a mix of both types of homes).

Another characteristic of a community is its openness or closedness. Would "outsiders" be easily acceptable in a community, or could this be called an ingroup community? The duration of time it takes for newcomers to be accepted, and whether newcomers could use the same services as do old-timers, both affect community characteristics.

The role of churches, synagogues, temples, mosques, and so on in a community is significant. Is organized religion an isolated and distant entity that primarily caters to older churchgoers, or is it an intimate part of the community, offering needed services to community members of all ages?

Different norms in the community and the role of morality also affect community life. For example, a small town in Florida, as in many other parts of the country, may view abortion as a controversial issue. Not long ago, the norm of protesting against abortion clinics was taken to an extreme when an antiabortionist killed a doctor who was performing abortion services in three small Florida towns. The laws of the state say that killing a human being is a crime, and thus the antiabortionist who killed the doctor went on trial for murder. Yet some prolife advocates believe there is little difference between killing a prochoice adult and killing a preborn child. The controversy still continues; meanwhile the norms and laws of our country do not allow us to kill anyone after birth.

To a large degree, a community is evaluated by its population, the income of the population, the services available in that community, and the influence of the media. The type of community life people lead is further affected by newspapers published in the community, local radio and TV stations, and the different cultural activities available. Various types of health and social services and civic and service organizations also affect community living. The community may also be very sophisticated, fairly sophisticated, or simple.

Community Linkages

Different types of communities develop linkages, and these become important networks in people's lives. What is a network? It can be described as a system of relationships that develops among people when individuals, groups, families, and others combine for friendship, work, school, and recreational purposes. Martin and O'Connor (1989) classify community linkages into the following six groups:

1. *Internal, vertical, top–down linkages* are present in communities where there is community-based authority. That is, some system in the community has authority to instruct another part of the community in how to engage in certain procedures, how to avoid certain types of practices, and how to abide by the rules created in the community. For example, the city office in a community has authority to require builders and developers to abide by rules by denying them permits and by giving occupancy permits. This office affects the whole economy and environmental conditions of a community. Here, a superordinate body has power over the subordinate element in the community.

2. *Internal, vertical, bottom–up linkages* function in a community where a subordinate subsystem is able to influence a community through lobbying and persuasion. For example, a group of parents may want extra police security when schoolchildren get out of school, because there has been a sudden wave of crime in that part of the community. This small neighborhood association has been able to influence the city and bring in more police officers to protect their children. This internal vertical linkage is created from the bottom up.

3. *Internal, horizontal linkages* occur between peer systems, in which subsystems communicate without an authority over them. In such cooperative and collaborative relations people of similar interest work together for mutual advantage. At times community people such as home builders and planners may get together to share information

and bring about changes in the community coding laws. One subsystem alone may find it difficult to carry out this task, but if subsystems combine efforts, they gain strength and also can better understand and support or oppose laws.

4. *External, vertical, top–down linkages* show a community's boundaries and involve the exercise of external authority. For example, state governments make laws that control local communities. Federal welfare programs make regulations that affect service delivery in communities. Today, with high technology and new, effective forms of communication, more external vertical, top–down linkages characterize American communities than ever before.

5. *External, vertical, bottom–up linkages* show a community's boundaries and involve the influence of authority. When a group of community welfare organizations get together and lobby for change in state or federal policies, then an external, vertical, bottom–up linkage has been made. Thus a group of voters who want pro- or antiabortion rights policies to be implemented in their communities try to influence an elected representative's vote in Washington, DC, by taking a matter of local concern and lobbying to a larger body outside of the community.

6. *External, horizontal linkages* also occur among peer systems in two or more communities. For example, two local communities may get together to build a regional hospital, an airport, an all-season recreational amusement park, and so forth. Thus a horizontal, external linkage is built between two communities, neither of which community has power or authority over the other. Collaborative efforts are used because both communities favor the results.

TYPES OF COMMUNITIES

W. S. Bernard (1973), a sociologist, has classified communities as locational, identificational, and interest communities. These categories are not mutually exclusive, because most people are likely to fit into several different groupings.

Locational communities have a common residence or territory. Such communities have developed with the evolution of nomadic groups that eventually began to settle in one place. Caring and attachment develop among people in such communities. The location of the community affects how members of the community communicate with each other. In some neighborhoods, there is a great deal of togetherness; in others, people simply find themselves together in a neighborhood due to necessity. Let us look at two different types of locational communities.

Majka and Donnelly (1988) define an ideological community as one where residents choose the neighborhood in part because it may be urban and diverse, and because they consciously seek a neighborhood that will serve as a community. A more homogenous community, for example, could be an older inner-city African-American neighborhood that provides a fertile base for organizing activity. About a generation ago, as Rubin and Rubin (1992) indicate, studies showed that African-American neighborhoods were both socially and politically integrated. More recently, Warcquant and Wilson (1989) and Wilson (1987) report that upper-income minorities tend to move out of poorer ghettos, and the African-American neighborhood thus becomes divided into two types of residential community. One type of ghetto is a community where people are poor but remain rich in networks and associations, although they may be cut off from the outside society. Another type is the *hyperghetto,* which does not have traditional organizations and institutions. Such a community is marginally economical. "Its activities are no longer structured around an internal and relatively autonomous social space that duplicates the institutional structure of the larger society and provides basic minimal resources for social mobility" (Warcquant & Wilson, 1989, p. 15).

Traditional communities that have existed in a particular location for a long period of time can organize easily when they need to deal with affective issues. For example, there was a great deal of unrest among the residents of one middle-class community because their cars were being robbed at night. So the informal community leaders got together and developed, with the help of the local police, their own night patrol system to watch out for delinquent boys who were breaking into the cars and removing whatever they could.

In middle-class urban America, people tend to mark their boundaries by walls, fences, and locked doors, which makes communication between neighbors difficult. Thus, even if they are located in a specific neighborhood, such people tend to be isolated and not familiar with each other unless a crisis occurs. However, in a crisis situation, the middle-class community just mentioned got its citizens to work together to keep their neighborhoods safe.

Identificational communities are based on a common identity (Bernard, 1973). In identificational communities, where people live is not as important as what holds them together, which includes affection and common identity. Identifiable community groups include ethnic and racial groups, religious groups, and groups based on sexual orientation. Also, identificational communities include communities that have a unique culture, in which each subgroup is accorded a certain status. For example, in the Native-American community, the elderly are seen as natural leaders. The idea of a group culture is usually associated with ethnic groups, but may be relevant to other kinds of communities. The subculture of some people in terms of values and norms may be related to their sexual orientation (gay, lesbian, or straight) rather than membership in a particular ethnic or minority group. Often ethnic minority groups and their members may experience unique problems. Such a group may be devalued in this country. For example, institutional racism results in high infant mortality rates, high minority youth unemployment rates, high morbidity rates, and low life expectancy among people of color. When they are overcome with problems, the oppressed may band together, because these circumstances evoke anger and resentment.

Interest communities have, as the term implies, shared interests with common goals and objectives. In ordinary communities, the interests of the community members may be broad, general, and less inclusive, whereas in interest-group communities the members care about each other because all members are focused on a particular interest. Such groups can be of various types, including professional and occupational groups. People belonging to a particular profession may come together to discuss their interests. For example, nurses, doctors, and social workers may derive a sense of togetherness from the helping profession. For another example, clustered around the controversial question of abortion are two types of interest groups, the prolife and prochoice groups. The prolife group believes that abortion is a crime and should be stopped, and works toward this end. Prochoice groups advocate freedom of choice with respect to decisions about one's body.

All the three different types of communities can be seen in the following example. Kwong (1987) reports that in New York the "The CCBA (Chinese Community Business Association) decided that the community should protest the city's closing of the local police fifth precinct. An order went out. Every store in the main Chinatown area was closed, and 20,000 Chinese turned out for the demonstration. As a result, the city government quickly rescinded the decision." However, Kwong continues, informal employee organizations cannot get a fair settlement of a labor–management dispute, because the Chinese elite will side with management. This community, located in a specific area, can effectively organize on the basis of solid links with its members. In this example, the members of a particular neighborhood (locational community) who are identifiable as Chinese (ethnic community) businesspeople (interest community) define common interests and work together to solve certain problems.

Racial and Ethnic Communities

From a social worker's perspective, let us look at some alternative types of communities that may develop based on the functions of a community. These may either be loosely knit or closed communities. People from different ethnic groups often get together because they gain community identity, competence, and self-direction with respect to human relatedness and a sense of belonging to a group.

A great deal of uneasiness may arise when race and ethnic issues are discussed. Mainstream society may verbalize nonprejudicial attitudes that stand in sharp contrast to the actual experiences of people of color. Depending on class, educational status, and family background, the types of prejudice that people face vary, but similar experiences and feelings may prompt racial and ethnic groups to organize communities to protect and insulate themselves from the majority culture. An ethnic group can be defined as a "community group based upon the ascribed status of a diffuse ancestry that is maintained by similarities of culture, language and/or phenotype [physical characteristics]" (Howells, 1971, p. 3).

What is a minority? In everyday use, a minority is a relatively small part of a group of people, whereas majority means more than half the group or community. Size is a factor in determining majority and minority status, but in the United States the term has more implications than just size. Louis Wirth (1945, p. 347), whose definition is most frequently quoted, says that a minority group is "a group of people who, because of their physical or cultural characteristics, are singled out from others in the society in which they live for differential and unequal treatment and who therefore regard themselves as objects of collective discrimination." Howard (1970, p. 3) states that the term *minority* is used to show the "fundamental fact of ethnic domination of one group by another. Members of minority groups experience stigma on categorical grounds." Thus women are referred to as a minority group even though they constitute a majority of the population. Newman (1973) postulates that minority status may be accorded to a person or group due to a number of reasons, including skin color, membership in an extremist religious or political group, or lifestyle. Recently members of minority groups have begun to reject the label, because it connotes inferiority as well as victimization.

From a social-work perspective, let us look at some issues of racism in this country. There are subtle ways by which specific groups are put at a disadvantage. Terms such as *disadvantaged,* and *oppressed,* and *discriminated against* are created and used for some groups, and in contrast other groups may be in an *advantaged* and *powerful* position. These terms are used freely by both groups of people, with little awareness of the stigma and impact they have on either group. It is also important to note that at times the label is worn proudly or even flaunted, and at times both groups exploit these status terms for all kinds of self-serving agendas.

Let us look at some of the problems ethnic groups have faced. For instance, spatial and temporal constraints on social or ethnic groups often cause many problems in such communities. Particularly in lower-income families, discriminatory physical and social settings harm the person. Georgia is a low-income resident of a high-rise public-housing project. The vandalism in her project is in part the residents' angry response to the outrageous dehumanization and depersonalization that the residents of this community experience. Crimes take place in semipublic spaces such as the lobby, elevators, and grounds where surveillance by tenants is impossible. Such settings become sites for drug dealing, as there are no boundary markers and often intruders cannot be recognized. In communities like this, people may create territories, such as the youth gangs who make several blocks or parks their "turf." In poor communities, turf boundaries are restricted because the tight space and physical settings do not allow territoriality to develop. Poverty and powerlessness may severely limit the youth in such places and may prevent the development of their own potentials. Children growing up in the inner-city communities have smaller areas to call their own. They have little exposure to the cultural attractions of the larger urban and rural environment (Germain, 1991). For example, a child from an inner city may not have seen a farm or farm animals, whereas children living in the rural areas irrespective of socioeconomic status can experience the attractions of a rural environment. Both inner-city and rural poor have very few opportunities to visit cultural attractions in cities and learn from them.

Institutional racism is prevalent (though often not documented) in both formal and informal policies, practices, and procedures in community housing, schools, workplaces, health care, and social services. These policies harm people of color. As Barbarian (1981) discusses, individual and institutional racism establish community environments where people of color live and create a circular loop that holds people in a condition of powerlessness. High unemployment rates, low life expectancy, and high infant-mortality rates are common among people of color. Moreover, institutional racism and anger, turned inward, often lead to violence within such communities.

Except for Native Americans, America is a nation of immigrants. However, groups that enter the country from places such as Great Britain and northern Europe become members of the dominant groups, whereas people with African, Hispanic, and even Native-American ancestry become victims of prejudice and discrimination. Racism is prejudice, discrimination, or oppression based on race. It encompasses various racial stereotypes, such as the stereotype that African Americans are only talented as athletes. Racism is a belief in cultural or biological (innate) superiority of a particular race over other races.

Institutional racism is structural and systemic in nature; that is, it is built into the economic, educational, health, social, political, and legal institutions of the society. It is pervasive because it affects many people rather than single individuals. For instance, because of institutional racism, millions of children of color suffer nutritional, medical, educational, and economic disadvantages, compared to Euro-American children. To what degree do the norms that govern economic, political, religious, and family life reward prejudice and discrimination on the basis of race and ethnicity? That depends on who is wielding power.

Formerly, the United States was more overtly racist in character. Federal policies worked to promote the well-being of immigrants from northern and western Europe, at the expense of southern and eastern Europeans. Non-Europeans were even more stringently discriminated against. This gap in services was more evident in immigration laws, voting regulations, and legal access to employment opportunities, housing, transportation, public accommodations, and education, among other areas of living. People of color were excluded from citizenship at various times, and a "separate but equal" philosophy justified discrimination against minorities (Longres, 1990).

The African-American community The African-American culture has a long history in the United States. The collective experiences of African Americans include slavery, economic deprivation, and institutional racism, coupled with an African heritage that has been modified due to continuous exposure to Euro-American cultures. This shared history has resulted in a unique blend of cultural and social values and a sense of connectedness and solidarity among its people (Queralt, 1996). However, it is important to remember that every African American is unique in terms of the extent to which that person shares the traditional values of the group. The individual's history depends on factors such as education, socioeconomic status, age, rural, urban or suburban status, and regional backgrounds such as the South and Northeast. Younger, well-educated, middle- or upper-middle-class African Americans are likely to be conversant with Euro-American mainstream culture and show that familiarity in their behaviors, values, and lifestyles, which are a unique blend of two cultures. But less educated, inner-city, or rural people, lower-income people, or those who are older may show a greater affinity to traditional African-American cultural values and less acculturation to mainstream culture (Queralt, 1996). Although Hatchett and Jackson (1993) state that the African- American community is held together by "white oppression and racism," there is strong evidence to show that African Americans stay together for more reasons than external oppression. For example, the African-American church does not exist because the white church is oppressive. African-American religion is qualitatively different from the white church and exists parallel to and not subservient to white religion (Billingsley, 1993).

During the massive African-American migration from the rural South, individual churches and clergy in northern cities helped migrants by announcing jobs from the pulpit or by posting positions on the church bulletin board. This tradition of finding employment through the church continues even today. Through African-American churches, mutual-aid societies, and fraternal lodges, African-Americans sought to create communities that would spread the ethos of economic uplift and self-help. A challenge facing the African-American church is deciding what kind of economic system will best serve the needs of the people with justice, equity, and fairness in the twenty-first century (Lincoln & Mamiya, 1990).

Lincoln and Mamiya (1990) note that the African-American families and churches constitute "enduring institutions" in African-American communities. These two major institutions share a special tradition of caring for young children. As the only communal institutions in urban and rural areas, African-American churches have been intimately involved in the complex network of African-American extended families. Some churches are dominated by one or a few kin groups, so that the phenomenon of family church or kin church is widespread, especially in rural areas. The relationship between African-American families and churches has been a dynamic one. Families have constituted the building blocks of African-American churches, and in their preaching, teaching, symbols, belief systems, morality, and rituals, the churches provided a unity that has wedded families and the community to each other (Lincoln & Mamiya, 1990). One of the most important functions that the African-American church has filled for young people is to provide a place where they can meet older adults, men and women who serve as role models for them. Thus socialization of children has taken place through observing, evaluating, emulating, and filing away for later use, behaviors that are valuable examples for the children (Lincoln & Mamiya, 1990). The church has also been a place for people to form their identity, receive validation, and develop a sense of belonging. And it is also a place where music, oratory, and other expressive functions flourish in the African-American community.

Extended-family kinship is a fundamental aspect of the African-American lifestyle and a major source of social and emotional support. African Americans across all socioeconomic levels tend to maintain stronger kinship bonds than Euro-Americans (Hatchett & Jackson, 1993). These ties are especially evident in times of crisis, illness, celebration, or death. Those who belong to the less mobile, lower socioeconomic class interact more frequently with a broad range of blood-related and non-blood-related kin. They include grandparents, adult siblings, boyfriends and girlfriends, uncles, aunts, grandchildren, neighbors, boarders, preachers, and deacons.

According to Billingsley, African Americans constitute a community in four respects. First, most African Americans live in neighborhoods where their neighbors are also African Americans. A national survey in 1989 showed that 80% of African Americans lived in neighborhoods that were predominantly African American. This concentration occurs because of economic and "racist exclusionary practices which prevent people from exercising their freedom of choice" (Billingsley, p. 72). African-American enclaves are found in every part of the nation. A second sense of community for African Americans is the shared sense of values that helps define them. A group of African-American scholars—among them John Hope Franklin, Eleanor Holmes Norton, and twenty-eight others—has summarized these values, which were published as a statement by the Joint Center for Political and Economic Studies in 1987:

> Blacks have always embraced the central values of the society, augmented those values in response to the unique experiences of slavery and subordination, incorporated them into a strong religious tradition, and espoused them fervently and persistently. These values—among them, the primacy of family, the importance of education, and the necessity for individual enterprise and hard work—have been fundamental to black survival. These community values have been matched by a strong sense of civic values, ironic in

> the face of racial discrimination—espousal of the rights and responsibilities of freedom, commitment to country, and adherence to the democratic creed. (Franklin & Norton, 1989)

Thirdly, most African Americans, wherever they live, continue to identify with their heritage to a large degree. People who move out of African-American neighborhoods return to visit neighborhoods in which their relatives and friends stayed. Others return to go to churches, barber shops, and beauty parlors. Even those who do not visit have a potential powerful connection to African-American causes and issues. In *The New York Times,* Roger Wilkins captured the spirit of the occasion when South African president Nelson Mandela was released after twenty-seven years of imprisonment: "there was a surge of pride when the world for the first time gave a black man his regal due during his lifetime. So when the day finally came, we clapped, cheered and cried at the sight of a king—our cousin, the king—walking in sunshine" (Wilkins, 1990).

Finally, the African-American community is seen in terms of institutions and organizations that grow out of the African-American heritage, identify with it, and serve African-American families. The African-American community has an organization, an agency, or an institution for every conceivable function. Sometimes these institutions survive as small but coordinated enterprises. At other times, they are small, uncoordinated, and uncooperative with others, and some shrivel up and dissolve too quickly. However, they anchor the community and can join together in collective action when circumstances or leadership inspire. Four organizations dominate the African-American community: church, school, business, and voluntary organizations.

Yet all these strong community networks do not alter the fact that poverty, unemployment, underemployment, and crime harm the African-American community, with the added burden of institutional racism, which exacerbates and perpetuates the other burdens this community labors under.

Help through primary prevention is important. As Bell and Jenkins (1990) indicate, "primary prevention refers to those actions that stop a problem from occurring" and is better than any form of remedy. He outlines a program of teaching conflict-resolution skills to young people, expanding community-based programs to encourage a sense of pride and belonging among lower-income African-American youth, providing professional help for African-American families under stress, establishing alcohol- and drug-free programs, and expanding community programs designed to enhance racial identity.

It is important to note that the African-American culture incorporates many coping and adapting strategies developed primarily to ward off racism, discrimination, and oppression and to survive under economic deprivation. When working with African Americans, a social worker needs to become aware of the built-in strengths of their community and culture.

The Hispanic community A common feature of all Hispanic cultures is the Spanish language. This is the second most widely spoken language in the United States (U.S. Bureau of the Census, 1992). It is easy for the Spanish-speaking people to maintain contact with their language, because the United States lies adjacent to several Caribbean and Latin American countries. This proximity has also enabled the Hispanic people to keep in close touch with their countries of origin. The Hispanic population consists largely of Chicanos (second-generation Mexican) and Puerto Ricans and a smaller number of Cubans. Together they form the largest ethnic minority. Most Chicanos live in the Southwest, most Puerto Ricans live in the Northeast, and most Cuban Americans live in Florida. The broad term *Latino cultures* includes all people of Spanish cultures who are an integral part of U.S. life.

Delgado and Humm-Delgado (1982) analyzed natural support systems in Hispanic communities. Family life is very important in the Hispanic culture. Although we have talked about three different groups of people —Chicanos, Puerto Ricans, and Cubans—Queralt (1984) observes that they are more alike than different, sharing similarities in terms of their Spanish language and Catholic religion. However, they may vary in demographic characteristics, cluster in different areas of the United States, and come from different socioeconomic classes.

Familism. The concept of familism—pride in the extended family—characterizes these families. The most significant aspect of familism is (1) the importance of the *compadrazo,* that is, the godparent–godchild relationship; (2) the benefits of financial dependency on kin; and (3) the availability of relatives as a source of advice (Schaefer, 1979). Within this kinship network, reciprocal support and obligation are the rule. The father is the patriarch, the official head of the family. He is the chief decision maker and the family's representative in the community.

As contrasted to Anglo men, Chicano men are described as showing greater pride in maleness. However, research data collected in Los Angeles and San Antonio suggests that this pattern is disappearing (Alvirez & Bean, 1976, pp. 277–278; Burma, 1970, pp. 23–24; Erlanger, 1976). The reasons why machismo is disappearing are discussed later.

The folk healers. Puerto-Rican communities have four types of folk healers: the spiritualist; the *santero,* who focuses mainly on emotional and interpersonal problems; the herbalist; and the *santiguador,* who focuses mainly on physical ailments. Mexican-American communities have the *curandero,* or *curandera,* the primary folk healer (Delgado & Humm-Delgado, 1982). It is important for the professional social worker to understand that participation in healing rituals or beliefs in supernatural or in folk-defined illnesses or the evil eye is an intimate part of such cultures. This belief does *not* mean a person is psychologically or emotionally distressed. For instance, a recent immigrant from Mexico may attribute not getting a job to the first woman who looked at her résumé and was shocked to see how high the immigrant's qualifications were. As months pass, and the new immigrant still does not get a job, she may blame the envy of the woman who saw her résumé and "cast an evil eye" on her. This is a common belief in Hispanic cultures, and does not indicate anything wrong with the person. Such beliefs should be understood within the cultural framework of the Hispanic culture. If such a client specifies that he or she has sought the advice of a priest or a folk healer, it is wise for the social worker to understand the importance of what took place between the client and the indigenous helper, so that help can be planned and carried out in accordance with the client's culture.

Religion. Most Hispanics can turn to their religious institutions for help. The Roman Catholic church is the primary religion of Hispanics; that is, approximately 85% of U.S. Hispanics are Catholic. The rest belong to Protestant denominations (Medina, 1987). However, the influence of the church on Puerto Ricans and other groups is declining (Delgado & Humm-Delgado, 1982). About four-fifths of all Puerto Ricans are Roman Catholic. The rest are Protestants, which is the result of Protestant missionary work after U.S. acquisition of land in Hispanic countries. Today the Puerto-Rican culture shows more eagerness to depend on individual solutions, preferring to get education and engage in other forms of self-improvement rather than go to public agencies for help (Schaefer 1979).

Cultural traits. Cultural traits of Hispanics may include machismo, fatalism, present-oriented behavior, close social distance, and strong orientation toward sociocultural institutions.

Hispanic men may display *machismo,* explicit pride in their own maleness. This show of male dominance and superiority is emphasized in many descriptions of Hispanic people. However, machismo has been misrepresented or exaggerated. Machismo means resorting to weapons or fighting, and can also mean being irresistible to women. However, men manifest these exploitive physical extremes only in certain situations. Research data show that common notions of machismo are disappearing (Alvirez & Bean, 1976, pp. 277–278; Erlanger, 1976). The feminist movement both in the United States and Latin America is changing the way men and women act toward each other. Also, urbanization and upward mobility and acculturation all combine to outdate machismo more with each passing generation (J. Moore & Pachon, 1976, pp. 118–120; E. Stevens, 1973). One reason why machismo is disappearing, particularly in the Puerto Rican culture, is that women are beginning to work outside the home, both on the mainland and in Puerto Rico. In the United States, similar factors are contributing to the decline of machismo.

Marin and Marin (1991) indicate five basic Hispanic cultural values that cut across the various Hispanic subgroups and that are undergoing modification as a result of acculturation: allocentrism, *simpatia,* familism, *respeto,* and *machismo* (which has been discussed earlier). Allocentrism or collectivism is a cultural trait associated with the preference for interpersonal relationships that are seen as nurturing, emphathetic, loving, intimate, and respectful and where members are willing to sacrifice for the welfare of the group. *Simpatia* emphasizes the need to promote and maintain harmonious and pleasant interpersonal relationships. In the Mexican-American culture, this social value is called *bien educado*. As mentioned earlier, familism stresses the importance of the family. *Respeto,* a term derived from high-power, high-distance cultures, accentuates the importance of, deference to, and respect for individuals who occupy roles of higher prestige, recognition, and power in society (Knight et al., 1993).

Like other ethnic groups, Hispanics have faced a great deal of prejudice directed at differences in language and culture, including social distance and patterns of touch. While working with Hispanics, the social worker should understand that their nonverbal interactions differ from Anglos. When interacting socially, Hispanics stand closer and touch more frequently (Henderson, 1989). Also, women tend to kiss each other on the cheek as part of greeting and saying goodbye. Usually men shake hands, but if they meet their friends or relatives after a long period of time, or when they wish to offer support in times of need, they may embrace.

In working with Hispanic Americans, note that—unlike Anglos, who emphasize individualistic democratic ideals of self-determination and so forth—Hispanics place considerable value on dealing with collective entities such as church and family. Such people derive their viewpoint from their own ethnic structure, and this sense of collectivity should be kept in mind when you help a Hispanic person, family, or community.

The Native Americans Any discussion of Native Americans must begin by emphasizing the diversity of the people. There are many tribes. As Wilkinson (who is Cherokee) says, "A tribe is a collection of people in which everyone has accepted duties and obligations to different people, and people operate in that kind of context. . . . A tribe is certainly nothing less than a big self-help organization that is designed to help people and meet the psychological, spiritual and economic needs of its members" (1980).

The Native Americans are split among those off and on the reservations, those who live in central cities and small towns, and those living on one coast or the other. In the last century, Native-American life has shifted from several hundred reservations to small towns and cities. Life for Native Americans in these contrasting social environments is quite different, but the similarities warrant some broad generalizations on the status of the Indians in contemporary United States. There are about thirteen different root languages and about 200 mutually distinct languages, about 130 major tribal groupings, and different levels of sociocultural development among all the Native Americans (Carpenter, 1980).

The history of the Native Americans is a painful one. Although natives of the soil, they have been outnumbered and mistreated by the Euro-Americans. Their history includes conquest and extermination, some slavery, removal of children from their homes to "civilize" them at boarding schools or to place them in non-Native-American foster homes, and continuous oppression (Sue & Sue, 1990). Their land was taken away from them, and they have been relocated over and over again. Their tribal way of living has been interfered with, they were forbidden to speak their languages, and a multitude of efforts were made to break up the Native-American cultural patterns and social organization. Assimilation by "appropriate social policy" became a fundamental aspect of Indian policy, and consisted of five components. (1) Originally, a variety of private organizations had dabbled in "educating" the Indians. This task was now shifted to the Bureau of Indian Affairs, which required Indians to abandon their languages, native dress, religious practices, and other traditional customs. (2) Traditional leaders and traditional procedures were undermined as the government simply bypassed them when dealing with questions of law and order and political issues. (3) The authority of tribal leaders was discouraged, and Bureau of Indian Affairs superintendents became the de facto government of many reservations. (4) Many missionaries were sent to reservations with the implicit mandate to "civilize" the Indians. (5) The Marginal Areas Act of 1855 ousted the jurisdiction of tribal authorities with respect to a broad range of criminal activity (Lewis, 1995).

Many Native Americans intermingled and became part of the mainstream American scene, but others have maintained their history and heritage. To some extent, the isolation of the Indian reservations has also helped preserve cultural continuity.

As a group, Native Americans are impoverished. About a third lives below poverty level, and the level of unemployment is nearly three times as high as Euro-Americans, as documented by the U.S. Bureau of Indian Affairs (1987). The data also show that about 62% of them live on or near reservations as marginally employed or unemployed.

To work with Native Americans, the social worker should understand their cultures and ways of behavior. Among Native Americans, as among other ethnic groups, understanding common threads allows social workers to be more helpful. Blanchard (Laguna Yaqui) and Unger (1977) comment, "Indian people derive their identity from relationships to their families, relatives, tribes and land base. Blood and clan ties are the strongest relationships between individuals. Every Indian person has the benefit of two relational systems, and the responsibilities of persons to each other are as strong and binding in either."

A great deal of racism has been wielded against Native Americans. In 1981, Barbara Cameron writes, as a child, in South Dakota,

> I was attending an all white (except for me) elementary school. During Halloween my friends and I went trick or treating. At one of the last stops, the mother knew all of the children except for me. She asked me to remove my mask, she realized I was an Indian and quite cruelly told me so, refusing to give me the treats my friends had received. It was a stingingly painful experience.

She continues,

> I told my mother about it the next evening after I tried to understand it. My mother was outraged and explained the realities of being an Indian in South Dakota. My mother paid a visit to the woman which resulted in their expressing a barrage of equal hatred for one another. I remember sitting in our pickup hearing the intensity of the anger and feeling very sad that my mother had to defend her child to someone who wasn't worthy of her presence. (Cameron, 1993, p. 203)

Prejudice and discrimination have permeated life for Native Americans, but this pattern is slowly changing. Being sympathetic to the needs and deprivation of Native Americans is not sufficient; rather the social worker must develop an understanding of their cultures to work with them in ways that can benefit them most. In particular, understanding family and relationships among extended families is crucial for working and understanding Native Americans.

The traditional Native-American family is extended and forms part of a much larger group of families and clans that trace descent to a common ancestor (Locke, 1992). The extended family is important and includes second-degree relatives—that is, aunts, uncles, and cousins—as well as those who are not kin. Usually various members of the family or clan, not just the parents, participate in child rearing, which is carried out in a permissive manner, without much punishment or guilt (Ho, 1987; Locke, 1992). The children may live with various family or clan members, not just with their parents. Elders in the families are honored and respected for their wisdom, and typically fill important positions on the tribal council (Lewis & Ho, 1989; Locke, 1992).

Native Americans see the world in a holistic manner and see mind, body, and spirit as being interconnected (Heinrich, Corbine, & Thomas, 1990). They believe everything in life has a spirit; that is, sky, waters, trees, rocks, animals, and people. Therefore, from a social worker's perspective it is not pathological when a Native American "feels," "sees," or "hears" spirits. Such visions can throw light on the meaning and purpose of life and the significance of certain events.

Important religious rituals for Native Americans are carried out by shamans, *sakims,* or medicine men, who help to look for the future through visions. Many traditional Native Americans would prefer to receive help from their own healers than go to a social worker.

A social worker needs to understand that Native Americans typically speak softly, use a gentle handshake, and are not physically demonstrative (Everett, Proctor, & Cartmell, 1983). Their traditional culture teaches them self-control, avoidance of emotional outbursts, observation rather than impulsive behaviors, and noninterference in the affairs of others (Lewis & Ho, 1989; Harrison, Wodarski, & Thyer, 1992). Social workers should give special attention to their nonverbal ways of communicating. They make little eye contact, and too much staring is considered aggressive. In some tribes children are taught it is disrespectful to look an elder in the eye. Also, traditional Native Americans do not measure time exactly and are not characteristically punctual. Usually events only begin when everyone is present, so that everyone can take part.

Social workers need to be aware that in recent times, a number of urban Native Americans are reviving Native-American culture. They may read books about Native Americans, attend local ceremonial pow-wows so that their children can learn about their heritage, and engage in traditional Indian handicrafts. While working with Native Americans, the social-work practitioner should be sensitive to their values of family unification, respect for nature, parental leadership, respect for the elderly, and collective family decision making. By understanding Native-American family lifestyles, the worker can help such families more effectively and efficiently.

Asian Americans There are many differences among Asian groups in culture, language, and religion. Asians include Chinese, Japanese, Koreans, Filipinos, Vietnamese, Indians (from India), and other Southeast Asians. Among these groups, many differences appear in social class, rural– urban histories and backgrounds, educational status, family status, and so forth. There are also different generational statuses, that is, native-born immigrants, second- and third-generation immigrants, and so forth. Historically, the newer immigrants appear to come from a higher socioeconomic class than their predecessors.

There are also a number of similarities among Asian groups. The members tend to be family-oriented, and respect for elders is a necessity. Wong (1981) wrote, "enhancement of community systems through community development and community organization activities improves individual and family support systems (p. 202).

As in other cultural groups, religious groups may often serve as a significant informal system in helping families maintain culture and other networks. Most East Asians practice Buddhism, Hinduism, Shintoism, or Taoism. A substantial number of Koreans, Vietnamese and Filipinos have converted to Christianity (Locke, 1992). Buddhism, which originated as a branch of Hinduism from India, is the dominant religion of the Chinese, Koreans, and Southeast Asians. Buddhism stresses the value of self-control, humility, generosity, love, and mercy as well as the importance of education and of cultivating a correct lifestyle, including "right views, right desires, right conduct, right occupation and right extinction of all cravings" (Henderson, 1989). Hindus and Buddhists believe in reincarnation; according to this belief system, each person's life goal is to perfect oneself so as to attain liberation from rebirth cycles. Shintoism is the national religion of Japan, although many Japanese practice Buddhism. Shintoism stresses respect for nature and the importance of harmonious social relations (Barnlund, 1989). All Eastern religions teach detachment and the importance of living a simple life.

Religion plays an important role in the life of Asians. For example, Buddhist monks often serve as significant natural helpers, and Buddhism may unify mutual-aid associations among Southeast Asians, Vietnamese, Cambodian, and other communities, promoting health and reducing stress and loneliness. These families highly value their mutual-aid networks, and this is often overlooked by agencies and professionals and social services, who may violate the cultural norms and patterns. For example, when one Vietnamese woman was distressed and began to complain, a social worker, meaning to be empathetic, put her arms around the woman. But this shocked her—the Vietnamese woman felt intruded on.

In Asian cultures, the transition from childhood to adulthood is relatively smooth, which facilitates the socialization process. Children are exposed to the companionship of adults and learn socially approved behaviors as well as what people think of them. American child rearing stresses the concept of guilt, whereas Asian cultures stress shame. Shame presupposes "that one is completely exposed and conscious of being looked at"—in a word, "self-conscious" (Erikson, 1963, p. 252).

The father is the head of the traditional Asian family household. He is its principal decision maker and chief disciplinarian (Locke, 1992). When offering help, a social worker needs to be aware of this pattern and work with such clients accordingly. Because of the concept of shame and family pride, many Asian Americans hesitate to seek professional help. They may do so only if all other resources have been exhausted, or if the family has already assimilated the mainstream Euro-American way of thinking.

Physical contact among Asian adults is usually limited in public, particularly among opposite-sex adults. For instance, couples from India, Japan, China, or Korea, who subscribe to the traditional culture, are much less likely to touch, kiss, caress, or hug in public than Euro-Americans. Yet in many Asian cultures mothers are very physically demonstrative with their young children. Also, in some East Asian cultures same-sex close friends may walk hand in hand in public, a behavior that has no connotations of homosexuality (Furuto, Biswas, Chong, Murase, & Ross-Sheriff, 1992).

In tune with their cultural traditions, many Asians value silence and reservation, and prefer to communicate indirectly, subtly, and nonverbally rather than openly, as is most common among Euro-Americans. For example, in Japan it is considered wise to speak as little as possible because "it is the shallow water that makes noise" (Haglund, 1988, p. 91.)

Traditional Asian cultures teach that it is the duty of each family member to preserve the family's dignity and honor. The entire family loses face if one of its members does poorly in school or work, or has emotional or mental problems. Family members are encouraged to act in society in ways that protect and enhance the family name and honor, and to avoid discussing personal and family problems in front of outsiders (Ho, 1976).

Asians have developed a large number of informal support systems, and social-work services, policy, and practice need to be directed to strengthening and sustaining them. Services that draw on social networks in community life, which have a greater cultural congruence than traditional services, are apt to be more effective than traditional "back-home"-mentality services. As there is rich and diverse history, language, and culture among the new and older groups of Asian Americans, social workers engaged in cross-cultural work should develop culture sensitivity, culture-relevant knowledge, and bicultural training on an experiential base (Pinderhughes, 1979).

Traditionalism has caused a great deal of unrest and conflict among the native-born Asian Americans. Particularly among the Chinese and other older immigrant groups, the generation gap has been steadily building. Children provide only limited assistance to their elderly parents because of separate living arrangements and geographic distance. They are taught that they are responsible for their parents, especially in health-care crises and in dealing with problems of old age, but due to geographic separation, work schedules, and lifestyle obstacles, second- or third-generation children may have to rely on ethnic-oriented public services on weekdays and fulfill their obligations to their parents on weekends or in the evenings (Lum, 1995). Other types of problems may arise between immigrants and their children born in the United States, too. The younger Asians grow up in a world where they find that their parental generation follows obsolete precedents and makes out-of-date responses, so they look to new models among their peers. Often "these peers present them with more practical modes than the . . . elders, whose past is inaccessible to them and whose future is difficult for them to see as their own" (Mead, 1970, p. 31).

Professionals need to be aware that Americanization among younger people of many ethnic groups tends to produce distinct generational differences. The younger generation has very little patience with parochialism. They are usually caught up in a spirit of idealism and restlessness. This change needs to be taken into account while working with younger people from different ethnic groups.

Recent immigrant groups The so-called new Americans are immigrants who enter under the immigration and naturalization quota system, and who are more likely to come from other parts of the world than Europe. These immigrants have occupational skills that make it possible for them to succeed more quickly than immigrants of the past (Longres, 1990).

Another sizable group of people are the refugees who (unlike immigrants) are forced out of their own native lands because of ethnic history, religious background, and so forth. Refugees also differ from people who are brought into the country by a conquering or colonizing group of people. In more recent times, these people included Russian Jews and people from Southeast Asia, including Vietnamese, Cambodians, and Laotians. Prior to 1975, fewer came from Southeast Asia, and most were affluent, urban, well-educated, and young. However, between

1980 and 1985 a larger number (250,000) of Vietnamese entered the country—more than half the total previously in the country. These more recent Indochinese refugees were not as educated or skilled as those who came earlier. Under the Migration and Refugee Assistance Act of 1975, the refugees received medical treatment, public-school education for children, and vocational training for adults. Many sponsors, such as churches and social agencies, were used to help these refugees. Some sponsors proved very helpful, whereas others exploited the refugees (Wright, 1980). The refugees now entering the United States are more like the "new immigrants" than like other immigrants, and they have benefited from government programs aimed at helping them make a smooth transition to life in the United States. Generally speaking, refugees have not been oppressed in the United States, and probably should not be thought of as subordinated minorities (Longres, 1990).

Another group of people who have entered the United States in more recent times could be called "entrants," for lack of a better name, as they entered the United states illegally. They have not received as much help as the Indochinese. These are the Haitians. Refugees receive help for three years, but the entrants receive far less help, although they have the same problems as other refugees. Unlike the earlier Haitians who entered the country in the 1960s and who were qualified professionals, the present group consists of people of peasant ancestry, who are fleeing from political repression and poverty. Often these people are held in detention camps and in some cases have been deported back to Haiti. They also suffer from constant fear of deportation, which includes not just fear of poverty but also fear of death. This fear is real, because they left their own country without permission. Under a new act called the Immigration Reform and Control Act (1986), entrants who are qualified aliens in the category of "Cuban/Haitian Entrant (Status Pending)" are eligible to apply for permanent-residence status. However, Cubans and Haitians who are people of color are discriminated against and treated very differently. As noted, Haitians have been held in detention camps, and a number of them have been deported. The fear of AIDS, which is rife in Haiti, plays a role, too.

Undocumented or illegal aliens constitute another group of people who enter the United States because they wish to better their lives. The actual number of illegal aliens in the country is not known, but about a decade ago it was estimated to be as high as 8 million. Bernard (1980) states that about 500,000 illegal aliens are arrested and deported every year, according to U.S. Immigration and Naturalization Service (INS) reports. According to the U.S. Immigration and Naturalization Service (1992) there was a total of 3.2 million illegal aliens from different African countries and this number is trebled when all the countries are taken into consideration. Often illegal aliens come because they want a better life in this country. Also, U.S. businesses—for example, the orange and grapefruit plantations owned by big corporations—employ illegal aliens in places such as Florida and California. It is not just big businesses who exploit illegal aliens, however. Most aliens are hired by labor-intensive, marginal, small businesses, such as clothing "sweat shops," or by upper-middle-class professionals for child care and household services. The employment of large numbers of these people is concentrated in Florida and southern California as well as other U.S.–Mexico border states, but the problem is nationwide and has reached epidemic proportions in some areas. Illegal immigration is encouraged because the workers are employed by big businesses, but they are exploited by being hired as low-wage workers without benefits. Lacking Social Security numbers, they are not eligible for any provision for their health or old age. Portes (1979) emphasizes that these people are not looking for a handout, but for honest work to fulfill basic needs. Illegal immigration is not always permanent, but may be cyclical: People are moving back and forth between countries as opportunities become available, being caught and sent back to their own countries, and then returning to the United States.

The majority of illegal aliens are from Mexico, although they are certainly not the only group. Others come from Haiti, the Dominican Republic, Guatemala, Honduras, El Salvador, Canada, Ireland, and Israel. Most Mexicans are legal residents. The large influx of illegal aliens are people from rural areas; faced with chronic unemployment and poverty, they may become illegal aliens as a last resort. Remember, they are welcome cheap labor. Cortes (1980) indicates that less than 4% of them had their children in schools and only 0.5% were on welfare. All types of special services are needed to help them understand, accommodate, and either adjust or return to their homelands. There is considerable exploitation of illegal aliens in the United States, where such people may live under inhumane conditions, make minimum wages, and depend on their employers in unfair ways.

A major problem is that different ethnic groups may not join each other to gain empowerment. Rather, they are fragmented and constantly fight with each other. Often such minorities are fighting for the same scarce jobs, so they see each other as rivals. The rivalry blocks mutual cooperation to fight racism. In the chaos, the larger problem of institutional racism is overlooked.

It is important to learn about refugees and undocumented aliens, as they are often brought to the attention of social services and other helping professions. The philosophy of our profession advocates that we help people by being sensitive to their history, background, and needs, without further alienating them from a people and a culture they do not readily understand.

Gay and Lesbian Communities

The recent emergence of the gay and lesbian communities into public awareness shows how communities develop in any social environment. A chief feature that distinguishes gay and lesbian communities and makes them unique is that for the most part, gays and lesbians are not socialized into the homosexual community as children, and therefore did not learn their roles, values, and expectations of the society in the process of growing up. Often they learn to become members of the homosexual society after they have "come out" and make a conscious choice to become members of that community. The stigma they face encourages them to be secretive and on guard in relating to heterosexual people (Warren, 1974).

The terms *gay culture* and *lesbian culture* refer to attitudes, experiences, lifestyles, behaviors, and a sense of shared history common to gays and lesbians in the United States (Cruikshank, 1992, p. 119). As we are well aware, homosexuals have been devalued, and have experienced hostility and powerlessness. There is a great deal of oppression of homosexuals because of homophobia—irrational fears, or hatred toward homosexuals. Examples of discrimination abound. One naval officer stationed in Virginia mentioned that he was gay, for example; he was promptly released from line duty and given a desk job. An even more extreme example is that of a sailor who was apparently murdered by a shipmate after he announced that he was gay. The belief system that supports such misconceptions and stereotypes is a constant life stressor for homosexuals.

Because of such disrespect and hostility, an estimated 10% of our population, or about 23 million people, live under the constant threat of being deprived of their human rights. They suffer real losses in jobs, housing, friends, and family. On July 12, 1996, the U.S. House of Representatives in Washington, DC, approved the Defense of Marriage Act by an overwhelming 342–67 vote; clearly, most lawmakers were united against legalizing gay marriage (Siegel, *The Daily Herald,* July 27, 1996, p. 1).

Gay bashing in public places is also increasing in some areas, such as some university settings. Gays and lesbians have asked to be recognized as any other minority group, but their struggle has been long and lonely. An early defender of homosexual rights, Core (1963), commented,

> Our minority status is similar, in a variety of respects, to that of national, religious and other ethnic groups: in the denial of civil liberties, in the legal, extralegal and quasi-legal discrimination; in the assignment of an inferior social position, in the exclusion from the mainstream of life and culture, in the development of the protection and security intragroup association, in the development of a special language and literature and a set of moral tenets within our group.

Altman (1993) notes that the objection to gays and lesbians is deeply seated: It is threatening because it challenges the conventional sex and gender roles in society. Asserting that one is a gay or lesbian clearly challenges the *apparent* naturalness of gender roles.

In 1993 there was a historic march of 1 million gay people in Washington, DC. According to *The Virginian-Pilot & Ledger-Star* (April 25, 1993), half a dozen officials took that opportunity to "come out"—to make known their own homosexuality for the first time. As the newspaper reports, from the Lincoln Memorial to the U.S. Capitol, there were thousands of homosexuals, demanding more spending on AIDS, honoring their military dead, and just plain having a good time.

Discrimination has been challenged in a strong civil-rights movement by gays and lesbians, supported by sympathetic heterosexuals. As Sen. Edward Kennedy (Democrat, Massachusetts) commented in *The Virginian-Pilot & Ledger-Star* (April 26, 1993), "We stand again at the crossroads of national conscience" (p. A1). Kennedy, who spoke by way of a taped audio message, likened the rally to the 1963 civil-rights march in Washington. Laws that prohibit discrimination on the basis of sexual preference have been passed in some states and cities. In Chicago in 1988, a "gay rights" ordinance was renamed as a human-rights ordinance and passed by a vote of 28–17. It provides protection against discrimination in housing, employment, and public accommodations that was not only extended to homosexuals but also to others whose marital status or parental status, military discharge, or source of income could have been a source of discrimination. Thus discrimination on the basis of race, sex, and age were also made illegal (Longres, 1990).

A "gay-liberation front" has emerged, supported by a number of gay and lesbian civil rights organizations, newspapers, journals, movies, magazines, and social and service clubs. Today the gay-rights agenda is pursued by well-financed gay and lesbian organizations that engage in sophisticated lobbying and other political activities. Its main purpose is to do away with all laws and practices in the United States that discriminate against gays and to extend to gay people the protections of the Civil Rights Act, which would make them equal citizens under the law (Queralt, 1996). High on their agenda are the following goals, as Cruikshank (1992) lists them: (1) to end housing and job discrimination on the basis of sexual orientation; (2) to repeal the remaining sodomy laws; (3) to stop discrimination in the military, in federal security clearances, and in areas of family law such as custody, visitation, adoption, and foster care; (4) to end the remaining traces of police harassment; (5) to stop antigay violence; and (6) to end AIDS-related discrimination.

Homosexuals are part of every racial, religious, and ethnic group, and of every socioeconomic status. The richness and diversity of the community has been described in a number of works (Bell & Weinberg, 1986). Highly talented gays and lesbians have been heavily represented in the arts and have made major contributions to literature, theater, and dance.

Although the social-work profession was a relative latecomer to more progressive views (DeCrescenzo, 1984), the profession has now taken a strongly affirmative stance, reflected in the National Association of Social Workers' (NASW) 1994 policy statement on lesbian and gay issues: "NASW shall support legislation, regulation, policies, judicial review, political action, changes in social work policy statements, the *Code of Ethics* and any other means to establish and protect equal rights of all people without regard to sexual orientation" (p. 163).

Social services to gays and lesbians and their families involve interventions with individuals, families, groups, communities, and organizations. Practice modalities used with gays and lesbians do not differ significantly from those used with other populations, but when providing services practitioners need to be aware of both their own internalized homophobia and their client's sexual orientation. Social workers need knowledge of gay and lesbian subcultures, social-work methods, and personal values and feelings about homosexuality, and they need a desire to provide services to an increasingly visible but legally ostracized group (Tully, 1995).

Women as a "Minority"

Of the 245 million people in the United States in 1989, 126 million (51%) were women. Of this female population, approximately 97 million, that is, 77%, were white, 16 million (13%) were African American, about 9 million (7%) were of Hispanic origin, and 4 million (3%) belonged to other races and ethnic groups (U.S. Bureau of the Census, 1990).

Sexual inequality, often overlooked or not understood by men, has been a major part of a woman's struggle to be an equal partner in the economics of living. Gender inequality and oppression of women has hindered the acceptance of women in society as anything other than wives, mothers, and sex objects. Women have been treated as inferior, and have been stereotyped as less able than men. The analysis of women by psychologists has been influenced by the father of psychoanalysis, Sigmund Freud, who viewed women as unequal to men. Seeing women as having meaning only in the *man's* life cycle, as Gilligan (1982) indicates, entails seeing women's lives as having economic place only as they relate to the economic life of man.

Women are socialized to be different from men. As Gilligan (1982) indicates, the early environment differs from and is experienced differently by both male and female children, and therefore basic differences occur in personalities. These are, however, the result of socialization, not genetics.

Life expectancy for women is longer than for men in all societies. On an average, white males born in 1990 are expected to live 72.6 years, and white women, 79.3 years. Expectancy for African-American women is 74.5 years, and for males, 66 years (U.S. Public Health Service, 1992).

This disparity between men and women's longevity has critical social consequences for women. Because they live longer, they need more retirement income for longer periods than men. However, the lifelong lower economic status of women leaves many women poor in their old age. Our society has failed to provide long-term care of the frail elderly population, and this impacts women more heavily than men (Gottlieb, 1995).

In terms of employment, even when women hold the same position as a man and spend the same amount of work time, they make lower wages and salaries than men. As the top of the promotion pyramid narrows, the chances of women getting to the top declines; men are more readily chosen for top executive positions.

The developing awareness in the general population of socialized differences between men and women's psychology is encouraging efforts to provide equality and equity for women. The feminist movement has made some progress in achieving gender justice. Change has occurred with reference to some occupations and professions. For the past three decades, there have also been changes in the elementary and secondary school curricula, in reproductive care for women, and in awareness and services for battered women and rape victims.

However, the position of women has a long way to go. *The Virginian-Pilot & Ledger-Star,* (February 22, 1993, p. A3) reports that women on Capitol Hill say they face harassment and bias. The *Washington Post* News Service reports that "women working on Capitol Hill say they routinely lose out on pay and promotions to male colleagues; a third of those women questioned in a *Washington Post* survey also report they had been sexually harassed by co-workers, supervisors, lobbyists or congressmen or senators." A majority of 603 female employees interviewed also said women working for Congress are less respected and valued than their male colleagues, problems that concerned these women even more than sexual harassment. They talked about a still-dominant male culture on the Hill that made even senior female staff feel like "outsiders" and even intruders. "You see it at meetings where women kind of vanish into the woodwork, even when their issues are discussed," said a legislative assistant. Often men view women as all being alike. For instance, a male junior executive will be viewed as such, whereas a female junior executive must prove that she is not *just* a woman or a "young thing," to be lumped together with a young receptionist—whose duties also may call for a stereotyped female role. The young female executive must prove that she is *not* "just" another woman but has different intellectual talents. "National polls repeatedly show that a majority of women—like female congressional workers interviewed by the Post—believe they are treated like second-class citizens. Studies show that female workers still lag behind men in terms of pay and opportunities for advancement on the job" (*The Virginian-Pilot & Ledger-Star,* February 22, 1993).

Race issues have different effects on how women feel about themselves. The African-American experience of being a woman has been different from that of white and Hispanic women. African-American women have worked outside the home for so many generations that the idea of women in the workplace has not been revolutionary for them. Moreover, African-American women continue to be at the bottom of the economic ladder. Also, African-American women have been heading families in large proportions for at least 60 years, so the balance of power in the family did not shift dramatically, as in white families when the wife went to work. Yet the women's movement, although frowned on as a product of white culture, has had its effects on African Americans as well. Many African-American men identify with women's demands and view them as an outgrowth of the civil-rights movement (Astrachan, 1991). However, the plight of African-American women is still one of surviving in a country where competition for jobs is high and one's ability to get a job may be blocked by discrimination.

Another ugly problem that plagues women is domestic violence, both emotional and physical. Definitive statistics on domestic violence are difficult to obtain, as women are reluctant to report it. Researchers estimate that at least half of all women are battered at some time in their lives (Walker, 1989), and that 1.5 million women are assaulted by their partners each year (Fagan, 1988). Some feel these estimates are too low (Strauss & Gelles, 1988). It is estimated that 90–95% of the victims of domestic assaults are women (Dobash, Wilson, & Daly, 1992). Domestic violence exists in all groups—ethnic, racial, religious, social, and economic. About 31% of all women killed in the United States are murdered by their husbands, ex-husbands, or boyfriends (Randall, 1990).

When women finally leave abusive husbands, it has been found they do not feel safe, because they have been followed and harassed for months or years. Most battered women (72% in one study) asserted that the emotional abuse they underwent was far worse than the physical abuse (Follingstad, Rutledge, Berg, Hause, & Polek, 1990).

Social workers have taken part in efforts to provide services that recognize sexism. A growing literature of feminist practice (Bricker-Jenkins, Huyman, & Gottlieb, 1991) describes interventions aimed at empowering women and counteracting the effects of bias and discrimination against them. These principles help enlarge the social-work profession's commitment to correct injustice and to understand the impact of society on individual women.

Feminist organizing is an example of a balanced form of macro practice. Feminist organizing is about changing power structures and processes in order to achieve gender equity. Both men and women can be beneficiaries and supporters of feminist endeavors (Hyde, 1996). As Newsome indicates (1997) "strategic planning has become the method of choice for social work organizations in their attempts to determine future direction. Complex organizational structures and fluctuating internal environments have often served as the stimuli for this type of social planning" (p. 1). Strategic planning is especially useful with reference to feminist organizing.

In working with women, social workers need to be sensitive to the social and economic position and needs of women in this culture. Often, women need help to become assertive and be able to take care of themselves, because being self-dependent goes a long way to ensure the growth and stability of a family. As an Eastern saying indicates, "When you educate a man, you have educated *him,* but when you educate a woman you have educated a *family.*"

IMPLICATIONS FOR SOCIAL-WORK PRACTICE

While working with people in communities, the worker must be sensitive to the needs of the individuals in the community and know how to bring about change. In working with members of communities, the worker needs to think in terms of empowerment of people and to take a strengths perspective.

The strengths perspective becomes particularly useful when we think in terms of identificational communities. Such communities are important to social workers because many patterns of behavior, attitudes, and values are derived from people's everyday experiences in communities. Some social and psychological problems experienced by individuals and families in communities are related to or originate from public issues in communities. For instance, if Social Security benefits are reduced suddenly for the new elderly, that would cause economic hardship for a large number of people. Communities generally support their members, so it is best to build strengths and resources in communities to help individuals and families cope and adapt. Social workers must be alert and attentive to the community context of client behavior (Longres, 1990).

The worker should be sensitive and empathetic to be an effective helper not only of the individual client but also of the community and its institutions. When things do go wrong in a helping situation, look at the cultural gaps. How do people talk and behave with each other? A white or an African-American worker may make mistakes in evaluating their clients, based on assumptions they make about each other. Similarly, a person from a wealthy Catholic background may not know how to deal with a poverty-ridden Southern Baptist family.

The worker needs to be aware of status differences in the social group he or she is dealing with. For example, a person belonging to a lower status may strive to reach a higher status by working hard, and a person of higher status who has faced a number of financial losses may strive to maintain what he or she has been used to. When resources and opportunities are limited, this striving can create conflicts. A person who is used to luxuries may perceive them as *necessities* and may be frustrated if he or she cannot have them. Building a relationship may also entail other differences than culture and status. It may also include attitudes and behaviors.

One purpose for understanding communities is to help social workers anticipate potential difficulties in working with clients. Clients may not communicate well due to differences in attitudes, values, norms, and traditions. As we saw, newcomers to this country have a special set of problems to deal with. Because of educational background and occupational skills, some are better prepared to achieve socioeconomic success. Social services may not be easily available to these people. And undocumented aliens, looking for work, may fear that they may be expelled from the country.

The task of the social-work practitioner is to help immigrants make the transition into this culture, keeping in mind the presence of institutional racism in our country and the feelings associated with it. The worker can help through advocacy, by providing appropriate services, as well as by making other needed services available.

In working with new arrivals, the worker also helps socialize the client to attitudes, values, norms, and traditions of U.S. society. New arrivals need not overlook their culture, but do need to develop a sense of *cultural pluralism,* because the United States is becoming culturally diverse. A similar value is the idea of *biculturalism*—being able to function competently within the norms, traditions, and values of both one's own culture and the culture of the United States. New arrivals, particularly refugees and illegal aliens, need to learn to function effectively in the American culture while holding on to positive aspects of their own heritage. They can be helped best by social workers who are themselves bilingual or by using translators and models from the same ethnic group to help clients develop an understanding of the majority culture while maintaining their own values, behavior patterns, and heritage.

When working with communities, we need to think in terms of people power. Workers in a community can aim for local empowerment. The worker should help people achieve their potential, improve their lives, and expand their sense of efficacy.

As Rubin and Rubin (1992) remark, people do not create all their own problems. Many problems are created for them in society. For example, sexism is a structural problem, a problem that women face and suffer because of their membership in a particular group. Thus the worker should help women clients to see the larger picture and to avoid blaming themselves for situations over which they have little or no control. In addition, the social worker must identify and intervene in aspects of problem situations that can be changed either in a specific case, or on a broader community level, through such measures as class-action suits and lobbying for legislative changes against gender discrimination. Of course, a worker cannot offer such solutions unless the community has an organized sense of shared problems and some degree of trust in the worker.

Another role the worker can take in working with people in communities is that of an advocate. The advocate-practitioner works for people such as the homeless and members from families of domestic violence. The worker's role as an advocate is to push for programs that enable people—such as the homeless, victims of domestic violence, the unemployed, and the ill-housed—to gain the resources they need to solve their problems. The worker can take the role of an empowerer, motivating people to realize that they can solve problems they face, and make effective decisions about their lives. Collective action is working together to solve shared problems.

People in communities are empowered when they work together to handle neighborhood problems that the authorities have not taken care of. Neighborhood members can join together to harass and drive drug dealers out, as seen in one community in Washington, DC: "Today, children are playing again on the sidewalks and in the yards of Fairlawn. People can walk to the market or stand at the bus stop without encountering whispering young men consummating drug deals" (Ayres, 1989, p. 14). Empowering people uses both personal and political links in the social network. When people are stepped on and exploited, they suffer from private fears, which may be reinforced by bureaucrats in unemployment offices and by other professions, such as some medical doctors in public clinics and hospitals, some bankers, the media, and some businesspeople. Empowering a person creates a bridge between the personal and the political spheres and reduces the humiliation that keeps people helpless (Rubin & Rubin, 1992).

In many situations, particularly when dealing with people of color, some disempowerment is caused by constant put-downs, subtle or overt, by people in authority. People may end up blaming themselves for their hurt and lack of success. Personal humiliation keeps people silent about their hurt and keeps them from joining together and fighting back. Embarrassment may take over; people pretend that it does not matter, that things do not really hurt them. Thus social manipulation leads to disempowerment; people learn inefficacy, which keeps them down. The worker can empower such people by helping them recognize that the personal hurt is socially caused and should be remedied through joint action. This is where the private and the public meet (hooks, 1989).

Thus the backgrounds of the people and the community are important factors in the helping process. At times, the worker helps a single person or family in a community to fight injustices or problems of living due to differences in culture and racial/ethnic background. At times, the whole community may need help, which may be as simple (or as complex) as helping it understand its own strengths and empowering it as a group to handle issues constructively and in an organized, efficient manner. Whichever group or person the worker deals with, the worker should be sensitive and empathetic, move toward empowerment, and build positive self-esteem through constructive help and action.

Other implications for work in communities include the following. Community work requires more than goodwill and good intentions. It calls for applying of a set of values, a body of knowledge, and a bagful of skills to work with specific, realistic problem-solving objectives. To achieve tangible results, a broad, abstract goal such as "empowerment" must be made concrete: for example, "driving the drug dealers away from Norfolk" or "developing a shelter and treatment program for victims of domestic violence."

It is important for clinicians as well as administrators and community organizers to understand communities. A worker should be able to intervene within a client's social environment—that is, family and community—as well as understand interventions with the individual.

Finally, it is important to recognize that an inevitable aspect of community dynamics is conflict—economic and political interests, social and cultural values, and personalities all conflict. In addition to having specific, realistic objectives, the worker needs to understand the opposition and develop a strategy for dealing with it. Community work, like individual or family work, is never smooth sailing, but the strategy of empowerment eventually pays off.

SUMMARY

A community is a group of people with common ties. Vertical communities consist of people with similar interests, such as professionals and businesspeople. In horizontal communities, people of different backgrounds and interests may get together in the same neighborhood to share common concerns or arrange a block party. Communities are created out of need; they evolve and eventually die, but they are more stable than other social systems and can survive for decades or centuries.

The five major functions of a community include: production-distribution-consumption, socialization, social control, social participation, and mutual support. All communities have a structure marked by degrees of differentiation, centrality, and solidarity.

The community is a holistic system, and is larger than the sum of its parts—people and places are interconnected and interrelated. There is also an interblending of individual and community problems. For example, AIDS, homelessness, preteen drinking, and drug use are becoming serious problems in a number of communities.

Bernard has classified communities as locational, identificational, and interest communities. Community characteristics include race, ethnicity, age composition, and socioeconomic status. The type of community life is affected by newspapers, radios, and TV stations and their influence on community members.

Communities develop linkages that become important networks in people's lives. Internal, vertical top–down linkages; internal, vertical bottom–up linkages; internal horizontal linkages; external, vertical top–down linkages; external, vertical bottom–up linkages; and external horizontal linkages all are prevalent in communities.

Some communities are based on community functions and may be either loosely knit or closed. For example, people of different ethnic groups often get together because a community offers identity, competence, and self-direction, with a sense of belonging to a group. One such community is the complex network of extended African-American families, its churches, and mutual-aid societies that support the ethos of economic uplift and self-help.

The Hispanic population, dominated by Mexican Americans, Cubans, and Puerto-Ricans, forms the largest ethnic minority. Although they have demographic and socioeconomic differences, these cultures share familism: pride in extended families, for which the kinship network offers reciprocal support and obligation. Folk healers, religion, social clubs, and machismo are also part of these cultures.

Native Americans are a diverse group with a number of tribes and cultures. They are split between those who live on the reservations and those who live in central cities and small towns. A major problem facing Native Americans is that a third lives below the poverty level. Their level of unemployment is nearly three times as high as whites, and about 62% live on or near reservations as marginally employed or unemployed people. Prejudice and discrimination have marred life for Native Americans, although this is slowly changing.

Asian groups differ a great deal in terms of culture, language, and religion. The most populous groups stem from China, Japan, Korea, India, and the Philippines. The newer immigrants come from higher socioeconomic classes than their predecessors. Although they differ greatly in history and background, they also share a number of similarities, such as family orientation and respect for elders. There is tremendous unrest among the younger Asians, and there is a large generation gap between the older groups and the younger members born in the United States.

The "new immigrants" enter under the quota system. They have occupational skills that make it possible for them to succeed more quickly than immigrants of the past. Another sizable group of people are the refugees, who, unlike immigrants, have been forced out of their countries by ethnic, religious, or political conflict. Another group of immigrants, called "entrants," enter the United States on their own, fleeing from political repression and poverty. A major problem of these minorities is that they often do not join each other to empower themselves; they are fragmented and constantly fight with each other for jobs. In the conflict, the larger problem of institutional racism is overlooked.

In some religious communities, 68% of the Americans belong to a church or synagogue, and 40% regularly attend church or some form of organized religion. The church has played an important role in the lives of Americans. It has been a source of support and comfort, and in some cases the center for cultural and social activities. A person often finds a mate in a church setting. Religion in many ways shapes life, attitudes, and philosophy for a large number of people, including the elderly.

The gay and lesbian communities have recently emerged into public awareness. Lesbian and gay communities are usually identifiable because their members have similar sexual preferences and share a common identity. Homosexuals have been devalued and have experienced hostility and powerlessness. In more recent times, such discrimination has been challenged in strong civil-rights movements by gays and lesbians.

Sexual inequality (often overlooked or not understood by men) has been a major part of women's struggle to be equal partners in economic life. Gender discrimination and maltreatment have hindered the acceptance of women as equal in society. The developing awareness of socialized differences between men and women's psychology has helped improve women's position, and the feminist movement has achieved some progress in gender justice. Race may affect how women feel about themselves, as among African-American and Hispanic women. Women are beginning to care about each other and look out for each other.

SUGGESTED READINGS

Bewley, C., & Glendinning, C. (1994). Representing the views of disabled people in community care planning. Special issue: Representation and disabled people. *Disability and Society, 9*(3), 301–314.

Drug use, drug prohibition, and minority communities. (1995, Summer). Special issue: Legalization of drugs. *Journal of Primary Prevention, 12*(4), 303–316.

Gougeon, T. D. (1993, December). Urban schools and immigrant families: Teacher perspectives. *Urban Review, 25*(4), 251–287.

Okocha, A. A. G. (1994, April). Preparing racial and ethnic minorities for the work force 2000. *Journal of Multicultural Counseling and Development, 22*(2), 106–114.

Sagiv, L., & Schwartz, S. H. (1995, September). Value priorities and readiness for out-group social contact. *Journal of Personality and Social Psychology, 69*(3), 437–448.

Shonholtz, R. (1993, Spring). The role of minorities in establishing mediating norms and institutions in the new democracies. Special issue: Developing mediating processes in the new democracies. *Mediation Quarterly, 10*(3), 231–241.

SUGGESTED VIDEOTAPES

America's war on poverty: City of promise. (1995). Blackside, Inc. Public Broadcasting System, 6360 La Pas Trail, Indianapolis, IN 46268. 59 minutes.

Biculturalism and acculturation. (1991). KLRN. Films for the Humanities and Sciences, 11 Perrine Road, Monmouth Junction, NJ 08852. 28 minutes.

Fire eyes—female circumcision. (1994). Soraya Mire. Filmmakers Library, 124 E. 40th Street, Suite 901, New York, NY 10016. 59 minutes.

Latino family. (1993). KLRN. Films for the Humanities and Sciences, 11 Perrine Road, Monmouth Junction, NJ 08852. 28 minutes.

Right to their own lands. (1993). CTE Ltd. Films for the Humanities and Sciences, 11 Perrine Road, Monmouth Junction, NJ 08852. 28 minutes.

Solving black inner-city poverty: William Julius Wilson. (1989). Public Affairs TV. KLRN. Films for the Humanities and Sciences, 11 Perrine Road, Monmouth Junction, NJ 08852. 29 minutes.

REFERENCES

Altman, D. (1993). Why gay men are so feared. In V. Cyrus (ed.), *Experiencing race, class and gender in the United States*. Mountain View, CA: Mayfield, pp. 69–70.

Alvirez, D., & Bean, F. D. (1976). The Mexican American family. In C. H. Mindel and R. W. Habenstein (eds.), *Ethnic families in America: Patterns and variations*. New York: Elsevier, pp. 271–292.

Astrachain, T. (1993). Dividing lines. In V. Cyrus (ed.), *Experiencing race, class and gender in the United States*. Mountain View, CA: Mayfield, pp. 86–91.

Ayres, B. D. (1989, August 20). Neighbors unite and score a victory in capital's drug war. *New York Times,* p. 14.

Backwell, J. (1985). *The black community: Diversity and unity*. New York: Dodd, Mead, p. 14.

Barbarian, O. A. (1981). Community competence: An individual systems model of institutional racism. In O. A. Barbarian, P. R. Good, M. Pharr, & J. A. Siskind (eds.), *Institutional racism and community competence*. DHHS Publication No. (ADM) 81–907. Rockville, MD: NIMH Center for Minority Groups Mental Health Programs, pp. 6–19.

Barnlund, D. C. (1989). *Communicative styles of Japanese and Americans: Images and reality*. Belmont, CA: Wadsworth.

Bell, C. C., & Jenkins, E. J. (1990). Preventing black homicide. In J. Stewart (ed.), *The state of black America*. Washington, DC: Urban League.

Bernard, J. (1973). *The sociology of community*. Glenview, IL: Scott, Foresman.

Bernard, W. S. (1980). Immigration: History of U.S. policy. In S. Thernstorm (ed.), *Harvard encyclopedia of American ethnic groups*. Cambridge, MA: Belknap Press, pp. 486–500.

Billingsley, A. (1992). *Climbing Jacob's ladder: The enduring legacy of African-American families*. New York: Simon & Schuster.

Blanchard, E. L., & Unger, S. (1977, May). Editorial notes: Destruction of American Indian families. *Social Casework, 58,* 312–314.

Blau, P. M., & Scott, W. R. (1962). *Formal organizations*. San Francisco: Chandler.

Bricker-Jenkins, M. (1991). The propositions and assumptions of feminist social work practice. In N. Huyman, M. Bricker-Jenkins, & N. Gottlieb (eds.), *Feminist social work in clinical settings*. Newbury Park, CA: Sage, pp. 271–303.

Burma, J. H. (1970). *Mexican Americans in the United States*. Cambridge, MA: Schenkman, pp. 20–24.

Cameron, B. (1993). "Gee, you don't seem like an Indian from the reservation." In V. Cyrus (ed.), *Experiencing race, class and gender in the United States*. Mountain View, CA: Mayfield, pp. 202–205.

Carpenter, E. M. (1980, October). Social service, policies, and issues. *Social Casework 61,* 455–461.

Corey, D. W. (1963). *The homosexual in America*. New York: Paperback Library, p. 24.

Corner, J. (1972). *Beyond black and white*. New York: Quadrangle, New York Times Books.

Cortes, C. E. (1980). Mexicans. In S. Thernstrom (ed.), *Harvard University encyclopedia of American ethnic groups*. Cambridge, MA: Belknap Press, p. 699.

Cruikshank, M. (1992). *The gay and lesbian liberation movement*. New York: Routledge.

DeCrescenzo, T. A. (1984). Homophobia: A study of the attitudes of mental health professionals toward homosexuality. In R. Schoenberg, R. S. Goldberg, & D. A. Shore (eds.), *Homosexuality and social work*. New York: Haworth Press.

Delgado, M., & Humm-Delgado, D. (1982, January). Natural systems: Source of strength in Hispanic communities. *Social Work, 27,* 83–89.

Digest of Educational Statistics. (1992). Washington, DC: Office of Educational Research and Improvement, U.S. Department of Education.

Dobash, R. E., Wilson, M., & Daly, M. (1992). The myth of sexual symmetry in marital violence. *Social Problems, 39,* 71–91.

Erikson, E. H. (1963). *Childhood and society*. New York: Norton.

Erlanger, H., with Persily, F. (1976). *Estrangement, machismo and gang violence*. Unpublished paper. Institute for Research on Poverty, University of Wisconsin at Madison.

Everett, F., Proctor, N., & Cartmell, B. (1983). Providing psychological services to American Indian children and families. *Professional Psychology, 14,* 588–603.

Fagan, J. (1988). Contributions of family violence research to criminal justice policy on wife assault. *Violence and Victims, 3,* 159–186.

Follingstad, D. R., Rutledge, L., Berg, B. J., Hause, E. S., & Polek, D. S. (1990). The role of emotional abuse in physically abusive relationships. *Journal of Family Violence, 5,* 107–120.

Franklin, J. H., & Norton, E. A. (eds.). (1989). *Black initiative and governmental responsibility: An essay on policy for racial justice*. Washington, DC: Joint Center for Political and Economic Studies, pp. 3–4.

Furuto, S. M., Biswas, R., Chung, D. K., Murase, K., & Ross-Sheriff, F. (eds.). (1992). *Social work practice with Asian Americans*. Newbury Park, CA: Sage.

Germain, C. B. (1991). *Human behavior in the social environment*. New York: Columbia University Press.

Gilligan, C. (1982). *In a different voice*. Cambridge, MA: Harvard University Press.

Gottlieb, N. (1995). Women: Overview. In *Encyclopedia of social work* (19th ed.). Washington DC: NASW [National Association of Social Workers] Press, pp. 2518–2528.

Gottschalk, S. (1978, Fall). *The community in America*. Lecture in general systems theory for social workers. School of Social Work, Florida State University, Tallahassee.

Hacker, A. (1993). Two nations: Black and white—separate, hostile, unequal. In *The state of black America 1993*. New York: National Urban League.

Haglund, E. (1988). Japan: Cultural considerations. In L. A. Samovar & R. E. Porter (eds.), *Intercultural communication: A reader* (5th ed.). Belmont, CA: Wadsworth, pp. 84–94.

Harrison, D. F., Wodarski, J. S., & Thyer, B. A. (eds.). (1992). *Cultural diversity and social work practice*. Springfield, IL: Charles C Thomas.

Hatchett, S. J., & Jackson, J. S. (1993). African American extended kin systems. In H. P. McAdoo (ed.), *Family ethnicity: Strength in diversity*. Newbury Park, CA: Sage, pp. 90–108.

Heinrich, R. K., Corbine, J. L., & Thomas, K. R. (1990). Counseling Native Americans. *Journal of Counseling and Development, 69,* 128–133.

Henderson, G. (1989). *A practitioner's guide to understanding indigenous and foreign cultures*. Springfield, IL: Charles C Thomas.

Ho, M. K. (1976). Social work with Asian Americans. *Social Casework, 57,* 195–201.

Ho, M. K. (1987). Family therapy with American Indians and Alaskan Natives. In M. K. Ho (ed.), *Family therapy with ethnic minorities.* Newbury Park, CA: Sage, pp. 69–83.

hooks, b. (1989). *Talking back: Thinking feminist, thinking black.* Boston: South End Press.

Howard, J. R. (ed.). (1970). *Awakening minorities.* New Brunswick, NJ: Transaction Books, p. 3.

Howells, W. W. (1971). The meaning of race. In R. H. Osborne (ed.), *The biological and social meaning of race.* San Francisco, CA: W. H. Freeman, p. 3.

Hyde, C. (1996). A feminist response to Rothman's "The interweaving of community intervention approaches." *Journal of Community Practice, 3,* 127–145.

Johnson, L. C. (1983). *Social work practice: A generalist approach.* Boston: Allyn and Bacon.

Johnston, L., O'Malley, P., & Bachman, J. (1993, April 14). *The Virginian-Pilot & Ledger-Star,* p. A5.

Kennedy, E. (1993, April 26). *The Virginian-Pilot & Ledger-Star,* p. A1.

Kwong, P. (1987). *The new Chinatown.* New York: Hill & Wang.

Lewis, R., & Ho, M. (1989). Social work with Native Americans. In D. Atkinson, G. Morton, & D. Sue (eds.), *Counseling American minorities.* Dubuque, IA: William C. Brown, pp. 51–58.

Lincoln, C. E., & Mamiya, L. H. (1990). *The black church in the African-American experience.* Durham, NC: Duke University Press.

Locke, D. C. (1992). *Increasing multicultural understanding: A comprehensive model.* Newbury Park, CA: Sage.

Longres, J. F. (1990). *Human behavior in the social environment.* Itasca, IL: Peacock.

Lum, D. (1995). *Social work practice and people of color* (3rd ed.). Pacific Grove, CA: Brooks/Cole.

Majka, L. C., & Donnelly, P. G. (1988). Cohesiveness within a heterogenous urban neighborhood: Implications for a community in a diverse setting. *Journal of Urban Affairs, 10*(2), 141–160.

Martin, P. Y., & O'Connor, G. G. (1989). *The social environment.* New York: Longman.

Martinez-Brawley, E., & Blundall, J. (1989). Farm families' preference toward the personal social services. *Social Work, 6,* 513–522.

McIntyre, E. L. G. (1986). Social networks: Potential for practice. *Social Work, 31,* 421–426.

Mead, M. (1970). *Culture and commitment.* New York: Doubleday, p. 31.

Medina, C. (1987, January–February). Latino culture and sex education. *SIECUS Report, 15*(3), 1–4.

Moore, J. W., & Pachon, H. (1976). *Mexican Americans* (2nd ed.). Englewood Cliffs, NJ: Prentice Hall.

Moses, A. E., & Hawkins, R. O. (1982). *Counseling lesbian women and gay men: A life issues approach.* St. Louis: Mosby.

Naisbitt, J. (1982). *Megatrends: Ten new questions transforming our lives.* New York: Warner Books.

National Association of Social Workers (NASW). (1994). *Lesbian and gay issues: Social work speaks* (3rd ed.). Silver Spring, MD: NASW Press, pp. 162–165.

Newman, W. M. (1973). *American pluralism: A study of minority groups and social theory*. New York: Harper & Row, p. 21.

Newsome, M. (1997). Strategic planning for the 21st century. *Social Work Education Reporter, 45*(1), 1.

Nisbet, R. A. (1966). *The sociological tradition*. New York: Basic Books.

Panzetta, A. F. (1983). The concept of community: The short circuit of the mental health movement. In R. M. Kramer & H. Specht (eds.), *Readings in community organization practice* (3rd ed.). Englewood Cliffs, NJ: Prentice Hall.

Pinderhughes, E. (1979, July). Teaching empathy in cross-cultural social work. *Social Work, 24,* 312–316.

Poplin, D. E. (1979). *Communities* (2nd ed.). New York: Macmillan.

Portes, A. (1979). Illegal immigration and the international system. Lessons from recent legal Mexican immigrants in the United States. *Social Problems, 26,* 425–427.

Queralt, M. (1984, March–April). Understanding Cuban immigrants: A cultural perspective. *Social Work, 29,* 115–121.

Queralt, M. (1996). *The social environment and human behavior: A diversity perspective*. Boston, MA: Allyn and Bacon.

Randall, T. C. (1990). Domestic violence intervention calls for more than beating injuries. *Journal of the American Medical Association, 264,* 939–940.

Rubin, H. J., & Rubin, I. S. (1992). *Community organizing and development* (2nd ed.). New York: Macmillan.

Sandoval, M. C., & de la Roza, M. C. (1986). A cultural perspective for serving Hispanic clients. In H. P. Lefley & P. B. Pedersen (eds.), *Cross-cultural training for mental health professionals*. Springfield, IL: Charles C Thomas, pp. 151–181.

Schaefer, R. T. (1979). *Racial and ethnic groups*. Boston: Little, Brown.

Siegel, T. (1996, July 27). Gay bashing. *The Daily Herald,* p. 2.

Stevens, E. P. (1973, September–October). Machismo and marianismo. *Society, 10,* pp. 57–63.

Strauss, M., & Gelles, R. (1988). How violent are American families? In G. Hotaling (ed.), *Family abuse and its consequences*. Newbury Park, CA: Sage, pp. 14–36.

Sue, D. W., & Sue, D. (1990). Counseling American Indians. In D. W. Sue & D. Sue (eds.), *Counseling the culturally different* (2nd ed.). New York: Wiley, pp. 175–188.

Tully, C. T. (1995). Lesbians overview. In *Encyclopedia of social work* (19th ed.). Washington DC: NASW [National Association of Social Workers] Press, pp. 1591–1596.

U.S. Bureau of Indian Affairs (1987). *Indian service population and labor estimates*. Washington, DC: Author.

U.S. Bureau of the Census. (1990). *U.S. population estimates by age, sex, race and Hispanic origin*. Current Population Reports, Series P-25, No. 145. Washington, DC: U.S. Government Printing Office.

U.S. Bureau of the Census. (1991). *Statistical Abstract of the United States: 1991* (111th ed.). Washington, DC: U.S. Government Printing Office.

U.S. Bureau of the Census. (1992). *1990 census of population and housing,* summary tape file 1C, CD 90-IC, limited stats summary. Washington, DC: U.S. Government Printing Office.

U.S. Bureau of the Census. (1993). *Hispanic Americans today*. Current Population Reports, Series P-23, No. 183. Washington, DC: U.S. Government Printing Office.

U.S. Public Health Service. (1992). *Health United States 1991*. Washington DC: U.S. Government Printing Office.

Walker, L. (1989). *Terrifying love: Why battered women kill and how society responds*. New York: Harper & Row.

Warcquant, L. J. D., & Wilson, W. J. (1989). The cost of racial and class exclusion in the inner city. *Annals of the American Academy of Political and Social Science, 501,* 8–25.

Warren, C. A. B. (1974). *Identity and community in the gay world*. New York: Wiley, p. 4.

Warren, R. (1963). *The community in America*. Chicago: Rand McNally.

Washington Post News Service Report. In *The Virginian-Pilot & Ledger-Star* (1993, February 22), p. A3.

Weinberg, M. S., & Williams, C. J. (1974). *Male homosexuals: Their problems and adaptations*. New York: Oxford University Press.

Wilkins, R. (1990, February 22). Mandela: Our cousin, a king: Black hands across the ocean. *The New York Times,* p. A23.

Wilkinson, G. T. (1980, October). On assisting Indian people. *Social Casework, 61,* 451–454.

Wilson, W. J. (1987). *The truly disadvantaged: The inner city, the underclass, and public policy*. Chicago: University of Chicago Press.

Wirth, L. (1945). The problem of minority groups. In R. Linton (ed.), *The science of men in the world crisis*. New York: Columbia University Press.

Wong, J. (1981). Appropriate mental health treatment and service delivery for southeast Asian refugees in America. In *Bridging cultures: South Asian refugees in America*. Los Angeles: Asian American Community Mental Health Training Center, pp. 195–223.

Wright, M. B. (1980). Indochinese. In S. Thernstrom (ed.), *Harvard encyclopedia of American ethnic groups*. Cambridge, MA: Belknap Press, pp. 486–496.

Zastrow, C. (1992). *The practice of social work* (4th ed.). Belmont, CA: Wadsworth.

Index